MOH

ESSAD BEY

MOHAMMED

Translated by

HELMUT L. RIPPERGER

First Published 1938

BRIDGES
PUBLISHING

PUBLISHER'S NOTE

It is, unfortunately, extremely difficult to transliterate Arabic words and proper names into English. In this book they have been transliterated according to what seemed the most familiar to English readers.

Further, our readers are kindly asked not to take offence by terms such as "Mohammedan", "negro" or "negress" but to take into consideration the time that this book was written. These terms were commonly used in years gone by and were not disrespectful or insinuating disrespect.

First published 1938
Second Edition 2014

Book cover: Rosi Weiss, Freiburg/Germany.
Illustration: *Mohammed on Mount Hira*, Istanbul 1595 (Hazine 1222, Folio 158b)
Layout and typesetting: Hans-Jürgen Maurer

This book is published by:
Bridges Publishing
Verlag Hans-Jürgen Maurer
Frankfurt/Germany

www.bridges-publishing.de

ISBN 978-3-929345-67-4

CONTENTS

IV. THE WORLD AFTER THE PROPHET

I.

THE WORLD BEFORE THE PROPHET

THE DESERT OF THE PROPHET

Come, that I may tell you how he crosses the
desert. Like the donkey bearing its burden, he
carries his bread and his water on his shoulders.
His back is bent. His drink is stinking water.

Papyrus Anastasi iv, 9

In the north-east of Africa lies Egypt, the land of the blue river, the green plain,
and the yellow desert which encircles both river and plain. A narrow tongue of
land joins Egypt with the world of Asia and a vast desert separates it from the
country of the two rivers, the Euphrates and the Tigris.

Pharaoh reigned in Egypt. On the Euphrates and the Tigris stood two mighty
empires, Assyria and Babylon. Between Egypt and Mesopotamia lay desert and
wilderness. The masters of this ancient world, which spread along the banks of the
great rivers, paid no attention to the desert. They erected buffer states on the edge of
the desert, sent out punitive expeditions from time to time, and recounted horror
stories of the miserable existence of the pillaging peoples of the desert. "Do not go
into the desert, my son," said a wise old Egyptian, "no one has ever found happiness
there. If you go into the desert you will soon be like a tree which has lost its bark and
is gnawed by the worm."

The Pharaohs disappeared. So did the empires of the two rivers. New kings came
and did the same as their predecessors. They built palaces, sent out hostile armies,
and erected buffer states against the desert. The wilderness and the barbaric solitude
which lay between the Nile and the Euphrates remained unchanged, indifferent to
the vicissitudes of the world about them. Speaking of the inhabitants of the desert,
a later ruler on the Euphrates said, "For us, they were always beggars and vagabonds."

On the Nile, the Tigris and the Euphrates, world empires appeared and disappeared. In the desert between the rivers apparently nothing appeared or disappeared.
The desert was always there and disturbed the cultural activities of the people of the
two countries. But it was not too great a hindrance. It was nothing but a dangerous
caravan route for trade, a land of demons for the teller of tales, and an unimportant
territory for conquerors and statesmen.

The name of the desert, *Jazirat al-Arab*, means "The Island of the Arabs". However, it is not an island but a world between Africa and Asia, related to both continents
and yet internally alien. It is a world by itself.

9

MOHAMMED

Arabia is a peninsula more than a million and a half square miles in size. Its coasts on the Red Sea, the Mediterranean and the Persian Gulf are rocky and inhospitable. Ships can reach it at but a few harbours. The sea, which connects other lands, separates Arabia from the rest of the world. The desert is even more isolated; in the North, in Iraq, there are the desert Nafud, *al-buhr billa ma*, that is "the sea without water," and in the South, *Rub' al-Khali*, and the terrible *Hadramaut*, the desert of red sand. Impenetrable, wild, sinister and poor, for thousands of years Arabia has been between the greatest cultural centres of the old Orient.

What manner of country is it? Old legends say: "When the Master of all the worlds created the earth, he distributed justly stone and water, valleys and meadows. Each country received some of these treasures of the Almighty and Arabia too was given its share. Then the Lord of the worlds decided to give each a bit of sand, for it would prove useful to man. He took the sand, packed it in a sack and sent out the Archangel Gabriel to apportion it correctly. But Satan, the evil one, envied mankind. As Gabriel swayed over Arabia, Satan approached him in secret, slit open the sack and all the sand poured down over Arabia, dried up its seas and forced the waters from its rivers." That was the origin of the desert.

This angered the Ruler of the worlds and he spoke: "My Arabia has become impoverished. But I will cover it with gold." And in his mercy, he made an enormous dome of glittering gold, which was to light the desert by night. But the evil one was determined to deprive man of this as well. He sent out his jinn and they covered the bright gold of heaven with heavy, black veils. The Master of the worlds was not to be outdone. He sent his angels who pierced the black veils of Satan with their lances, and so appeared the Arabian stars, the godly gold which smiles at man when he lies sleepless at the entrance to his tent. But by day the land is in the power of the evil one.

For months on end, the heavens are steel blue over the earth. In the time of the torrid heat, they become dull and ashen grey. The heavens choke the land, incessantly they pour down glowing flames of heat upon the parched ground. Yellow, dry, unchanged, the land lies under the grilling sun. Mountain walls and blocks of stone crack open in the eternal, scorching sun. Slowly they are ground to powder like everything else that dwells beneath the Arabian sky. Between heaven and earth there is nothing but dust. Carried by the wind in great clouds, it covers the horizon, darkens the sun, and falls down upon man like stinging rain. Arabia is the slave of sun and desert.

In Hadramaut, Nafud, Dahna and Rub' al-Khali the grey, sterile plain turns into a terrifying sea of red sand. Two-thirds of the Arabian country is ruled by death. Sand swamps which suck in man and beast lie between the red hills. Slowly one sinks into the depths of the soft sand. Sly Bedouins know how to vanquish their hostile neighbours by luring them into the treacherous Rub' al-Khali.

Nine-tenths of Arabia is made up of barren desert. And where the desert ends, the steep rocky mountains peopled by demons begin. At night one can hear them whimper and howl in their caves. Theirs are the voices of hell, from the mountain *Jabal Selbal*.

No river worthy of the name runs through this land.

Only at a few points in Najd, in the adjacent Yemen and in Hejaz, and at the foot of the mountains, can human habitations appear and flourish. There, cities and villages arise, and there the peasant tills his sparse fields. Along the broad valley – or is it a river-bed? – one finds human dwellings. They belong to an industrious, impoverished people who are afraid of the desert. All of these cities, villages and fields are purely accidental, fortuitous landmarks in the monotonous grey of the everyday life of the desert. In them occurred the few attempts at a state-like civilization with the benefit of a modest influence filtered in from neighbouring cultural centres. But it must be remembered that these were accidental influences. The bursting of a dam sufficed to destroy a civilization, a surprise attack by night to wipe out a state.

And again the sand covers everything. Canals dry up and buildings decay. The spreading desert alone is the decisive factor in Arabia. It gives the land its stamp and the great majority of the people are dependent upon it. The desert is the alpha and omega of the Arabian world. It was there before the cities of Arabia were founded, and it will be there when the last Arabian field is buried in sand. The desert is the cradle and the grave of all things Arabic.

Arabia is subject to the rivalry of two elements and the Arab must needs fight with both. They are the powers of sand and water. Even without ever having seen a desert, everyone knows what sand is. But who in the western world can even begin to suspect what water is? For us it exists like the air or the earth. In the Orient there are both air and earth. There is water too, but not in the riverbeds for the rivers are dried up, not in the lakes for there never were any. What water there is, is carefully hoarded in leather sacks or in the bellies of camels. Long and bitter struggles have ensued over a tiny spring. A stream may assure the existence and prosperity of an entire tribe.

When the summer comes, the nomad may cover as much as sixty or seventy miles through sand and dust to reach a well. Water is the treasure of the desert, for the angels spit it out upon the earth when they wish to assure man of their goodwill. That is why each bit of water tastes differently, according to the angel from whose mouth it came. Whoever has the good fortune to discover a spring or a water source, never speaks of it. Carefully and jealously he guards his secret for the benefit of his tribe. Arabia is a world without water.

For long periods the skies are the colour of ashes as if they were covered with a crust of sand. Simooms course through the land and hot winds blow over the desert.

The inhabitants crouch down beside their tents and with tired eyes look towards the horizon. Fantastic dreams arise out of the sand, always the same, water, water, water! Rarely, perhaps once in many months, a cloud appears upon the horizon. The heavens become overcast and then the Arabian cloudburst begins. The waters come from the sky, fall upon the hot sand, are mixed with it, and turn suddenly into a catastrophe.

The desert valleys in which the Bedouins camp are filled with water. Suddenly they change into rivers. Old, dead riverbeds pulse with life. Tents are destroyed and camels carried away by the rushing torrents. The desert tribes take refuge on the hills of sand which are turned into riverbanks. Then the rain stops and the desert is a huge mud pond. None can approach it, not man nor beast. Two, three hours pass and desert moss makes its appearance on the slimy sand. Again the sun shines down in all of its power and pitilessly absorbs the water, the gift of heaven.

Rapidly the desert takes on its old aspect; it is empty, dry, bare and lifeless. Slowly the Bedouin gathers up the few belongings he was able to rescue from the fury of the storm and slowly the tribe makes its way through the solitude and wilderness. Again the winds whirl up the sands. For days and days the nomad wanders across the lonely steppes. His camel covers from six to ten miles an hour. Slowly the senses become dulled. One sees nothing but the blue world of sand and sky and soon it becomes difficult to know where the heavens end and the skies begin. Half asleep, half awake, the way continues over the desert and between dream and reality lies always the same: the grey, endless, monotonous desert – the sand.

In the desert nothing stimulates the imagination. It was in the desert that oriental sluggishness was born, lulled by the interminable marches of the caravans in the implacable solitude. It is the desert, too, which gives birth to the outbreaks of temper, the sudden tempests of Bedouin energy. The brain of the dweller in the desert is disturbed by but little, for he has time for repose, thought and meditation. His brain is dry and clear like the desert air, like the desert sand. He has room for only a few thoughts. But those few are deeply and securely implanted in his soul.

From the beginning of time one thought has been rooted in him: the incalculability of things. The desert is unfathomable. Today it may give man a fig tree and a little water. Tomorrow, a simoom will kill his last camel.

No one knows what the desert will bring. For the desert is nothingness, and nothingness is very powerful, more powerful than the nomad. Obediently, man submits to the inexplicable desert. Helplessly he suffers its dominion. The terrors of the desert enslave him; they are an incomprehensible riddle, a supernatural fate. Powerless, he bows to the events suspended over him.

Nine-tenths of Arabia is desert and the remaining tenth can easily become so at any moment. The Arab must have the piety of the desert – he is a fatalist.

The man who lives in the desert is like the sand itself. Insignificant for the rest of the world, he has remained unchanged throughout the centuries. Since the beginning of time, the Arab has been immutable. He has remained rigid and constant like the sand from which he sprang, in which he lives, and from which he cannot separate himself.

But what sort of people are they?

THE PEOPLE OF THE DESERT

For us, the Arabs were nothing but beggars and
vagabonds.

Jesdegerd III

When Isaac was born, Abraham cast out his slave Hagar and her son Ishmael from his tent. The mother and child went into the desert. The Bible does not know what happened to them. But sages say that Ishmael met the daughters of Lilith in the desert. From these daughters and from the son of Abraham sprang the Arabs. The people increased rapidly, but the desert in which they lived was sterile and desolate. Their habitation conditioned the existence of the inhabitants. They wandered from oasis to oasis, allowed their cattle to graze until the meagre pastures became barren. When the time came in which the people had increased to such proportions that the pasture lands were insufficient for the needs of their herds, a part of them emigrated. On the Nile and the Euphrates these emigrants were soon known either as courageous conquerors or as mercenaries in the service of strange princes.

Every twelve to fifteen hundred years, these emigrations from the overpopulated desert were repeated and, from the beginning of time, they always followed the same route. The way led to Mesopotamia, through the fruitful country of Syria and Palestine. In these countries, blessed with water, the people of the desert became sedentary. They founded states, built houses and began to fight their wild brothers who had remained in Arabia. And so, out of this Semitic invasion from Arabia ensued the empires of Assyria and Babylon, the cultural Centres of the old world.

The Chaldeans who founded these empires were followed out of the depths of Arabia by the many peoples mentioned in the Bible. In the time of Rome, the Arameans came as well. Again and again, the original home of the Semites sent out their warring tribes into the world of cities and agriculture.

At longer intervals, the small occasional emigrations which never entirely ceased were followed by great expansions until, at the beginning of the 6th century, a new desert people appeared upon the horizon of the old world, the Arabs.

The people were made up of two large classes. One, those who live in the desert according to the demands of the desert, the nomads, and the other those who try to live in the desert as one lives in Mesopotamia, in Syria or in Egypt, the sedentary Arabs. Each hates the other violently and bitterly. To the Bedouin, the stay-at-home is nothing short of a slave, a man who is less dependent upon his victorious sword than upon his plough. The other hates the Bedouin, the wild robber of the desert, with all the rancour of the renegade who was yesterday a free Bedouin himself.

"When the Almighty created the world," the Bedouin will tell you, "he took the wind and said, 'Be man' and out of the wind God created the Bedouin. Then God took an arrow, and out of the arrow he made the steed of the desert. Then the Almighty took a bit of earth out of which came the donkey. And it was only out of the first donkey dung that the Master of the worlds, in his great mercy, created the sedentary, the city-dweller and peasant."

But the latter, in turn, does not remain silent. Because of a certain practice of the desert, he maliciously calls the Bedouin "the man who cannot tell the difference between a woman and a virgin," and that suffices in his opinion to differentiate between city and desert.

Nevertheless, the best and most valuable part of the Arabs dwell in the desert. Life there is hard and filled with danger. He who lives in it must submit to rules of iron. He must take precautions that are unknown to the cities. The individual, isolated as he is, can accomplish but little alone. In order to combat the forces of nature, he must have associates. The first and also the majority of the persons he sees around him belong to his family. With them he concludes a life-long alliance. This alliance is the tribe. Most Occidentals today ignore the meaning of this term. They know families, associations and the state. One must care for the family, serve the state, and belong to an association. But none of these ties exclusively absorbs the existence of the individual. The tribe alone does this. The tribe which dominates the free son of the desert is a pitiless force to which he is more slavishly allied than the European is to family, state and party. For to the Arab, the tribe is family, state and party in one.

The tribe represents an enlarged family, the members of which cannot separate from one another. The tribe has its laws which must be blindly obeyed. Imperatively it determines the role of each member of the community. It orders its members to march to war, or to starve. To it belong all the camels, sheep, children and wives of each individual member. By means of thousands of laws and varied traditions it exercises unlimited power. All in all, it is the prototype of the primitive, communistic state. One cannot conceive of an Arab outside his tribe. It is only membership of a certain party which lends him individual importance and human dignity. Thousands of persons belong to one tribe. They are all related and each one knows the exact degree of his relationship to the others.

When the tribe rides through the desert it is led by its chief, the sheikh. His principal duty is the maintenance of the laws of the tribe. If he fails in this he is deposed. Anyone breaking the laws of the tribe is expelled from the community which, above all else, is the worst thing that can happen to a person in Arabia. The outcast is free as a bird, and he is exposed to pillage and murder. He is a man without a tribe and no one will help him, no one will protect him. The Arab is safeguarded not by the state, for it does not exist, but by the consideration in which his particular tribe is held. In theory, the member of an important tribe can travel through the desert without danger, for no one would dare to attack him who is backed by a powerful tribe. If this tribe is wealthy he may incur debts. If he does not repay them the tribe will make good. If a young man wishes to marry and is poor the tribe will provide the dowry. If he is taken into captivity the tribe will ransom him. Obviously it is beneficial to belong to a mighty tribe in Arabia. All the comfort and security which the modern state can offer its citizens, and much more beside, is possessed by the Arab member of an important tribe. And all is lost to him if he is expelled by, and from, his tribe. The mightier the tribe, the more secure is the life and wealth of the Arab who belongs to it.

But how can a tribe become mighty? The method is simple, primitive and available to all. By increasing the number of its membership as much as it can! The more children that run around in the tent of an Arab, the greater the assurance that his tribe will continue to be great and honoured.

The father of a large family enjoys particular esteem. Nowhere more than in the camps of the nomads of the desert procreative virility is appreciated and publicly exalted. "I am poor and simple," says the Bedouin to the effeminate city dweller, "but I have produced twenty children and I shall produce twenty more." Of the wise and of people in good repute, the Bedouin will declare, "He can procreate as many children as he pleases. He is in God's favour." There is no argument as impressive to a Bedouin as the number of one's children. Ten to twenty children in an Arab's tent are not a rarity. But child mortality is high and the only effective measure against it is to continue to have as many children, and as quickly, as one can.

Obviously, the great number of children necessary to the Arab in order to maintain the power of his tribe is not compatible with having just one wife. Life in the desert and tribal life demand polygamy. The process of acquiring a wife for the Bedouin is far from complicated. He merely robs her from a neighbouring tribe. He does not like to take a wife from his own tribe for he is afraid of in-breeding.

It is in the spring, when several tribes are camped about an oasis, that the Bedouin does his wooing. He may meet the chosen one in the camel pastures, at the well, or at night around the open fire. During his long winter wanderings the Bedouin becomes amorous and his advances must make rapid progress. When the tribal camps break up he must have made his decision. Either he buys his bride from her people or merely steals her. If he does neither, he composes a melancholy love poem, a *gasidah*, and goes on with his tribe, alone. It may also happen that an energetic Bedouin maiden will kidnap her lover by force and make him a member of her own tribe.

This happens in tribes where there is a dearth of men.

The marriage of Bedouins is governed by numerous laws. In addition to normal wedlock there is also temporary marriage. One can marry for a year or a few months and it is not at all dishonourable for a woman to enter into such a union. Any father will permit his daughter to move into a neighbour's tent for a few months. This practice makes life more agreeable.

Among the Bedouins, divorce is not complicated by difficult regulations. If a man grows tired of his wife he returns her in all honour to her original owner, her father. Her standing is in no way affected by this. Eroticism plays but an indifferent role among people whose sole idea in life is the procreation of children. In ancient times the nomads even practised polyandry. Ten or twelve young men bent on marrying some local beauty might form an association, if the price asked by her father was too high for the individual. They were married and each of the men given a wooden staff. Each had the right to enter the tent of his one-tenth wife whenever he desired to do so. The little wooden staff was placed outside the tent, so that the remaining husbands would not disturb them.

The basic, realistic reasoning of the Bedouin is manifest in the theory that it is better to have a one-tenth interest in a good business than to be in entire possession of a poor one. Experts are called in to determine the fatherhood in such cases. Judgments of this sort have developed into a regular science in the desert where each and every man wishes to be a father. No matter how much the Arab may incline to romantic love, the purpose and goal of his marriage is the begetting of children.

In this connection another usage has sprung up which is considered equally decent. If a Bedouin is not blessed with children he will look about in his own tribe to find a man from whom one might expect healthy progeny. He enters into a contract with him. The man chosen may be paid, for example, two camels and five sheep, and agrees to produce a child by the wife of the less fortunate individual. The contract also stipulates that the substitute father may have no rights whatever in the child. The child belongs to the husband.

Although children mean wealth and importance to the tribe, they must be of the male sex. Boys will be future warriors and sages, but the tribe has no use for girls, who are only a burden. They cannot go to war, they cannot protect the sheep of their tribe, nor can they conquer new pastures. When a girl is born in the tent of a nomad it is looked upon as the punishment of God. And if too many girls are born to him the Bedouin has recourse to an expedient which is as simple as it is brutal. There is a horrible custom in the desert which permits the burying alive of unnecessary girls, so that they may not become a burden to the tribe and drink the mother's milk destined for the boys. These are the naïf eugenics of the desert.

Boys and men are the wealth of the tribe. When a man dies the tribe becomes poorer. If a man is murdered, then the murderer, if he belongs to another tribe, must also die, so that the equilibrium between the tribes be maintained. From this resulted the complicated law of Arabian blood vengeance, the supreme law of the desert.

Every non-Oriental holds that blood vengeance is a bestial law based on a cruel desire for revenge, a primitive instinct of the wilderness. This is a mistake. The law of blood vengeance is much more complicated than most of the laws of Europe. It is not enacted in a fit of sudden passion, but subject to many regulations and restrictions which are engraved in the memory of every nomad from the time of his earliest youth. The much-maligned blood vengeance of the Arabs, when seen in its proper light, is the only protection against anarchy, against war on the part of all against all. Peace is temporarily maintained in the desert merely because this menace is constantly present among the tribes. It is solely the fear of vengeance which permits peace to flourish at times. The loss of a family member, a warrior, weakens the tribe, leaves a void, and strengthens the tribe of the opponent. It is of no consequence whether the murder was deliberate or happened by chance.

The idea of sin, of crime, was unknown to the ancient Bedouins. They simply felt that damage done had to be repaired. Blood vengeance is really reparations *á l'orientale*. So, for example, it is entirely logical that blood vengeance is applied only to strange tribes. The murderer, *per se,* is not punishable, but the damage done is. For this reason a murder which is committed within a tribe hurts the murderer just as much, for he has become poorer by the loss of a blood relation. If one were to punish the murderer beyond this the tribe would be weakened by the additional loss of a second of its members. Blood vengeance within a tribe is, therefore, a contradiction in itself.

Blood vengeance is not provoked by murder alone. It may come into play as the result of a robbery, an insult or a simple injury. In short, where any damage is done, either moral or physical. Ancient traditions govern its accomplishment, and they consist for the most part of guerrilla warfare, pillage and massacre. Officially these feuds last until the original parity has been restored, but in actuality they are endless. The grounds which may lead up to a blood feud are more than insignificant when compared with the shocking results which ensue.

The following incident gave rise to a war between two powerful tribes lasting for more than ten years. A worthy sheikh named Kulaib was walking one day in the pastures in which his herd was grazing. Suddenly he saw a lark which had just laid its eggs and was guarding them anxiously. Kulaib had a soft heart and spoke, "Be quiet, O lark. I, the Sheikh Kulaib, promise that nothing shall happen to you." Having spoken, he went his way.

An hour later an equally worthy sheikh of another tribe, Jassas, rode past the same spot and, not seeing the lark, his camel stepped on the eggs. The day after, as Kulaib went through the pasture, he saw the broken eggs before him. Filled with rage, he ran through the camps and saw to his horror that the feet of the camel of Jassas were covered with egg-yolk. Now he knew who the evil-doer was. He sought out Jassas, and it happened that he had just turned his back upon Kulaib. Kulaib was too noble to step into the sight of Jassas and Jassas was too noble to turn around for anyone. "Turn around or I will kill you," cried Kulaib. "Come before me," shouted Jassas. The result was that the two sheikhs murdered each other and the ten years of warfare already mentioned began.

Practically every Arabian tribe has blood enemies which it must fight, and every Arab is constantly on the look-out for one. Consequently, it would appear as if the life of the Bedouin was a perpetual battle, not only against nature but his fellow-man as well. But the desert has its own rules for peace, and they must be obeyed by all. They are very ancient, these laws, and no one knows their origin, but they are obeyed as the laws of God. Having been instituted for all, irrespective of tribal affiliation, the slightest infraction of them brings dire punishment – expulsion from the desert. In speaking of such banishment the Bedouin only does so with horror. No one will have anything to do with the criminal or his tribe. He is avoided and shunned.

And what are these laws? They are like the remnants of some ancient, forgotten constitution of the desert. They do not say much, but without them existence in the desert would be impossible. In the heat of battle, in war, in the intoxication of exacting blood vengeance, it is forbidden, for example, to cut down the palm-trees of an opponent, or to destroy his wells. Palm-trees and water sources are sanctuaries. Cursed is he who harms them, for they are there for the good of all, serving one tribe today and another tomorrow. Whoever commits such an act ceases to be a man. Turned into a wild beast, he should be killed when encountered.

Hospitality is also governed by these laws. Were his mortal enemy to kill the first-born of a nomad and then appear with the child's head in his hands at the tent of the father, he must be received hospitably, offered sheep's milk and fat. The father must serve the murderer with all humility and thank him for the honour of his visit. Such is the law of the desert.

But the laws alone would not be enough to make the lives of the Bedouins bearable. Pillage and cattle-raising could not suffice to still the demands of the nomad. From time to time he must make trips to far-off annual markets where all the tribes are assembled and where he can exchange his leather, camels and sheep for the merchant's stock of arms, cloth and other necessities. But how is it possible for many tribes to come together in one place when they are all entangled in blood feuds? Another law of the desert provides for this. The Arabs have declared four months of the year to be holy, and in that time no wars may be waged, nor may blood enemies attack one another. Peace reigns in the desert. The people journey to the market without fear. All sing and dance while blood enemies sit side by side and praise the gods who allow one-third of the year to pass in peace.

But these outbursts of piety are not voiced with too much enthusiasm. There are few things to which the Bedouin is as indifferent as he is to matters of faith. The trot of his camel is more important than all problems of religion put together. The Arab, the Bedouin of the 6th century, believes all that is placed before him in questions of faith, but at heart he believes nothing. He sees the stars and believes them to be gods. He sees the endless, flat desert plain before him and bows before it reverently, for the desert is powerful. He sees fire and prays to it also, for the Persians do and they are a great people.

The Arab of the 6th century ignores all religion in the European sense of the word.

No doubt the sight of the vast desert gives him an inkling of the puissance of some godhead which rules over all things. But the religions of his neighbours, the Christians and the Jews, teach the same thing, and some of the tribes were converted to Judaism or Christianity. Only on rare occasions does the Bedouin think of a great divinity. Much closer to him are the pieces of stone or the crudely carved statues which his tribe carries with it. The stone is the divinity for home use, it has no laws and makes but few demands. Each tribe has its own tribal god and its own tribal stone which accompanies the tribe wherever it goes and suffices for the primitive, religious needs of the desert. When it fails, the sorcerers, soothsayers and saints have to help, which entails the summoning up of the entire demonic underworld of the desert. The ordinary son of the desert is more than satisfied with his religion; it helps him without asking any services in return.

The Arabs are divided into tribes which look upon themselves as nations, as states, which from the very beginning have been hostile to every other tribe, nation or state. Each tribe has its god, its past and its customs. Unity is entirely unknown among the tribes of Arabia and for them an Arabian nation simply does not exist.

And yet it was not always thus. It is a moot point, but it might well be that the customs, life and laws of the Arabs of the 6th century were the last vestiges of a flourishing culture of earlier days. Perhaps the Arabs were once wealthy and powerful with states of their own, magnificent cities, written laws and established religions. Perhaps decadence had swept that all away, and now it lives on, buried by the desert sands in the form of inexplicable customs and traditional usage. Perhaps. No one can be certain.

But we are certain that these people had once accomplished great deeds. When the great trade routes of the Orient still crossed Arabia, and when King Hiram and King Solomon sent their caravans to the fairyland of Ophir, the Arabians were rich and mighty. The Queen of Sheba, who brought the rulers of the Jews one hundred and fifty talents of gold, reigned in the South. The empire of the Nabataeans flourished in the North. Media was also known as a country of gold. But little has come down to us concerning these countries. They were there, flowered and disappeared, buried in the sands of the desert. In Roman times Arabia was sufficiently united to accomplish a great rebellion. The empire of Palmyra unified nearly all of Arabia in an uprising against Rome. The armies were led by a woman, the admirable Zenobia. At a later time she was destined to ornament, in chains, the triumphal train of her conqueror.

But all of this belongs to the past.

Now, in the 6th century, the past lies deeply buried under the desert sands. There is no more unity among the peoples of Arabia and nowhere are independent states to be found. Not in the south, in what was Arabia Felix, nor on the gold coast of the north, in Media. It was only in the extreme north, where the deserts touch the confines of Byzantium and Persia, that the great powers of the era, like their predecessors, erected buffer states. The only state-like groups of the Arabs were the empire of the Sassanids in Trans-Jordania which paid tribute to Byzantium, and the Achaemenides who were vassals of Persia.

In the desert, however, in the barbaric wilderness, lived the free people of Arabia. Tribe fell upon tribe and blood feuds harassed the land. One tribe hated the other, fought it, but spared its palm-trees and wells. They praised the free existence of the Bedouins, the men of the desert, who know no force, need no state, and belong to a tribe for which they go to battle, procreate children and pray to an idol of stone.

So lived the youngest under the Semites, the Arabs. Moses and Christ were born to the Semites. And now in the great desert between Iraq and Egypt, a prophet was to be born to the latest branch on the Semitic tree – Mohammed, the Messenger of God.

THE SINGING DESERT

My tent, through which the wind blows, is love-
lier than a sumptuous palace.

Umm-Jesid, Mother of the Sixth Caliph

Were the Bedouins, who knew neither state nor restraint, actually a unified people? What held them together? Why did these countless tribes,
which constantly fought one another, feel from time to time that they
were members of one nation?

The reply is found in an ancient Arabian poem. *"In His bounty, God gave four gifts
to the Arabs. First, the simple turban of the desert, which becomes him better than a
crown; then the tent, which is more comfortable than a palace; the sword, which affords
more protection than the highest wall. The fourth and best gift of Heaven, however, is the
lovely art of free song. That is the Arab's most precious treasure."* Possibly this answer
may seem strange but nevertheless it is a true one. The unity of the rude Arabian
tribes depends upon the force of the Arabic word, the Arabic song.

Song rules the desert. Even in our day, there is no nation as enthusiastic about
the beauty of words, about lyric impression as the Arabs. The simple desert folk command an unheard-of wealth of language. Language is to the Arab, what architecture,
painting and music are to other people.

The Arab is the master of his language. He knows all of the hundred synonyms
for the word camel, or sword, and delights in using the most complicated forms of
expression. At the same time he heartily pities the less fortunate people who are
poorer in idiom than he. He takes meticulous care to preserve the purity of his
speech. From his infancy the Arab is initiated in the art of beautiful words. A simple
Bedouin woman of the desert will chastise her children for using a wrong grammat-
ical construction. For the word is holy; it joins all the Arabs and makes them into
one people.

Whoever would rule over the Arabs must first master the word. Although every
tribe has its own dialect, which is only understood with difficulty by neighbouring
tribes, the poetry of the desert reigns over all dialects. It is the literary language of
the Arabs, and the member of every tribe must be thoroughly familiar with it if he
wishes to be known as an Arab. It is the language of the poets, and the Arab loves his
poetry more than he does turban, sword and tent. Every Arab, without exception,
can make poems, and they all have the greatest interest in literary questions. To the

Arab poetry is what sport, politics and newspapers are to the moderns. For poetry expresses the sense of the beautiful, public opinion and political information. In short, it represents all that is of interest to the Arab.

Every Arab is a poet. Perched on his camel during his long rides through the flat countryside the hours are monotonous and grey. The animal moves through the desert with rhythmic steps. In order not to be alone, not to fall asleep, to escape the terrors of the desert, the Arab begins to describe the plains of sand which lie before him, the camel on which he rides, the skies which spread endlessly over him, and his own power. At first he speaks slowly and in a monotone, freely and without restraint. Gradually his speech assumes a regular form, it becomes co-ordinated and adapts itself to the even rhythm of the walk of his camel. It is the basic cadence of all Bedouin lyrics, and it has been said that the complicated metre of the Arabic verse is nothing but the variations of the individual pace of the solitary camel as it strides through the great desert.

The Arab places unusual importance upon his poetry and the beauty of words. The word is magic, it is powerful, and whoever masters it is mightier than the warrior. The true poet can make charms of his words, he can conjure up sickness or exorcize it. Even if he fails in this, his power is still great. A successful satire on the part of a poet can suffice to ruin the reputation of an Arab among all the tribes of the desert. The poet's ridicule is more to be feared than the sword of the hero.

Each tribe has its own poet who accompanies it in battle. Before the conflict between two tribes, the poets step forth to praise their own and to belittle the prowess of the opposing tribe. The Arabs listen attentively. It has happened that the tribe whose poet was vanquished silently withdrew from the field without even attempting to fight with its weapons. What good is the sword when the poem is of no avail?

Poetical tournaments were the greatest events of the desert. Unheard-of honours were bestowed upon the prize-crowned poet. His song was embroidered upon cloths of black in huge letters of gold, and hung up at the entrance to the temple.

It is rare that an Arabian poet can read and write. He must improvise his verses. If they are good, his hearers will learn them by heart. And the more quickly the lines of a poet are memorized, the greater his glory. The poet's words are decisive in many things in the desert, and he who is without the true gift of speech can never reign there. Only he who can sway and hold his people through the magic of his eloquence, annihilate his enemy with a well-turned phrase, magnify the reputation of his tribe with felicitous words, can be a leader in the desert. For there poetry takes the place of newspapers, cinema and the books of our day. The ear of the desert belongs to the poet, who, incidentally, must also be an able warrior.

Bedouin lyric is filled with love, blood hatred, romantic encounters, pride of tribe, as well as numerous descriptions of life in the desert, of camels and noble Arabian steeds. But of greater importance than these wonders in verse, which are best under-stood by the Arab, are the poets themselves. Their romantic adventures are the actual incarnation of all Bedouin ideals.

One of the most famous of the old Arabic poets was Amr ibn al-Abd, called Tarafah. He lived among the Sassanids at the Court of the King of Hirah. Here he sang joyous songs about wine and women, but particularly about his camel, which he loved more than anything else in the world. Tarafah was fond of ridicule and he made fun of wine, women and God. The king smiled at him. One day, however, he made a poem which made fun of the king. The king ceased smiling. His face became grave, and he began to ponder in what manner he should discipline this *lèse-majesté*. Finally he decided to punish the rash poet with death. But one may not execute the favourite of the gods. His blood is too precious to be spilled by the executioner. Not even the king himself could dare to ordain his death. He summoned Tarafah to his presence and gave him a letter saying, "Go, take this letter to my satrap in Bahrain. There you will receive much honour and reward."

Tarafah was a poet and could not read. He took the letter and went out into the desert. On his way he met a wise old man, a man wise enough to know how to read the written word. The sage read the letter, for letters were not private in those days. "Oh, Tarafah," he said, "do not go to Bahrain, for this letter says that the satrap is to bury you alive as a punishment for the poem in which you ridiculed the king. Tear up the letter and throw it into the river." And Tarafah the poet replied:

"Reading is a great art, and a great art writing.
The running waters are not worthy to bear what is written.
In the future, the songs of Tarafah will be written and read."

I will not suffer anything written to be destroyed through my fault. Rather death!" He continued on his way and suffered a painful death in honour of the art of writing.

More romantic still is the life of the poet Antarah ibn Shaddad of the tribe of Abs. His mother was a negress and it was only because of his heroic deeds that his father accorded him equality with his white brothers. Nevertheless, the white tribes of the Arabs made fun of the black son of a slave. But Antarah used to say, "My soul is like the bodies of my white fellow-men, but my body is like their souls." To those who did not get the point he would add, "Half of me is honourable by birth, the other half is covered by my sword." All his life Antarah battled against his enemies, gave gifts to foe and friend alike, and rhymed his verses to the steps of his white camel. The Arabs honoured him because he was a poet, but they gave neither friendship nor love to the black son of a slave.

It was Antarah's habit to give others, even if they were strangers, whatever he had that they liked, considering as his own property only that which he had secured through his sword. Although the Arabs did not love Antarah, because of his wisdom, his courage and his pleasant nature they decided to call him Antarah al-Haki, which means, Antarah the Happy One. But Antarah refused. "I have an enemy," he said, "and I may not call myself happy until I have found and destroyed him." "So destroy him quickly," answered the people, "for we are impatient to call you the happy Antarah." For a long time Antarah searched for his enemy. Day and night he rode through the desert, questioned all whom he met, and begged the gods for vengeance. But the enemy knew how to hide himself, and for this reason Antarah named him "the happiness which flees." Finally the gods had pity on Antarah and pointed out his enemy to him on the horizon. Antarah trembled with joy and thought that at last his longing would be stilled. The enemy, too, had recognized Antarah and had recourse to the way of all cowards, flight. But Antarah's camel was strong. Soon he had overtaken him and soon he was brandishing his spear over the head of his foe. But the enemy turned around and said, "O, Antarah, give me your weapon." Antarah could not resist the request, and throwing his spear at the feet of his enemy, he galloped away lest "the happiness which flees" slay him with his own weapon.

When the Bedouins heard of this happening, some praised the generosity of the enemy in permitting Antarah to escape, but the majority laughed at the black man with the white soul. But when the Month of the Feast had come, the women of Arabia wove a great, black cloth and the wise men placed thereon in letters of gold the name of the joyous poet, Antarah. And they ordered the warriors to place the cloth at the entrance of the temple, in front of the holy Caaba. But from that time on Antarah was called Antarah the Fool, which means, Antarah the Poet.

These and similar stories were often told in the desert. They all deal with heroic poets who battled the world and vanquished it with the power of their songs. They were the symbol of Arabian virtue.

The most important and the most genial among the poets, however, was the king's son, Imru'u 'l Qais ibn Hujr. His life was an adventurous one. Because of his frivolity he was cast off by his father and journeyed with his friends into the desert. There he sang songs and captivated the good graces of the women. When his father had been murdered by the tribe of Banu Asad, none of his brothers would avenge the father's death. It was Imru'u 'l Qais, the banished son, who dedicated his life to the task. For decades on end he roamed restlessly through the desert, fought the Banu Asad, secluded himself in the romantic fortress of the Jew, Samuel, and finally reached the court of the Emperor of Byzantium. There great honours were bestowed upon him and he was appointed phylarch of Palestine. He died at Angora, poisoned by the emperor whose niece he had seduced. His life has furnished much material for romantic legends which centre around him and his friend, Samuel. One of these tells how

Imru'u 'l Qais had buried five coats of mail, which made him unconquerable, in the fortress Ablaq, which belonged to Samuel. When Imru'u 'l Qais went to Byzantium, the King of Hirah demanded that the Jew Samuel give up the coats of mail. But Samuel al-Waffa, the Faithful One, refused to do so, and after a number of Homeric battles he suffered a painful death. Even to this day, the Bedouins have not forgotten Imru'u 'l Qais and Samuel.

Imru'u 'l Qais, Antarah, Tarafah and many more of the knightly poets fill the history of Arabia. They were symbols of the ancient, romantic Arabia, the Bedouins, the tents, the stone idols, and of blood vengeance. Arabia was poor and looked down upon by the rest of mankind. Arabia was a desert and barbaric wilderness, pitied by none and neglected by all. Only the Bedouin loved his country, like a child its mother, loved the chivalrous combats of the desert, the poetical tournaments, and the countless songs of the wandering poets. It was no wonder that when the Messenger of God was given to the country many held him to be a poet.

THE WORLD ABOUT ARABIA

Eraclius vor do mit groteme here im Persyam he stret mit deme jungen koninge Cosdra unde sloch ludes vele he veng oc viftich dusend unde makede ledich manegen cristenen man.

Saxon Chronicle

(Heraclius went to Persia with a great army. He fought the young king, Cosdra, and killed many men. In all he took fifty thousand prisoners and freed numerous Christians.)

Two states governed the history of the world around the year A. D. 600, Persia and Byzantium. Both were large, rich and powerful. Both could look back on an ancient past, and both fought each other constantly. Byzantium was the Roman Empire of the Orient, the heir to the *imperium* and the *pax romana*. Persia's ancestors were the Achaemenides who once ruled over all of Asia, had fallen under the sword of the great Macedonian and, later still after the fall of Rome, had re-appeared as one of the great world powers. Byzantium and Iran, Orient and Occident, Christianity and fire-worship – two worlds, two cultures, two empires which were always alien to one another. Peace was impossible between them.

Byzantium. Its walls on the Bosphorus encircled its palaces and churches. But its power extended over all of Asia Minor, Syria, Palestine, Egypt, Iberia, North Africa, over the Grecian islands and the Balkans. Byzantium was mighty, rich and proud. It was the heir of Rome; but a late heir, it is true. It still contained the people who had once been conquered, Roman law was still in force, and people still trembled at the commands of the emperor. But the emperor himself was no Roman, no Imperator. On the shores of the Bosphorus, behind the thick walls of the marble palaces, the face of Rome was changing, slowly but inevitably. With the new faith a new world broke in, which had nothing in common with Rome. "I am the Roman Emperor, sovereign of the Romans," spoke the ruler of Byzantium. But he was not a classic emperor, nor was the land classic which obeyed him. In Byzantium the classic visage of Rome took on an oriental stamp, and soon the Roman form disappeared under the oriental robes.

Byzantine sovereignty rested on a number of civilizations. Asia Minor, Egypt and Rome all bowed the knee before its throne. The throne itself was secure, but only a few were able to sit securely upon it. *Porphyrogenites* the Byzantines called the few emperors who rightfully succeeded to the throne. All races and peoples furnished emperors for Byzantium, amid the acclamations of the praetorian guards and the populace. For it was the strange guard and the noisy populace, avid for spectacles, who gave the Christian Roman Empire of the Orient its sovereigns.

The power of the emperor was great. From Rome he inherited the great art of militarism; from the Oriental world, his slave, he received the much greater arts of poisoning, lying and treachery. Byzantium called this inheritance politics. It was defended by the brutal strength of the mercenaries: it had much to defend and its enemies were not weak.

In Byzantium, the centre of Oriental Christianity, the emperor was the protector of the Christian religion, the Holy Sepulchre and the true faith. Everyone in Byzantium knew what this true Christian faith was, but each one interpreted it in his own manner. Innumerable sects, with their combats and their hatred for one another, shattered the empire. In the bazaars, the assemblies and the markets the sects were discussed just as one now discusses political parties. The simplest merchant would employ the finest dialectic in order to overcome his adversary. They centred round abstract things, and abstract discussions are well liked in the Orient. But when the discussions were ended the manifestations of the differences of opinion were very concrete. The opponents fell upon each other, killing and plundering. For, even more than abstract discussion, the Orient enjoys the free play of violence.

The spirit of Byzantium degenerated more and more. He who could no longer tolerate conditions as they were, bade farewell to the proud city on the Bosphorus, to its palaces, its intrigues and the poisonings of the court, and retired to the desert to mortify the flesh and seek salvation. The Byzantine world was full of ascetics. So, for example, St. Simon Stylites stood motionless and in prayer for seven years on the summit of a pillar to manifest his surrender to God. Others preferred to lie half buried in a grave, and still others laid themselves in chains. There were men who surrounded themselves with pupils in the desert, and from them new sects sprang up.

Thus Christianity was spread in the Orient through the number of its sects. The spiritual life was nothing but sectarian disorder. The danger, however, did not threaten from within, but from without. Many greedy hands were stretched towards the golden throne and the crown of the emperor, towards the treasures of the palaces, towards the wealth of the cities and the fields. Wild, greedy eyes leered at Byzantium.

The old world was disarranged. People became uneasy. In the Balkans, behind the great walls of the Caucasus, in all corners of the empire, hordes of nomads made their appearance. They knocked violently at the gates of Byzantium. Without ceasing, year in and year out, the emperor was forced to protect the Christian world of the Orient against barbaric invasions. But the great danger which threatened Byzantium was not the savage nomads, not the Alani, the Huns, the Slavs of the North. The great enemy was Iran, Persia, the land of the Shahinshah, the Great King of the pious Persian, Sassanian dynasty.

Sacred Iran, the land of the eternal fire, of Ahura-Mazda, the good, and the wicked Ahriman, was but little known to the European world. It was only known that Iran was the powerful eastern neighbour of the Roman and Byzantine Empires, that for decades it had carried on bloody warfare with Rome, that it had been frequently vanquished and as frequently victorious, and that it was not open to any Christian influence. But what went on in its interior, no one knew.

It was a large, beautiful and quiet country. It stretched from the borders of Byzantium to the depths of Central Asia, from the coasts of the Persian Gulf to the summits of the Caucasus. It was the green and mysterious country of the holy fire, the prophet Zoroaster, the priests of Atropatene and the Great Shah.

Many centuries ago Zoroaster had founded the religion of fire. Surrounded by his disciples, he wandered over the fertile country of Iran. Where he appeared temples were erected, sacred flames burst forth from the earth, people knelt down, and priests chanted hymns in honour of the god of fire. On the shores of the troubled Caspian lay Atropatene, an Iranian province. This was the country Zoroaster chose. It became the holy land of Persia. Priests ruled it, prayed to the sacred fire and, from the coast of the Caspian Sea, determined who was to be emperor of the great expanse between China and Byzantium. The priests were mighty and endowed with much wisdom.

A story is told of an offering made by the priests to the Emperor Shapur, who ascended the throne of Iran when he was a child. It was a game of polo. An artificial green was placed on an iron table and little iron horses raced across it. A complicated mechanism moved the ball about, while another piece of machinery made it possible for the artificial horses to attend to their artificial wants while coursing around the artificial table. The present was given to the young emperor so that he might not only enjoy the game but also have respect for the priests who gave it to him. Later, when he bad grown up and no longer needed toys, they built two men of steel for him, two robots, who accompanied him wherever he went.

Another emperor, Qubad, tried to break the power of the priests. A heretic by the name of Mazdak appeared before him and spoke to the emperor as follows: "No man should be richer than his fellows. Equality must reign in the land of Iran and no priest should have anything to say over the people." The emperor was impressed with what Mazdak had to tell him. He distributed the wives of his harem among the people, took the wealth away from the wealthy, and left their poverty to the poor, for such was the teaching of Mazdak. The priests rose up to save the land of Iran. Prince Khosrau Anushirvan, of the immortal soul, brought about the defeat of Mazdak who, when the women of the harem had been distributed, had received the mother of the prince. From that time on, no shah attempted to disregard the words of the priests.

The emperor of Iran resided at Ctesiphon, on the banks of the Euphrates. The sacred land of fire which lay around him weighed heavily upon his shoulders. It was from Ctesiphon that Khosrau the Just, the heir of Qubad, carried on his war. He destroyed half of Byzantium, destroyed Antioch, and defeated the army of the Emperor Justinian. For decades the war raged between Persia and Byzantium. It was not a war between two states, but the conflict between the young Christianity and the ancient faith of the god of fire. When, for example, the Negus who ruled Ethiopia occupied Yemen, he was attacked by the Great Shah merely because the Negus was a Christian and the Shah would not endure a Christian victor in the world.

Incessant battles, campaigns and pillages bled the states of Byzantium and Persia. The cities became depopulated, the fields remained untilled and deserted. Because of a lack of men, Khosrau the Victorious was forced to employ women in his army. Men were needed to wage war and settle the land. The sorry, empty fields, the sparsely settled farms, the run-down country places, the armies of both states, sighed for inhabitants, for men who could fight.

The men came. They were Arabs. Arabian tribes came out of the wild desert, settled down in the deserted villages and filled the armies. Long before Mohammed, long before the campaigns of Islam, the worlds of Byzantium and Persia had called the Arab people into their midst.

The greatest victories were won by Persia over Byzantium at the time when Khosrau conquered Damascus and Jerusalem and finally even besieged Byzantium itself. The Roman Empire of the Orient seemed lost. Heraclius sat on the throne. He left it, the capital and the country. With a handful of warriors he crossed the rugged mountains to the holy land of Atropatene. There he attacked the priests and destroyed the temples. Frightened, the priests recalled their emperor. The emperor consented. He raised the siege of Byzantium, evacuated Jerusalem, returned home and rescued the eternal, holy fire of Iran.

This occurred in the year 628, when the rulers of Persia and Byzantium, Heraclius and Khosrau, were forced to conclude peace between the two countries.

Heraclius entered into liberated Jerusalem and Khosrau went to Ctesiphon. It appeared as if the world again desired peace. While Heraclius was celebrating the liberation of Christianity in Jerusalem, Khosrau was building a throne for himself in Ctesiphon such as the world had never seen before. A replica of Heaven was fashioned out of gold, silver and precious jewels, with sun, moon and stars. At will, the skies could produce thunder and rain. The throne was placed on top of the skies, and the whole thing was worked by horsepower.

This was the last act of homage paid to the emperor by his priests. Shortly after he had mounted his new throne for the first time, and while Heraclius was still celebrating his triumphs in Jersualem, an event occurred which was noted by but a few, and the few who had the time laughed at it.

In Ctesiphon and in Jerusalem two Arabs, both wild of aspect, appeared simultaneously and demanded to be led before the respective emperors. It is not known whether their requests were granted. It is known that they finally succeeded in bringing to the attention of the emperors written messages which they had brought with them from the desert.

Both letters were the same in content. In simple but courteous language the two rulers were asked to relinquish their faiths and to acknowledge an obscure Arabian divinity, as well as a newly founded cult known as "resignation." Naturally, the writer of the missive was entirely unknown to the emperors. He called himself, simply, "Mohammed, Messenger of God." In the intoxication of his triumphal inarch, Heraclius did not find time to formulate a reply. Nor could the Emperor of Byzantium, who was served like a demigod, enter into correspondence with an Arab! Khosrau, who had by no means been indemnified for the loss of Jerusalem by the gift of the priests, was in a bad humour. He tore up the letter, trod upon it with his feet, and ordered his satrap in Southern Arabia to decapitate the "Messenger of God." This order could not be executed because, before it reached Arabia, the mighty Great Shah was himself dethroned and beheaded.

Neither of the two emperors had heard the name of Mohammed up to that time. Ten years later, the army of the same Mohammed had conquered all of Persia, half of Byzantium, and had put out forever the holy fire of Iran. And finally, it hoisted the green flag of the Messenger of God – upon the grave of Christ.

This army, this faith, this prophet, had arisen out of nothing, out of the desert of Arabia, out of the land of beggars and vagabonds. Ten years sufficed to create a world out of that nothing.

The letter which bore the name of Mohammed had come from a small city in the centre of the Arabian desert. Both emperors may have heard its name by chance. The city was called Mecca. When the army of Khosrau had gone to Arabia, Mecca had been too small to be worthy of an attack. In ten years it had become the focal point of an entire world which extended from the shores of Gibraltar to the tops of the Himalayas.

THE CITY OF THE CAABA

All Arabs are merchants.
Strabo

A long time ago the patriarch Abraham wandered through the deserts of Arabia, through the rocky valleys of Hejaz. Mountains, naked rocks, ravines and precipices barred his way. Behind each rock sat a demon who, with tears and wailing, sought to entrap the patriarch in his spell. Courageously, Abraham strode through the barren, arid desert. When the demons got too bold he took a stone and threw it at the evil ones. Thousands of years have passed. Millions and millions of people have continuously imitated Abraham's gesture in the desert of Hejaz by throwing little stones at the three "devil's pillars," the rocks behind which the demons hid themselves.

For a long time the patriarch wandered through Hejaz. Finally he reached the bottom of a valley which was surrounded by bare and rugged crags. Here, in the midst of the wild country, the Master of all the worlds manifested His grace. He sent down from Heaven a white stone, white as the wings of an archangel. Here the Caaba, the sanctuary of Arabia, was erected. Set in its walls, placed there by the hands of Abraham, rests the brilliant "Hajaru-l-aswad," the stone of God. Abraham travelled on, praising the Lord, but the relic remained in the midst of the valley of solitude and wilderness.

The Bedouins of the land heard about the relic, for the wind and the sand carried the news to the desert. Soon everyone knew that whoever kissed the white stone of the Caaba could appear without fear in the presence of the Almighty. All sins are taken by the stone, upon itself. The Bedouins arrived in great caravans. Each one kissed the white stone and each one gave to it his sins. The stone carried many sins. They were large and heavy sins. The more their number mounted, the blacker the stone became. And the sins of mankind are so great and so numerous that the gleaming, white stone of the Almighty became jet black, black as the night, black as sin. But when the Day of the Last Judgment arrives, and the Almighty calls the just and the unjust to His throne, the stone will have two eyes. It will again become gleaming and white and, resting in the hands of the Almighty, it will give evidence for all those who, having had confidence in Him, confided their sins to it. So at least old legends tell.

About the Caaba extends the country of Hejaz, which means frontier. The country is bounded by the endless plains of Central Arabia and the territory of the ancient

and mighty kingdom of the Sabeans. Through the bare, fantastically formed mountains nature has fashioned two deep valleys. Through these valleys the caravans pass,
in a southerly direction by way of the coastal region of Tihamah to Yemen, and north-
west to Syria. Both ways cross at the Caaba, at the Makurabah, "the sanctuary" of
the country. Encircling the Makurabah, the city of Mecca was founded. The desert
people called the city of the Caaba "al-Munawwarah" – the shining one, "Umm-al-
Quva" – mother of cities, "al-Mushar-rafah" – the noble one. The proud emperor of
Iran had not deemed the city worthy of attack, so unimportant had it seemed to him.
But in the camps of the tents the Bedouins had many songs to sing of the power, the
beauty, and the wealth of the city of Mecca. For there was no other city like it in the
desert.

Caravans from foreign lands crossed each other in Mecca. Where caravans meet,
permanent buildings spring up. There the merchants live and flourish, there wealth
and power are born. And merchants began to settle in Mecca as well. They sent out
caravans through the desert, built large fortresses and accumulated riches. Mecca, the
capital of Arabia, was at the same time the commercial metropolis of the country.
But the merchants who lived in Mecca were Arabs, almost Bedouins still, and so the
city differed from all of the other trading cities of the world.

At that time many tribes competed for the leadership of Mecca. Bloody conflicts
ensued, for whoever ruled over Mecca could be sure of wealth. In the 5th century
A. D., the city of Mecca came into the hands of the tribe of the Quraish. Old, romantic legends tell of the crafty courage, of the wisdom and power of the great hero,
Qusayy, who founded the power of the Quraish in Mecca. Now, in the 6th century,
the lofty tribe of the Quraish had been split into a series of small tribes and families
who, but loosely joined together, shared the rule over Mecca. The mightiest, richest
and noblest of these families were the Umayyah.

Mecca was a remarkable city. Around the Caaba rose the houses and forts of the
individual families, one pressing close to the other. The richer, larger and more powerful the family was, the closer their houses and forts lay to the Caaba. According to
the custom of the desert, each family lived together in a fort. Each family obeyed no
one but the head of the family and thought itself an example of virtue if it undertook nothing that was harmful to its neighbours of other families. Each family carried
on its own business affairs, and it was only in cases where the chances of gain meant
large investments of capital that several families joined together for the duration of a
transaction.

Naturally, each merchant was also a warrior. At that time the merchant in Mecca
was nothing but a better sort of knight of the desert. Whoever could not protect his
wealth by means of his sword was soon a poor man. For this strange republic of desert
merchants knew nothing of law, government or central power. One lived in a fort,

obeyed the commands of the family elders and in return, like the Bedouin of the desert, was protected and defended by the family. For the same reason there were no courts, no jails, no punishments in Mecca. Important family members were safe-guarded by the family. However, if a Meccan committed too many transgressions he was banned from the family. The inhabitants of Mecca were nothing but Bedouins suddenly become rich, and they lost nothing of their previous primitive character because of the change.

Nevertheless, Mecca was a flourishing city, a city rich in trade which desired naught else but peace. But peace could only be assured if there was some feeling of solidarity. A council was formed, called "Mala'" which decided all questions concern-ing the entire city, its welfare and its wealth. From time to time, the elders of Mecca assembled in a special building not far from the Caaba, called "Dar-n-nadwah," where they discussed affairs. Every Meccan who had reached the age of forty had the right to attend these meetings. But this institution by no means implied that a democracy ruled in Mecca. Important decisions lay in the hands of the few Batha families, the families who lived in the district of Batha near the Caaba. These families were the bankers and merchants of Mecca. They lent money, sent out caravans, and led a life that was almost civilized in the style of the great men of the cultural worlds of the times.

In addition to the Ummayah there were the tribes of the Makhzum, the Naufal, the Asad, the Zuhrah and the Sahm. These families and their representatives, Abu Sufyan, Abu Jahl, Utbah and a few others were the leaders of the city by inheritance. Since ancient times, members of the noble Quraish tribe held the few official posi-tions there were, such as chiefs of the army, or leaders of the caravans.

Mecca was a merchant republic, created to increase the welfare of the Quraish families. It was like a great bank or a corporation in which the various stockholders might not agree with one another, but nevertheless they all were united in one desire, higher dividends. In addition to the small caravans which each merchant sent out at his own risk, two big trade caravans were assembled each year in which practically every Meccan participated. The caravans were made up of two or three thousand camels and were escorted by an army of from two to three hundred men. They were under way for six months and the profits were usually between fifty and one hundred per cent. Precious metals, pearls, spices, cosmetics, perfumes, weapons, slaves, in short everything that the old world had to sell came to Mecca, was stored there and ex-changed for leather, women, dates, and other products of the desert.

Mecca, the queen of the desert, had many attractions for the stranger. Year in and year out, endless caravans passed through its streets. The camels marched with soft, pensive tread, covered with the dust of the desert and their eyes filled with nostalgia for the steppes. Little bells hung from their necks and their tinkling sounded like the call of the desert. Gravely, the cameleers walked by their side, as calm, proud and silent as their camels. Their great bewildered eyes seemed to say, "This is Mecca, the queen of the desert." Innumerable camels stood about the large place of the Caaba, surrounded by a curious throng. The street urchins crept under the camels' bellies and through the slender labyrinth of their feet. The crowd was made of negros, Christians, Jews, slave dealers, prostitutes and magicians.

All languages and all faiths were represented in Mecca. Wine and women were the recompense of the caravan leader after his long journey. A fashionable merchant, dressed in silk with amber in his hair, steps out of the Caaba. With wise eyes he looks upon the motley crowd, upon the camels and the dust of the desert. Slowly the camels sink to their knees, their backs heavily laden. The merchant, perhaps he is of the Ummayah or the Asad, strokes his perfumed beard with his delicate, fine fingers. He issues instructions to the leader of his caravan. And again endless caravans wander through the streets of Mecca. The merchant returns to the Caaba. He must go to the money changer who determines the rate for Persian and Byzantine currency. He must discuss discounts with the Bank of Ummayah, or perhaps he wishes to visit a lady where, stretched out on a soft carpet, he will drink wine or talk of the latest Bedouin campaigns, and complain of the heat. If the merchant is very wealthy he owns a villa surrounded by date palms in the oasis of Ta'if. He will spend the summer months there. But the villa too must bring him an income and for this reason the dates from his villa are sold in the bazaars.

With amazement and wonderment, with almost mystical fear, a story was told in Mecca of a very rich Quraishite who owned a garden in Ta'if which he maintained merely for pleasure and without deriving any commercial profit from it. This moved the perfumed merchants more deeply than news of the bloodiest warfare of the people of the desert.

All Mecca flourished under the blessings of the great caravans. Yet still the city was surrounded by rocky deserts. No grass, no flowers grew there. Barren, crude rocks encircled the city. During the day, they took in the heat of the sun only to send out hot blasts over the city at night. Demonic lunar landscapes looked down upon the Caaba. A wise Arab once said, "Were it not for trade, not a single soul would live in Mecca." The negro el Haiqatan, a Himyarite poet, sang of Mecca, "If Mecca had any attractions to offer, Himyarite princes at the head of their armies would long since have hurried there. There winter and summer are equally desolate. No bird flies over Mecca, no grass grows. There are no wild beasts to be hunted. Only the most miserable of occupations flourishes there, trade."

Truly, trade did flourish and the Quraishite aristocrats prospered with it. Despite all the dreariness and hardships of their country, they possessed sufficient means and attractions to lure and hold the Bedouins within their walls during the times of the great markets. Obviously the nomad needed weapons, slaves and amber, but it was not impossible for him to procure them elsewhere, possibly even cheaper and better.

It was not trade only, then, that drew the Bedouins to Mecca. It was something else, an irresistible force which attracted them. For the Caaba stood in Mecca, the mystical sanctuary with its black stone. And the Quraishites knew how to profit by it.

Numerous festivities occurred each spring, at the time of the great market, in honour of the Caaba. Every Arab had sooner or later to come to Mecca, for these festivities were the most sensational events of the desert. And Mecca feared no competition.

To which god was the Caaba dedicated? The Arabs of the 6th century hardly knew. It was the supreme god of the Arabs, "II" or "Allahu ta'ala," the father of all gods and of all men, really the only true god. But among the Arabs belief in him had begun to pale. One had only the vaguest of recollections about him. Each tribe had its own god, and there was therefore little reason to bother about the great god of the Caaba, Allah. The name of the crafty Meccan, who succeeded in making the Caaba the religious centre of Arabia, was Amr ibn Luhayy.

It had been his idea to erect symbols of all the Arabian gods in the courtyard of the Caaba. Inasmuch as the god of each tribe was thus represented, it was possible for each tribe to worship its own divinity there. There were three hundred and sixty idols in the Caaba, and the fame of Mecca eclipsed that of all other cities. Flattered by the knowledge that its god was also there, each tribe travelled to Mecca when the time of the great peace had come. The great fair was the rendezvous of both idols and people. It took place upon the return of the great caravans. And simultaneously the solemn festivities set in, in honour of the three hundred and sixty gods, which were visited by all the tribes of the desert.

In questions of religion the Meccans were tolerant. Every idol meant more visitors, assured greater incomes to the inhabitants of Mecca. Next to the barbaric gods and goddesses of the Arabs, such as Hubal, al-Lat and al Uzza, stood statues of Christ, the Blessed Virgin and Moses, for there were tribes in the desert who had been converted to Judaism or Christianity. The Meccans themselves were fairly indifferent to all the gods. They were only too happy to offer everything that might make the market more successful.

In ancient times, human sacrifices were offered up in the courtyard of the Caaba. Later, human blood was replaced by that of a hundred camels.

The plan of Mecca was as follows. The Caaba stood in the centre. It was surrounded by all the gods, no matter who they were or where they came from. Around the gods sat the merchants who protected them. Every merchant had his fort-like habitation and these made up the city. On all sides was the vast desert, out of which poured the tribes during the sacred months to pray to their gods, envy the rich merchants, make purchases and spend their money. The only ones to profit by all this were the merchants. And for this reason they tried to avoid warfare and blood feuds and to maintain the pious, tolerant belief in three hundred and sixty gods, and possibly a few more.

The old Semitic spirit was revived in the narrow, crooked streets of Mecca during the sacred months. Processions of pious Bedouins went around the holy edifice seven times, and each one of them kissed the black stone. Racing between two ancient pillars, monuments to two half-forgotten Semitic symbols for man and woman, was an old custom. All that remained was the belief that the pillars had been a pair of lovers who, having violated the Caaba, had been punished by the gods by being changed into stone.

Bloody sacrifices without number were brought to the idols of the Caaba. The old Semitic gods, the cruel Moloch, the lascivious Astarte and the infamous Baal awakened to new life in their old home.

Persian and Greek girls wandered through the streets, goddesses of love attracted by the fame of Mecca. Orgies were held in the houses of the merchants where the women, native and strangers, showed themselves without veils, drank with the men, and gave their civilized, Persian-Byzantine favours to the ardent passion of the sons of the desert, hungry for love.

Mecca revelled in the frenzied throes of the great market, and a brutal joyous life was led amid the cruel, barbaric gods. Tournaments were held, goods were sold, and the buyers shamelessly cheated. A sort of primitive court sat permanently in the Caaba. Its members were the principal merchants of the city. Before it appeared those who wished to end some old, bloody conflict or prevent a new quarrel. Those who cared little for peace could announce in the courtyard of the Caaba that their tribe intended to attack and destroy such and such a tribe upon the expiration of the sacred months.

Thousands of soothsayers, prophets, magicians and doctors strolled about the courtyard. They were prepared, for a small fee, to predict the outcome of the conflict which had been announced, or to call down the wrath of the gods upon the tribe of the opponents.

Slaves, women and camels were bought and sold. Love affairs were started and broken. There were games of all sorts, singing, and throwing of dice. Huge bonfires were started and games of chance lasted all through the night. Whoever had lost all but his freedom (and one could lose that as well at dice), was cared for by the city fathers free of charge, lest he might despair and start trouble.

All the poets of Arabia assembled during the sacred months to take part in the poetical tournaments which took place in the Caaba. For days on end they sang of their tribe in well-rounded verses, of their beloved, or of the carefree existence of the desert. Stinging epigrams were composed with lightning-like rapidity which inflamed the tribes to new feuds. The victor in the tournament was given princely honours. His poems were embroidered in letters of gold on black cloths which hung for a year at the entrance to the Caaba. Now and again poetry was used for purely business reasons. The poor father of many homely daughters could commission a poet to sing of the beauty of his daughters in all of the bazaars of the city. If the poet was talented, the father was able to get rid of his daughters before the fair was over.

The revelry lasted day and night. But one had to take care not to participate unarmed. Strangers were attacked and robbed in the narrow, quiet, dark streets. This caused but little stir, for everyone was occupied with his own amusement. It was only when the victim happened to be a famous poet that one would hear of the incident in the "Arabian press."

The city of Mecca was joyous, brutal, alive, barbaric and rich. Here Mohammed was born, Mohammed, the Messenger of God.

This occurred on 29 August in the year A. D. 570, in the fortieth year of the reign of the great Emperor Khosrau Anu-shirvan and in the year 880 of the Seleucidaean era.

II.

THE MISSION

Arabia was a nothing, not country, not state, not culture.

Overnight a world emerged out of this nothing.

This world extended from Morocco to the Indies and it has

    not yet disappeared.

The world out of the nothing was fathered by the Spirit.

The Spirit was Mohammed.

THE BIRTH OF THE PROPHET

> I place him under the protection of the Only
> One, that he will protect him against the evil of
> the envious, and I call him Mohammed.
>
> *Aminah, mother of the Prophet*

I n the land of Yemen, in the south of Arabia, ruled the tyrant Abraha, the viceroy of the Negus Negasti, the Christian emperor of Abyssinia. His soul was as black as his body. He was filled with great envy.

A great distance separated Mecca from Yemen, and Mecca was rich. People made pilgrimages to the gods of the Caaba and no one paid any attention to the glorious city of San'a, the residence of Abraha. So Abraha built a magnificent church with walls of marble and cupolas of gold. Nowhere in Arabia had one ever seen such a marvel. In the future, he thought, the Arabs would journey to San'a and not to the Caaba. But the people of the desert laughed at the envious Abraha, for they wished to remain faithful to their Caaba. They mocked him and wished to show him their ridicule. A young Meccan came to San'a and acted as if he were overcome with the beauty of the church. "Let me into the church, Abraha," he said, "and I will spend the entire night there in prayer." When the night came, the Meccan profaned the church and fled. Abraha was beside himself with rage. He collected a mighty army, at the head of which, seated on a large white elephant, he rode towards Mecca to destroy the city. The army of Mecca had never seen an elephant and fled in terror. The people of Mecca, however, said, "The Caaba does not belong to us, but to God. Ours are the camels, the sheep and the gold. We must rescue our property, for God can take care of his." They took their possessions and retired to the hills near Mecca. Only a few warriors remained in the city. Riding on his great white elephant Abraha appeared before the walls of Mecca and began to besiege it. Mecca seemed doomed. A miracle happened. From the direction of the sea, thousands of swallows appeared and covered the heavens. Each swallow carried three stones, one in its beak and two in its claws. Thousands of stones fell upon the army of Abraha and panic broke out in its ranks. Warriors fled, tents were destroyed and the big white elephant knelt down before the Caaba. A death-dealing desert wind annihilated the army. Abraha retreated with the remainder of his followers to San'a where his end was obscure and miserable. Thus did God shield His house, the Caaba.

The Meccans called the year of the miracle, 570, the "Year of the White Elephant."

The same year, the Prophet Mohammed was born at Mecca. His full name was Mohammed ibn Abdallah, ibn Abdalmuttalib, ibn Hashim, the Quraishite. When Qusayy, the legendary founder of the Quraish fortunes died, he left a son, Abd al-Maraf. He it was who ruled in Mecca. Among his sons was one named Hashim, who married a woman from Yathrib and founded the tribe of the Hashemites, which was that of the Prophet. At one time the tribe was rich and powerful. Part of its inheritance was the wells of Zamzam, near Mecca, which God had once disclosed to the thirsty Hagar and her son Ishmael. The tribe had been renowned for its liberality in giving alms. But of all this, nothing certain is known. We do know that at the time when the Prophet appeared, the tribe was neither rich nor held in great esteem. Mohammed's grandfather, Abd al-Muttalib, was said to have been the last great man of his tribe. It was also said that he ruined himself by his generosity to others, which at first did not harm his reputation. In the eyes of the Arabs it was more important that he had no sons. This showed that he was not in God's favour. Thereupon, Abd al-Muttalib swore that if twelve sons were born to him, he would sacrifice one to the Caaba. Twelve sons were born in succession and he took one of them, Abdallah, to the Caaba. At the moment that he lifted his knife, a voice was heard from heaven commanding him not to slay his son, and to sacrifice a hundred camels in his stead. And so it happened that Abdallah remained alive and married a woman called Aminah, who in the Year of the Elephant bore him a son named Mohammed, which means, *He who is Praised.*

So much for the pious legend. No one knows how much of it is true. We do know that the army of Abraha actually set out towards Mecca and that it was destroyed by an epidemic of smallpox. We also know that at the same time a man named Abdallah which means no more than *Slave of God*, who belonged to the impoverished tribe of the Hashim, had a son whose name was Mohammed.

Many pious legends surround the birth of the Prophet. Great joy reigned among the heavenly angels on the night of his birth. The birth of the Prophet was being celebrated in the celestial regions. The spirits of darkness, the demons and the jinn noticed that there was festivity in heaven but no one could explain the reason for it. Sneaking to the gates of heaven, the evil spirits sought to learn the secret of the heavenly powers. But they were not to succeed, for the archangels appeared at the heavenly gates and threw burning torches at the evil ones. Men saw it and called them falling stars. But the sages knew that whenever a star fell from heaven, the angels, with torch in hand, were driving the evil spirits away. In the night Mohammed was born the eternal fire, which had burned in Persia for hundreds of years, went out. The land was visited by an earthquake. The palace of Khosrau in Ctesiphon collapsed and only fourteen of its pillars remained standing. This was the number of infidel rulers who were to rule Iran until the true faith conquered. Countless were the miracles which occurred on the night of his birth.

And yet it was only a poor child who was born in a lowly house in Mecca, which had been visited by disaster two months before his birth. On a trip to Yathrib through the desert, Mohammed's father, Abdallah, had died, and his son's inheritance was a meagre one. It consisted of a little house, five hungry camels, and an old slave.

We know that Mecca lay in an arid valley, surrounded by torrid rocks. The streets were narrow and piled high with filth. The air was heavy in Mecca, and the children there grew up pale, weak, and sickly. All about Mecca was desert. The air of the desert was limpid and its people were noble, chivalrous and robust. To call oneself an Arab in the true sense of the word meant that one had breathed the air of the desert. For this reason, it was customary in Mecca to place the suckling babes in the care of a Bedouin tribe. Together with the milk of a Bedouin woman, they drank in the laws of the desert and the free, chivalrous thinking of the Bedouins. In the desert one became an Arab.

Twice a year, tribes came to Mecca seeking such babies, for they were much sought after in the desert. The parents gave presents to the wet-nurse and her family, and in addition, the bonds of milk-relationship with a noble Quraish tribe might always prove useful to a Bedouin.

In the year of Mohammed's birth, people of the tribe of Banu Sa'd came to Mecca, but no one wished to have Mohammed. His family seemed to be too poor to make it worthwhile for anyone to take the orphan. When all of the tribe of Sa'd had been given foster-children and were on their way home, a poor woman by the name of Halimah who had not been given a charge decided to take the boy with her.

And so Mohammed came to the desert, to the tribe of Sa'd, where he was to receive mother's milk for a period of two years according to the practice of the Bedouins.

Yellow sand, sterile steppes, the arid domain of the poorest of the tribes, small black tents, camel's milk, Bedouins, and a vision of eternity which began at the flaps of the tents, these were the first things to present themselves to Mohammed's eyes.

The Sa'd were pure Bedouin, and so it was that the first thing which the ears of the Prophet heard were long, wise discussions about the force of the word and of the finely turned phrase of the finest of all languages.

The life of a poor tribe is rude, brutal and filled with danger, and the children, too, are confronted with these dangers. But Mohammed did not belong to the Sa'd, for he was a noble Quraish. Behind him stood the great city of Mecca which he only knew from stories he had heard. His first impressions were the desert, the infinite with all its dangers, and the deeply rooted consciousness that if things came to the worst, he was certain of mighty protection far, far away on the other side of the steppes. For the Sa'd, too, he was a chosen one, a person who, thanks to his birth, belonged to the queen of cities, to the powerful Quraishites. And so the child Mohammed was only vaguely aware of the infinite, the fear of danger, the protection of an unknown hand, and the feeling that he stood above the other helpless members of the tribe of Sa'd.

It was customary for the foster-children to return to their families when they were two years old. But the Sa'd begged that they might keep Mohammed for another year for he had brought them luck. The nomads, too, have many legends about the life of the Prophet. Sheep bowed down before him when he passed, the moon came down to him, grass grew on the spots where he had stood. There is a lovely legend connected with the Prophet's sojourn in the desert. Once, when he was four years of age, he was playing with his foster-brother, Masruh, on the edge of the desert. Suddenly two angels appeared, Gabriel and Michael, garbed in gleaming robes of white, and gently laid the boy on the ground and opened his breast. They took out his heart, cleaned it on all sides and pressed out the drop of original sin which every person since Adam carries in himself. So they prepared him for his future mission.

Mohammed was four when he was brought back to his mother from the desert, and he was six when his mother, Aminah, died.

Mohammed was left behind, poor and abandoned. His mother had died near Yathrib, and there was no one in the desert who wished to bother with him. Finally the old slave, Barakah, brought him to his grandfather, Abd al-Muttalib, who lived in the lovely city of Mecca. Here Mohammed lived as the youngest and poorest among the Hashim. Abd al-Muttalib had grown old and feeble and he did not know that a prophet was growing up among them. However, before his death he thought of Mohammed and ordered his son, Abu Talib, who was now to rule over the Hashim, to take care of the child.

Abu Talib was also poor and blessed with many children. He took his nephew into his house, gave him food and drink but was unable to do more for him. As master of the Hashim, Abu Talib carried on trade and travelled with his caravans to Syria and Yemen. On these occasions Mohammed remained behind, alone in Mecca. Once, when Abu Talib was again preparing his caravan, Mohammed approached him, and nestling close to him said, "Take me along, O Abu Talib, for there is no one in Mecca who will look out for me." Abu Talib granted his request, and Mohammed the Prophet was taken along as a cameleer into the desert of Syria, into the desolation of Iraq. Endlessly, the caravan wandered across the steppes, passing through the great country, and among the people of the Emperor of Byzantium and the holy monks who sought out their salvation in the desert.

A number of times Mohammed and his uncle travelled through the world between Syria and Yemen. Then the caravan returned to Mecca. Mohammed grew up and continued to remain with his uncle, as the poorest of the Hashim. Then war came, a typical Bedouin war. The tribe of Kinanah, relatives of the Quraishites, had been attacked. The rich merchants did not hesitate for a moment to set out in the field to defend their blood-brothers. Mohammed, at the age of sixteen, accompanied them as a carrier of arrows for the Hashemites. Returning from the campaign, he joined a Meccan association whose purpose it was to maintain the honour of the merchants of Mecca.

His success as a merchant was far from extraordinary. On the contrary, business was poor and one day Abu Talib was forced to place his nephew in the service of some rich Meccans as a shepherd. Mohammed pastured his flock outside the gates of Mecca and received but meagre wages. Later on he became a petty merchant, but this, too, brought him but little profit. On the other hand, he gradually earned the reputation among the Meccans of being an honest and just man, a merchant on whose word one could always rely. This accounted for his being called al-Amin, which means, the Reliable.

In the merchant city of Mecca, reliability was counted as the greatest virtue of man. Whoever possessed it did not have to go hungry. Influential people soon began to take an interest in the honest youth. When in his twenty-fifth year a period of poverty set in, he was offered the post of superintendent in the house of the rich widow, Khadijah. Upon the advice of his uncle, he accepted.

So the Prophet of God became a travelling merchant who led strange caravans through the world, bought goods and sold them, and acquired riches.

KHADIJAH

The caravan passes through the desert. Twenty, thirty camels majestically follow one another. Their eyes are sadly proud, their steps are rhythmic peace. Steadily and without emotion the camels advance, but if the cameleer carelessly comes too close to the leading camel, it will stretch out its neck and bite him cruelly. The camel is dangerous, cunning and brutal. It is like the desert, like the world through which it passes. A young man sits on the back of the first camel. He wears a silken turban and is carefully dressed. His eyes are painted with aromatic oil so that they will not be harmed by the heat of the desert. The young man is twenty-five years of age, and his beard, the pride of the Arab, is still very short. His face is grave. The camels are heavily laden and it will be the young man's task to see that their burdens become heavier still. The eyes of the young man are dark and sombre. His hands are as soft as those of a scholar and his mouth is like a stripe of blood across his face.

Hours pass. The young man gazes into the distance. Here again, he is first among all the others, and again the unseen city of Mecca protects him from afar. But who protects the people of Mecca? The young man does not know. Unerringly he leads the caravan. He sells his goods, argues with crafty dealers, buys wisely and so increases the wealth of his mistress.

Again the desert, the camels, the lonesome hours and the lonesome thoughts. What does the man of the desert think about? About the eternity of the sand, the infinity of the heavens and the invisible powers which reign over both. He thinks of God. Thoughts about God and religious problems were very popular in the world which spread itself before Mohammed. God held the place occupied by politics today. Everyone thought about the divine power and everyone opposed the thoughts of his neighbour. Mohammed's caravan passed through Yemen and Syria. In both countries, God was the real problem. The sole discussions in the bazaars, in the churches, in the baths and gardens, were about God. The sectarians preached in the open places, praising the truth of their faith and condemning the heresy of others. Monophysites, monophilites, Gregorians, Copts, Christians, Nestorians, Jews of all kinds, fought with and among each other. They all referred to one thing, God's revelation, the Bible, which was the same for all but interpreted by each in his own manner. Even those who travelled peacefully with their caravans through desert and cities were drawn into these conflicts of faith. In the bazaars they were surrounded by fanatic preachers. In the desert, they were met by ascetics who questioned them about their religious thoughts, swore that the world was soon to come to an end, and quoted holy revelation. In short, everything turned on religion.

The young stranger from Mecca knew that religion could be the focal point of many interests. The great city of the desert was built around a sanctuary. The wealth of the city rose with the number of its gods. Even in the great courtyard of the Caaba discussions were held about the gods, and the tribes disputed over the power of Hubal, al-Lat and al-Uzza. Christians and Jews came as well, boasted of the revelations they had received from God, and preached their faiths. These discussions were very welcome to the merchants of Mecca, for they made the city more famous than it already was.

But the merchants themselves had but little faith in the publicity idols of their gods. The old religion was dead. All that remained was advertisement, meaningless ceremony, outmoded ritual, nonsense and barbarity. Many in Mecca felt this, many knew it to be so. The gods who reigned in Mecca were dead. But inasmuch as these gods meant wealth to the city, they were not to be offended. The merchants were definite and decided about that. Whoever felt the urge for the true faith and sought the divine truth, left Mecca. These seekers after God were numerous, but it did not disturb the Meccans. One could seek one's salvation where one chose, but the pillars of Mecca's wealth were not to be shaken. These seekers after God, called *hanifs*, were disregarded with respectful irony.

Nor was the truth to be found outside Mecca. In Syria, Palestine, Egypt, and in most of the neighbouring countries of Arabia, the Christians were in bitter strife. The simple soul of the man of Mecca intent upon finding God, could not find itself in all the confusion. The Christians, the Jews, the sectarians, could not bring peace of mind to most of the Arabs. The *hanifs* wandered through the desert, read divine scriptures and were plagued with scruples. Nearly all of them condemned the dead gods of Mecca. Nearly all of them remembered a great, mighty godhead called Allah, who had once ruled over the people of Arabia. No one knew the way to this divinity, for the monotheism of the Arabs lay dead, buried in thousand-year-old legends. The passionate faith of the *hanifs* was turned towards the old, great god, Allah. But none among them dared to resurrect him. ... Restless, decrepit old men, they wandered through the desert, and the people of the desert looked upon them either as insane or saints.

Mohammed, the Hashemite, saw and experienced all this during his long rides. He, too, knew that the gods of the Caaba were dead, and the reason why they were still worshipped. He, too, knew that there were revelations, that the world fought over them, and that they must have come from a mighty, holy god. The eyes of the Hashemite took it all in: desert, infinity, and men who fought about the truth. But Mohammed was young, and the burdens the camels bore heavy. It was his duty constantly to increase the revenue of his mistress. Khadijah paid him two young cows and this was considered a good wage.

In everyday life, Mohammed was both able and experienced. Day after day, he dealt with the merchants and increased his gains, all of which sharpened his wits. For three years he travelled with the camels of Khadijah, and there were but few managers who combined honesty with success in a like manner. The wealth of Khadijah grew, and with it the reputation of her twenty-eight-year-old manager. But Mohammed's fortune did not increase. He was still unmarried and childless which meant, according to the Arabs, "a man without a tail."

Suddenly, unexpected good fortune came to Mohammed.

Historians know but little about the past of the widow Khadijah, the daughter of Khuwailid, of the tribe of the Quraish. Apparently there was little to tell of her. She had been twice widowed, was rich, no longer young, and belonged to the noblest of tribes, the Quraish. Like all the others in Mecca, she too carried on a business, lived a retired life, collected wealth and longed for happiness. From the corner window of her house she could see her young manager and cameleer enter in with his goods. Mohammed was young and handsome. He won her heart. Many men had wooed Khadijah, but there were but few in Mecca who could equal Mohammed's virtues and personal appearance.

One day, Maisarah, a slave belonging to Khadijah, appeared before Mohammed. "Why do you not marry?" he asked. "At your age all men have at least one wife and several children." And Mohammed replied as most men in his condition would have replied, "I earn enough money to support myself. But my income is not enough for wife and child." "But if a woman could be found who was rich herself, and beautiful, and noble as well?" asked the slave. "There are no more such women," Mohammed answered carefully.

The day after, Khadijah in person came to Mohammed and said, "Mohammed, I love you because of your loyalty, because of your honesty and your good life. You are in good repute among the people, and you, like myself, belong to the noble tribe of the Quraish. I would like to be your wife." And Mohammed accepted her proposal.

Thereupon followed scenes, truly grotesque, in Arabian fashion. The marriage with her poor manager was obviously a misalliance for Khadijah. It was not to be expected that her father would give his consent.

Khadijah arranged a banquet to which Mohammed and the leaders of the Hashemites were invited. In the seat of honour sat Khuwailid, the father of Khadijah.

He was old and given to drink. Khadijah filled glass after glass for her father, and he emptied each in succession, gladly and thankfully. After a while, beautiful slaves appeared, who danced for the old man and played cymbals, so that he was in excellent spirits. But when the head of the old man began to sink upon his breast and his hands began to tremble, Khadijah ordered that a wedding garment be brought in. Abu Talib, the eldest among the Hashemites, began to praise the virtues of his nephew in flowery language, and begged for the hand of Khadijah for the lowly price of a few camels.

The old man did not understand much of the speech. When it had come to an end, Khadijah made her father straighten up, stretched out his hands in front of him and made him give the paternal blessing. According to custom, a camel was slaughtered for the poor and a slightly intoxicated uncle of some sort mumbled the marriage formula. The next day, when Khadijah's father learned the humiliating truth, he at first wished to declare a blood-feud against his son-in-law and the entire tribe of the Hashim. It was only with difficulty that his anger was appeased.

And so Mohammed married Khadijah.

The marriage lasted for many years, and up to the time of her death Khadijah never once regretted that she had chosen the poor cameleer from the tribe of the Hashim.

MOHAMMED'S GOOD FORTUNE

I am but a man like you.
Mohammed

Through his marriage, Mohammed became a member of Mecca's highest aristocracy. His prestige grew. He was happy. He went about his business quietly, frequented the courtyard of the Caaba from time to time, and led the life of a well-situated, happily married merchant. We have already said that Khadijah had no cause to regret her choice. During the twenty-four years of his married life, Mohammed was an exemplary husband. Time passed by tranquilly and without incident. Throughout the city one spoke of the well-groomed appearance, the pleasant manner, the righteousness, the God fearing bearing, of Mohammed. He once said of himself, "Agreeable scents, women and, above all else, prayer are the most beautiful things on this earth."

Then, as later on, he took great pride in his unusual virility, which made him popular among all the tribes of the country. The pious sages of Arabia said reverently, "God gave him the seed of thirty men." The Orientals knew no better proof of God's favour. In later years, Mohammed had many opportunities of proving his manly prowess. It is the more astonishing, therefore, that he who was the most manly of all the Arabs, remained scrupulously faithful to a wife many years older than himself, as long as she lived.

His was the straight and narrow path and none could find the slightest fault with him. It was from the circle of his closest friends, who knew every intimate detail of his life, that the warmest and the most faithful of his adherents were recruited for his future mission.

Pleasant scents were Mohammed's joy. He constantly used all the perfumes of the Orient, amber, musk, pomades, salves and hair oils. At night, Mohammed anointed his eyes to heighten their brilliance and to increase their power. His black, perfumed hair hung down over his shoulders in two braids. A turban of silk was elegantly wound around his head. He washed himself several times a day, constantly chewed a piece of wood to keep his teeth snowy white, and wore a full beard. His features were accentuated, his complexion a yellowish brown, and he was sensitive to odours of every kind. For example, he was annoyed if anyone ate onions or garlic in his presence. Thus was Mohammed before his mission, and so he remained until the end of his life. One of the chief characteristics of Islam was a delight in the body, in strength and in beauty. The ascetics and Christian penitents who condemned the flesh and the pleasures of the flesh were deeply hated by Mohammed. They were like spirits from another world and he could not understand them.

Nevertheless, this elegant, fastidious, rich gentleman who apparently abandoned himself to the pleasures of life was serious to the point of austerity. It was not merely chance that in addition to scents and women he also preferred prayer.

When he was forty, Mohammed began to attend the council of Mecca and the assemblies which took place in the Caaba. There he was looked upon as reliable and just, even though he was a man of but few words. The gift of facile speech, the polished phrase, the art of poetry so valued by the Arabs were apparently not his. On the other hand, one could always count on his sense of justice. If a dispute arose among the merchants, if anyone felt himself injured or abused, Mohammed was called. Gravely and objectively he judged the cause and gave his decision.

He was not too pious a devotee of the gods of the Caaba, but that was not to be expected of a Meccan merchant. Like all the rest, he appeared at the usual ceremonies and spoke the usual prayers. He preferred to wander through the fields around Mecca, alone, lost in thought, and possibly in prayer. Because of his good reputation, none chided him for this. Mecca was unusually tolerant in such matters.

Even at that time Mohammed had one strong antipathy. He hated the prophets, the magicians and the soothsayers who constantly paraded about in the courtyard of the Caaba. But after all, that was his personal affair, for no one was obliged to believe in necromancy. That is, with the possible exception of the wild, superstitious Bedouins.

In society, Mohammed was always pleasant and friendly. Whoever did him a service could count on his gratitude. When his uncle, Abu Talib, was in need, Mohammed adopted his son, Ali, and kept him in his own house. Ali was a handsome youth, rather simple, but courageous, noble and enthusiastic. A great future was his, for he was to be the fourth Caliph of Islam.

In the summer, when the heat of Mecca became unbearable, Mohammed withdrew to Ta'if like other fashionable Meccans, or put up his tent near Mount Hirah, whose valleys were always cool. Mohammed loved the bald mountain so close to Mecca, for one could see the wild, rude landscape from its summits, and the gardens of Ta'if in the distance. Even when his family had returned to Mecca, Mohammed preferred to revisit the caves of Hirah.

So Mohammed lived until the time of his mission. Peaceful, unobtrusive, tranquil was his life; simple, honest, unobtrusive were his deeds. He was a man like all the others. Mohammed never failed to stress this throughout the rest of his life.

The idea of immortality was unknown to the Arab. He replaced it with an earthly succession through the creation of a new branch on the tree of his tribe. Mohammed wanted children, and Khadijah bore them for him, three sons and three daughters. Mohammed's measure of happiness was filled to the last drop. He offered great gifts to the gods. Qasim, Abd Manaf and Atakhair were the names of his sons. This shows best how little Mohammed was given to religious scruples, for Abd Manaf means "The slave of Manaf," and Manaf was a prominent idol in the Caaba. According to Arabian custom, Mohammed called himself Abu'l-Qasim, which means, "father of Qasim."

Filth lay upon the streets of Mecca and men were surrounded by evil spirits. Sickness and death nested in the narrow byways. Year after year, many children died in Mecca and among them were the three sons of the Prophet.

Again Mohammed was a "man without a tail," a man without immortality, a man who could not live on in others. Despite his loss, Mohammed remained calm. It was probably the greatest sorrow of his life, and possibly the impetus for his spiritual transformation.

Gradually, almost unnoticeably, Mohammed's mode of life began to change. His usual high spirits left him. His appearances in the great courtyard of the Caaba became fewer and fewer, and fewer and fewer his offerings to the gods. But this did not attract attention. To the eyes of the stranger, Abu'l-Qasim, Mohammed al-Amin, the Hashemite, was still a happy citizen. Though his own sons had died, he had adopted the son of his uncle. His oldest daughter was married to a capable man, and his second daughter was engaged. Hi wealth increased steadily. There was obviously no reason to believe that Mohammed had fallen a prey to despair.

And yet there was a visible change. The conscientious and able merchant suddenly did something that no Meccan before or after him had ever done: he began to neglect his business. He ceased earning money. Instead of making his appearance in the bazaars, to bargain about prices or to send out caravans, he wandered about in the vicinity of Mecca, neglected his companions and appeared to have succumbed to an internal unrest. Often he was seen wandering through the countryside with feverish eyes and sunken cheeks. He was a rare guest in his own palatial house situated at the northern end of the Caaba. Something was happening inside him, yet he could tell no one the reason for the change. Perhaps he himself did not know what it was. But one thing he did know: the greed for money, the empty life of Mecca, the faith of his fellowmen no longer satisfied him. He sought a higher aim, spiritual peace. The Meccans respected this. Even Khadijah, for whom the change in Mohammed had come unexpectedly, did not think she had the right to stand in the way of her husband who had given her so much happiness throughout the years. She left him alone, perhaps hoping that he might some day find himself again. The desire for solitude and religious introspection was nothing new to Mecca. One knew these feelings of inner emptiness, of religious unrest which from time to time befell the wisest men of the city. The time spent in solitude was called "the months of penance," and one thought nothing of these phenomena of the soul. At first Khadijah, too, saw no cause for anxiety.

It was on Mount Hirah, in the eastern part of the city, that one met with Mohammed most frequently. It was from there that one had an unobstructed view of Mecca, of the stony desert and the endless steppes. The mountain had many caverns, and at the entrance to one or the other one could see Mohammed, crouched down and speechless in profound meditation. When his daughters brought him food, he paid no attention to them. He stared into the distance. The shadow of Mount Hirah covered him.

Occasionally the merchants of Mecca passed by him. Thoughtlessly they glanced his way and said with indifference, "Our Mohammed has joined the *hanifs*."

IQRA'

Stand up, O Prophet – see and listen – announce me from place to place. And wandering over land and sea, enflame all hearts with the Word.

Pushkin

What did Mohammed see in the desert? It was not empty of men. Mohammed was not the only one to seek deliverance from earthly misery amid the barren rocks and the eternal, grey country near Mecca. Like him, many *hanifs* wandered about. Robed in wide mantles, they sat in the shadow of the rocks. They meditated over the eternal truth, read old strange books and prayed to an unknown God. Mohammed met them, talked with them, heard their doubts, and read with them the ancient writings. But he did not find the truth for it was no more disclosed to the *hanifs* than it was to himself.

"Did I but know, O Lord of the World, how to pray to thee, gladly would I do so," spoke Sa'id ibn Amr, the unhappiest of the *hanifs*. And others like Ubaidallah, Umar, Ummayah, could do nothing but speak of their doubts to Mohammed. The world lay before them full of suffering and sin, governed by countless gods. Man trod the short path from cradle to grave in filth and misery, without faith and truth. When the heart of a *hanif* was filled with despair, he had recourse in a refuge old as the world, song. But the songs were banal and of the earth, for the truth was unknown. "They were stuck to the earth," the Koran says of them.

The most important of the *hanifs* was blind, old Waraqah ibn Naufal, a cousin of Khadijah, who from his youth had sought God and had not found him. Waraqah had confessed all faiths, read all the books, and prayed to all the gods. But he had never found the truth. He had been a heathen, then a Jew and then a Christian. He was the first to translate parts of the Holy Scripture into the language of the Arabs. Towards the end of his life he knew but one thing and that was that some man would discover the truth. Who the man was or when he would come, Waraqah did not know. It was through him that Mohammed learned of the Bible of the Jews and of the Christians, of the belief in the prophets and despair at human enigmas.

Mohammed's heart became more and more obscure. Grey was the world before him, and steel blue the heavens. There was no truth between them. Without ceasing, Mohammed roamed from mountain to valley. His clothes were torn. There was nothing left of the elegant merchant of Mecca. His hair was unkempt, his gait halting, and he stared about him with big, crazed eyes. For days at a time he went without food. Whoever saw him thought that things went badly with the husband of Khadijah. No one knew what had happened to him, and he himself knew least of all. He was nothing but a simple, uneducated tradesman without the gift of words. He could not say what misery drove him through the desert nor what miracle he sought. Night and day he hid in dark holes in Mount Hirah.

Around him lay the fantastic country of Hejaz. Pointed rocks glowed in the eternal sun, and at twilight they gleamed in all the colours of the rainbow. The dry, clear air opened up wide, infinite horizons. From a mountain top Mohammed saw the great sands of the world, saw the shepherds pasturing their flocks, saw the tribes go off into the distance on their majestic camels, and saw the sharp contrast, almost without transition, of night following day. For months Mohammed did not speak. No person, no living thing crossed his path. He saw nothing but stones, rocks, sand and, through the dry, desert air, the eternal stars which seemed quite close.

Slowly the inanimate world, the stones, the rocks and gorges began to come to life. In the still nights and in the endless, hot days, the stones began to speak. Mohammed fled from them but they followed him. He heard howling and calling, the stones and rocks were turned into voices, and the voices closed in around him. He covered his face and threw himself upon the ground. His body began to tremble. Foam appeared upon his quivering lips, for he heard voices that were not human. Sweat covered his brow and he seemed paralysed. Cowering close to the ground, he sat in his cave. His eyes stared into the distance and they saw neither rocks, sand nor heavens. Perhaps they saw far off symbols like those employed by the peoples of the Bible, perhaps it was a flame, the flame which replaces all images of God for the Jewish people. Old scenes, half-remembered memories of wise monks, of caravan journeys, and the discourse of countless sectarians appeared and disappeared. And again it was day. Again the stones glowed in the sun, and again voices wild and terrible, strange and terrifying, filled Mohammed's ears. Again he ran through the desert, hid his face in his hands, and stumbled over the stones. Renewed came the distant, thunderous call. Incomprehensible sentences, voices and visions came to him. Exhausted, Mohammed sank to the ground, looked at the rocks, shuddered and heard, carried by the dry air, the same tones and words, "I am He who is here; listen to me."

Image and thought became confused in the torrid air of the desert. Heaven and earth were filled with visions, and like the distant sound of waves, like the whirling of the winds, a mysterious voice seemed to caress Mohammed, "You are the chosen one, proclaim the name of the Lord." Numerous are the voices of the desert, countless the eyes that pierce man. Demons, jinn, evil spirits, pursue man in the desert, and no one knows which tone, which voice, which aspect, the evil one assumes. Mohammed was a simple man, an uneducated merchant of Mecca. He could not discriminate between the voices. He only knew that man is surrounded by many demons who try to ensnare him. And so he thought that he was possessed, one of those who wander through the bazaars, proclaiming evil truths with foaming mouths, and unable to loose themselves from the earth.

Mohammed had always hated magicians, soothsayers and those who were possessed. Now he was afraid that he himself had fallen under the spell of a demon. "All my life I have abhorred the magicians and conjurers, and now I fear lest I become one myself," he said to Khadijah. But he did not know which demon pursued him.

He was afraid of being possessed, afraid of the terrible madness of the desert. And so he fled through the desert, staggered as if intoxicated, stared like a madman with fierce, unseeing eyes, sought refuge and found it not. He sank to the earth, his body covered with sweat, quivering and trembling. Days, weeks and months passed by in misery and anguish.

Then came the night el Qadr – suddenly, unexpectedly and terrifyingly.

What is the night el Qadr?

When the Oriental speaks of pious miracles, of the special grace of God, of the blessed who may look at the world through God's fingers, he says that such a thing is only possible in the night el Qadr, in the great night of miracles. The night el Qadr is in the month of Ramadan, the month of fasting and penance. Ramadan has thirty nights, but no one knows which the night el Qadr is. In that night, nature falls asleep. The streams cease to flow, the winds are still and the evil spirits forget to watch over the wonders of the earth. In the night el Qadr, one can hear the grass grow and the trees speak. Nymphs arise out of the depths, and the sands of the desert lie in deep slumber. Those who experience the night el Qadr become sages or saints, for in this night man may see through the fingers of God.

In the night el Qadr, in the month of Ramadan, the Word of God came over Mohammed.

Exhausted by the voices, by the tricks of the evil one, and worn out by misery, suffering and despair, on this night Mohammed lay at the entrance to a cave hewn out by the sword of Satan, on Mount Hirah. He slept or perhaps he was deep in thought. Suddenly he saw a vision. Its outlines were not clear. A man? A demon? A being? It seemed as if two eyes of the size of heaven pierced through him and he heard a voice, as distinct and clear as any he had ever heard, say "Iqra" – "recite." And as the voice was clear and easily understood, and had nothing terrifying about it, Mohammed answered truthfully, "I cannot recite." Unseen hands grasped him, threw him to the ground and began to choke him so that Mohammed thought he would suffocate. And again the voice commanded, "Recite." In deathly fear, Mohammed answered, "What shall I recite?" Then the vision spread out a great cloth before the eyes of the prophet and in fiery letters Mohammed read the first lines of the Koran:

> "In the name of the merciful and compassionate God. READ, in the name of thy Lord! Who created man from congealed blood! Read, for thy Lord is most generous! Who taught the pen! Taught man what he did not know!"*

Suddenly the vision disappeared and all was silent about Mohammed. Night lay over him and the desert slept, like the world in the night el Qadr.

Mohammed arose, stepped out of the cave and climbed to the top of the mountain. He saw the stars of Arabia, the fantastic pointed rocks and the city of Mecca with its house of God, the Caaba. And again a voice, like the faintest stirring of the desert wind, came to his ear and spoke: "Thou art the messenger of God, O Mohammed, and I am Gabriel, His archangel." Then the voice was silent. Two great eyes looked at him. Mohammed looked to the right and to the left, up and down, and all round him was the piercing glance of the archangel. Dizzily Mohammed ran down the mountains, sharp stones scratched his legs and the dry stumps of the desert wounded his feet. He felt nothing. Like a madman, like one pursued, he ran through the rocky ravines. Until noon of the next day he roamed through the valley and always the eyes of Gabriel followed him.

Exhausted, Mohammed returned home and calling Khadijah told her all that had happened. "I do not know," he said, "if it is a good spirit or a demon which pursues me." Khadijah was wise and wished to help her husband. "Sit down upon my left knee," she said to him, "do you still see the spirit?" "Yes," answered Mohammed. "Sit down upon my right knee," she commanded. "I still see him," replied Mohammed. Thereupon Khadijah sighed, disrobed herself and pressed Mohammed closely to her flesh. "Do you still see him?" she asked. "I no longer see him," said Mohammed. "Then, O Mohammed, it is a good spirit, for an evil spirit would rejoice at seeing us thus, whereas a good spirit would retire in shame."

Since Mohammed was a man, he was comforted by the words of Khadijah, and fell asleep. But Khadijah was a woman. She knew no peace and wished to know what had befallen her husband.

There were many wise men in Mecca who knew about all kinds of trade, about prices and wares, but few who knew of good and evil spirits, or of the things of heaven. Softly she got up from the bed, crept out of the house and went to her wise

---

* This and all subsequent quotations from the Koran are taken from the translation by C. H. Palmer (Oxford University Press).

cousin, the blind *hanif* Waraqah ibn Naufal, who knew all the gods, had confessed all faiths and still had not mastered the truth. Khadijah told him about the spirits who had surrounded her husband. When Waraqah had heard all, he lifted his hands to heaven and deeply moved, cried out, "By Him who holds my life between his hands, if everything occurred as you have related it to me, then it was indeed the great archangel who appeared to Mohammed, just as he once appeared to Moses and to all the prophets of this people. Tell your husband to remain steadfast."

Reassured, Khadijah returned home. Waraqah was a wise man: he could not err. On the following day Mohammed, still doubting and unbelieving, went to the Caaba. According to custom, he encircled the holy edifice seven times, and at the seventh time he came upon the blind Waraqah. "Tell me what you have seen and heard," Waraqah bade him, and when Mohammed repeated what Khadijah had already told him, he said with trembling voice, "Verily, you are the Prophet of this people, the greatest of all archangels has appeared to you. Men will not believe you. They will call you a liar, will maltreat you, condemn you and oppose you. Remain steadfast, however, for you have been called to be the Prophet of the people." And the old man bowed down before Mohammed and kissed and blessed him.

"I am the Messenger of God," said Mohammed.

He now stood alone in the courtyard of the Caaba. Innumerable idols looked down on him, silent statues hung with jewels stood about him. Priests, merchants, cameleers, the whole city of Mecca stood against him. He was alone, the messenger of an unknown God that he was to proclaim. A vision was the only weapon with which he was to fight three hundred and sixty gods, the might and power of his opponents, the ridicule and shame which was to come down upon him. There was the memory of severe eyes, a vision not to be obliterated, and a few short, unforgettable sentences which were to move the world:

"Say, 'He is God alone! God the Eternal!
He begets not and is not begotten!
Nor is there like unto Him any one!'"

THE MISSION BEGINS

O thou who art covered! rise up and warn! And
thy Lord magnify!

Koran, LXXIV

Mohammed believed in his mission. The vision which he had seen was too
clear, and the words he had heard too indelibly impressed upon his memory, to permit of doubt. They were the key to the truth. But the truth
itself was still hidden. The revelation still lacked outline and had merely pointed the
way. The spirit which had announced it had not completed his task.

Mohammed waited: day after day he roamed through the bare fields in the vicinity
of Mecca, seeking the spot where the spirit had first appeared to him, repeating the
unforgettable verses which had been revealed, and awaiting a miracle. Through a
small space which had been opened for but a moment, he had been permitted to
look into another world. Whoever had been accorded such a privilege, ceased being
a man like others. But the space had closed up long since, and the miracles ended.
Passionately, the Prophet awaited their return. But they did not come again, and Mohammed began to doubt and to seek some other way out. He recalled the opportunity
which had been given him, but now he no longer knew which of the powers dominated him. It was as if jinn, evil spirits and demons had taken possession of him.

In order to put an end to the tortures, the despair, and the torments which racked
his soul, the Prophet decided to climb up on a high peak and to cast his body possessed by demons into the depths. "I wanted to find eternal repose and rid my soul
of its pain," he said later. The Prophet approached the edge of the precipice and saw
the yawning void below. He bent down and saw little stones, which his foot had dislodged, crash down into the deep. Only one step separated him from everlasting
peace. Suddenly he heard a voice, low but audible, in his ear. Mohammed stood
rooted to the spot. His eyes swept the horizon and, high above his head, he saw the
Indescribable One.

The vision drew near. Standing on the top of the rock, on the edge of the abyss,
Mohammed received the second revelation, the famous *Sura* called "The Chapter of
the Forenoon." The verses of this *Sura* are of matchless beauty. They were the first to
make clear his future mission to the Prophet. "By the forenoon, and the night when
it darkens," Mohammed heard, "thy Lord has not forsaken thee. ... Did He not find
thee an orphan, and give thee shelter? And find thee erring, and guide thee? And

find thee poor with a family and nourish thee? ... And as for the favour of thy Lord discourse thereof." Then Mohammed knelt down and prayed to his Lord, and descended from the rock.

He had found everlasting peace. He knew that he was a prophet.

And so the revelations of the Koran began, and endured for twenty-three years, ending with the death of the Prophet. Peace had now come to Mohammed, and he was sure of his mission. The way lay straight before him.

But was the way free? It was filled with statues and idols, kingdoms and wild tribes. World empires barred his path. Merchants, priests, magicians, sages, warriors, all obstructed the road which led to the truth. And opposing them, in obedience to a few beautiful lines spoken by the vision, was a simple, untutored merchant who came from the rude, desert city of Mecca.

Mohammed was a merchant. All his life he had bought and sold wares, increased his wealth, journeyed with his caravans, and traded with strange dealers. It was a strange background for the prophet of a new faith. On the other hand, it was his early training which made it possible for him to think logically, and to reason calmly. There had been many prophets before Mohammed, and like him they had been filled with zeal for their cause. Like him, they wandered along the path of suffering unafraid, and either perished or conquered. But none of them had succeeded in creating a world empire, a state. That called for a sound merchant, one who could transplant the experiences derived from practical business to the visionary existence of a prophet, the leader of a new world.

Sure of his mission, and having regained his peace of mind, Mohammed again took up his former mode of existence. He returned to his house, paid visits to the Caaba, resumed his elegant clothes, and gave evidence of his earlier good humour and friendliness. To all outward appearances he was again the rich merchant of Mecca. The Meccans welcomed the return of Mohammed to civil life. Apparently, the months of penitence were over. It did not cause much stir, for in Mecca one was accustomed to see great merchants overcome with attacks of religious enthusiasm. It passed like sickness and fever. Mohammed had recovered. At least, so one thought in Mecca. However, none knew of the knowledge which Mohammed had brought with him from the desert. None knew that during the quiet, Arabian nights, the Archangel Gabriel appeared in the house of Mohammed, and that the carefree merchant fell upon the ground, his lips covered with foam, and received revelations of a new faith, and that he was gradually turning himself into the prophet of that faith.

Mohammed did not disclose the revelations, his faith, or anything concerning his inner life, to his fellow citizens. He believed himself to be an inspired prophet and not *Rasul*, the representative of God. Carefully, Mohammed began his work, the spreading of the new faith.

Mohammed was fully aware of the situation. He had no intention of entering the Caaba alone, to proclaim the new teaching to an astonished and sceptical crowd without a following or adherents. Before announcing it publicly, he wished to lay a secure foundation, to attract a circle of followers who would support the future battle of the Prophet in word and deed, and obey him blindly.

Mohammed began to seek out his future companions. But since he was careful, collected and prudent, he sought them in the intimate circle of his own family.

Khadijah, his wife, was the first believer in the new faith.

She adopted the creed of her husband without question or hesitation. She believed in the word of her wise uncle, Waraqah, and she believed in Mohammed's revelations. Mohammed taught her his prayer, and through the prayer he won his second follower. Once, when he was in his room praying with Khadijah, Ali, the ten-year-old son of his uncle, Abu Talib, came in. The melodious voice of his cousin and the solemn ceremonial of the prayer pleased the child. He knelt down on the rug, repeated the verses of the Koran, and so entered upon the way which was to lead him to the throne of the Caliphs, and make of him the ruler of Egypt, Syria, Palestine, Persia, Mesopotamia and North Africa. A third member of the family was soon added. Zaid, a slave given to Mohammed by Khadijah, who had been freed by him and, like Ali, adopted by him, was the new recruit. Later, when Zaid's own father, a rich Arab, appeared, Zaid refused to leave the house of his adopter. He was the first adult adherent of Islam, and although he was the servant of the Prophet and no one is a hero to his own servant, he became a steadfast and loyal member of the new communion.

Mohammed now had three followers. All three were members of his own household. It would have been difficult to impress the people of Mecca with three members of his immediate family. Slowly, Mohammed widened the sphere of his activity. Step by step, he looked for new members among the leading families of Mecca, called on those whom he was sure were religiously inclined, talked with them carefully and at length, and gradually dispelled their numerous objections and doubts. He dealt with them like a merchant with his wares, and did not disclose himself until he was certain of success. When he had satisfied the proselytes that logically there was the necessity for a new faith, he went over to the supernatural proofs, to the word of God, the Koran.

Mohammed was an able propagandist, and had been one ever since he had first travelled for Khadijah. Now his experience came in good stead. Gradually he collected a small community of believers about him. There were not only slaves, beggars and servants who had run to Mohammed because he had been the first in Arabia to preach the equality of all in the sight of God, and because he aided his people with advice and money, but also members of the noble families of Mecca who, like Mohammed, had been troubled with religious scruples, and had wished to find a means of escape.

There were young, enterprising, rich persons among them, who thought that the way of Mohammed was the way to freedom.

His greatest acquisition however, was not due to Mohammed's gift of persuasion or to his logical explanations. "I have never called anyone to Islam," said Mohammed, "who at first was not filled with doubt, questions and contradictions, with the exception of Abu Bakr, the Faithful. He had no objections, no scruples."

Abu Bakr was certainly not the man to devote himself to anything without forethought. He was of humble origin and came from poor surroundings. Through his own labours, he had amassed a great fortune, and enjoyed a still greater reputation. He was a born society man, well versed in the complicated relationships of Mecca. He was a teller of jokes and beloved as a happy, jolly fellow. His character was as hard as granite, but internally, like many others, he was plagued by doubts and given to meditation and introspection. This rich banker, who had no need of further worldly goods, went over to Islam and unquestioningly trod the path of truth, like a child going to its mother. Among all of Mohammed's followers, this teller of obscene stories, this cunning merchant, was the most devout. For the Prophet was the first person ever to be taken seriously by Abu Bakr, and Abu Bakr was destined to be the heir of the Prophet of God, to be the first caliph of Islam.

Mohammed's prudence in proceeding about his task was not without some inconvenience. The first year of his mission brought him but eight adherents. They assembled in the house of the Prophet and prayed piously. But they were not the world which Mohammed wished to conquer. Mohammed decided to be more daring and to enlarge his operations. Despite all the precautions which had been taken, the assemblies which were held in his house, the prayers of the eight faithful, the endeavours of the Prophet to secure new followers obviously could not be hidden from the world. Slowly the news spread throughout the city, that Mohammed was conducting meetings in his house, that he taught some sort of new faith and that he sought converts.

Little attention was paid to these rumours. Perhaps Mohammed had become a Jewish or a Christian sectarian, and one was accustomed to many gods.

One day Mohammed invited all the members of the tribes of the Hashemites and the Abdal-Muttalibs to his house. His relatives came, perhaps because they thought that he wished to discuss some business with them, or because they were eager to secure news of his secret assemblies. They were served with mutton and camel's milk. When the repast was ended, Mohammed arose, told them of the principles of his new religion, and invited them all to believe in Islam. "Which of you wishes to join me in my undertaking?" he cried. A painful silence set in.

The relatives looked at each other in astonishment. What were they to think? Was it a joke or was he in earnest? Much to the amusement of all, young Ali, the first Moslem, sprang up and confessed his faith in Islam. But Mohammed stroked the child's hair and said, "See, my brothers, this is my vizier, my satrap." Neither he, nor Ali, had any inkling that these few friendly words would become the turning point in the history of Islam, that the world of the faithful would be split into two parties. Two parties which, to this day, have not ceased opposing one another, the Sunni and the Shi'ites.

Breathlessly, Mohammed awaited a reply. Finally his uncle, Abdal-Uzza, whose son Utbah had married Mohammed's daughter, got up. He was a great personage whose wife belonged to the aristocratic Ummayah, a fact which influenced his opinions. "Go to the devil!" he cried angrily. "What means this nonsense?" And he picked up a stone to punish his nephew. Thereupon such a tumult and shouting set up among the relatives that Mohammed could not continue speaking.

The assembly was dispersed. Mohammed named his uncle Abdal-Uzza, Abu Lahab, which means "father of the flame," and he and his wife became two of the bitterest enemies of Islam. On the same day, Abu Lahab forced his son to send Ruqaiyah, Mohammed's daughter, back to her father in disgrace. This insult confirmed the breach between the relatives. For Mohammed as well as for Ruqaiyah, her return was fortunate, for when the scandal in the Hashemite family was noised abroad, Uthman, the most handsome youth of all Mecca, called upon Mohammed. For years he had been in love with Ruqaiyah. He seized the opportunity, was converted to Islam, and received the hand of his beloved in return. Obviously he could not have known that this trivial step would later make of him the ruler of a world empire, and that he would be the third Caliph of Islam.

For three years Mohammed remained a silent preacher. His flock counted hardly twenty members. The Archangel Gabriel appeared to Mohammed as he had so often done before, and commanded him, "Step forth and preach the new faith to the world." It was an ordinary, calm night, when Mohammed sat in his house and conversed with the archangel. No one in the world knew that in this night the wheel of world history had begun to turn and that the ashes of the world had begun to tremble; that a new epoch was setting in.

Stories tell that in Byzantium a boy was born with the head of a pig on that night; that the crosses on all the churches began to sway; that two horrible monsters arose out of the waters of the Nile, most terrifying to behold. On the next day, the sun was but one third its size. Bloody lances shone down from a moonless sky and the Emperor of Byzantium had bad dreams.

In that night, Mohammed decided to show himself to the peoples of the world. It was at the beginning of the fourth year of his mission.

THERE IS NO GOD BUT ALLAH

> There is in the world a single way, which no one
> can go but you; do not ask where it leads, but go.
> *Nietzsche*

The faith which was revealed to Mohammed in dreamlike visions, the faith which he preached to mankind and with which he conquered it, is called Islam. Many have tried to translate the word Islam. None have succeeded. It has been said, "Islam means submission to God," forgetting both the philology and the inherent sense of the word. Islam is derived from the verb *salm* or *salama*, which means peace, relaxation after a duty performed, peaceful existence. The verbal noun *Islam* means peace, refuge, rescue. In the mouth of Mohammed it meant the striving towards a higher peace, towards godly piety. So much for philology. But what is Islam?

The faith which Mohammed proclaimed is dry and overpowering like the sands of the desert. There is no clearer faith in the world, nor is there any other which contains religion, *Weltanschauung* and justice in the same measure. Islam is all-embracing.

In his innumerable meditations on Mount Hirah, Mohammed found a single dogma which moved him. He discovered that, since the beginning of time, all the peoples of the world had known but one truth, had constantly received one and the same truth from God, and that due to their miserable earthly existence they had forgotten it, neglected it, and obscured it with errors. This discovery of the primitive, pure and only truth is called Islam. Mohammed was not the creator of a new religion, nor did he wish to discover a new truth. He merely wished to resurrect the old in a new glory. He was a reformer, and the Islam which he preached was for him but a resurrection of the primitive faith of the world.

For thousands of years, for millions of years, there has been but one truth in the world. God the Incomprehensible, the Unrecognizable, had sent it to mankind. Throughout the entire existence of the world, through all peoples and all cultures, through all times and all countries, there has been a steady procession of prophets, of holy ones, commanded by God to preach the primitive truth to humanity. A prophet is no saint, no worker of miracles; nor is he possessed, but merely the mouthpiece through which God speaks to man.

The succession of prophets is endless, and they have preached in all languages to all peoples. Their message was the same at all times: the sole unchanging word of

God. There is not a hair's breadth of difference in the revelations of the prophets. It is only rarely that people wish to follow their words. Most of the prophets were disowned, opposed, slandered and banished. And it was only occasionally that mankind bowed before the teaching of a prophet, and, believing, accepted the word of God through his mouth. When a prophet died, man forgot the important points which he had taught, forgot the word of God. A religion remained, but like a splinter of gold in a haystack, merely splinters of the primitive dogma were retained in that faith. In this manner, the differences in religions ensued, for although each religion goes back to the words of its own prophet, they are all the same: the word of God.

Faith in the prophets is the corner-stone of Islam. It is the basic dogma on which the entire foundation of its teaching is developed.

The most important of the prophets who appeared to the world were Abraham, Moses and Jesus. The people have remembered their words.

For Mohammed, the peoples of the world were divided into two parts, those who had received the Scriptures and those who had not. The people of the Scriptures are the Jews and the Christians. In God's mercy, they had received the truth through Moses and Christ. Since the words of the prophets were not immediately written down, sects and trends developed out of the original unity, and each one contains a part of the truth but denies the whole. All in all, Judaism, Christianity and Islam were identical to Mohammed.

Inasmuch as all the words were forgotten and were misinterpreted, God finally sent down another prophet who was to repeat all that which the prophets of olden times had preached. He was to lead the religions back to their original unity and purity, and leave behind him a unified kingdom of God on earth. The last in the long line of prophets, the final seal, as it were, of all of the prophets, is Mohammed, the Messenger of God. For this reason his teaching contains nothing which was not known to the old religions, to the old world. Islam, therefore, in its doctrine underlines everything which coincides with that of Jewish and Christian teaching, for Moses and Jesus only preached the true faith.

Just as Columbus did not know that he had discovered a new world, so Mohammed did not realize that he had called a new religion to life. Up to the time of his death, he constantly repeated that Islam had no desire to bring anything new to the world.

How was this strange, sober, positive, edifice of Islam created? On Mount Hirah the Prophet received from God the command to preach the truth. For twenty-three years the Archangel Gabriel appeared regularly to him and gradually taught him the eternal truth, the entire Koran. The Koran is, therefore, the final word of God which, having been put down immediately, could not be lost or misinterpreted.

The miracle of the Koran will always remain a riddle to a sceptical world. A simple, uneducated man, who had never made a poem, who did not have the gift of facile speech, suddenly preached a literate, aesthetic, miraculous piece of work, to say nothing of its content. Up to the present day, the Koran has never been surpassed as the greatest product of the Arabic tongue. The intoxicating beauty of its verses was ample proof of its divine origin for Mohammed and for all the Arabs.

The Arabs were a race of poets, of literary experts. They lived in a world of poetry, and both friends and foes were forced to recognize the beauty of the verses of the Koran. The entire book, which is a marvellously constructed piece of logical thinking, contains one hundred and fourteen chapters, called *Suras*. The verses of these chapters are the world in which the life of three hundred million persons moves.

Even in Mohammed's day, there were numerous attempts to imitate the Koran. But all were to fail miserably. Poetically, the Koran has no predecessors and no successors. It is also characteristic of the Arabian world that Islam was first forced to appeal to aesthetic proofs to prove its divine origin. Only he who masters the rhythmic word can rule in the desert, and in the final analysis the force and spread of the new faith is not to be derived from the beauty of the Koran itself. The power of expression, the magic of the word, the steely rhythm of these verses cannot be translated into any other language. When, amid the poetic Arabian people, the prophet recited the verses, a sort of spell came forth from him, for the word was alive in the people. Mohammed was fully aware of the magical power of the Koran. But he knew also that the Koran was no work of his own making. It is not Mohammed who speaks to mankind through the Koran, but God. In the Koran, "I" is always God, and "you" is Mohammed. Each *Sura* was revealed in reference to a particular event, to a particular question which troubled the Prophet.

How did the revelation of the Koran occur? The Archangel Gabriel was the intermediary between God and His prophet. Suddenly, without warning, he appeared to the Prophet. Sometimes in the form of a strange wanderer, sometimes as a youth, sometimes merely a voice understood by the Prophet alone. When the angel appeared to the Prophet as a voice, when Mohammed first heard the verses, the excitement which filled him was terrifying. He turned pale, his brow was covered with sweat, and mad, disconnected sounds issued from his lips. His face was like a bolt of lightning and none dared to look at him. Sometimes he sank to the ground, his body trembled, his lips were covered with foam, and he cried out like a young camel. Then he slowly composed himself, fell asleep and awoke to proclaim a new, captivating verse to the world. Never did Gabriel appear to the Prophet in his own form. For Mohammed was but human and could not have endured the sight of an angel. Only once did Mohammed beg the archangel to show himself to him in his proper person. Gabriel fulfilled his request, and Mohammed fell into a deep faint as if struck by lightning. For a mortal the sight of an angel is terrible and unbearable.

For twenty-three years Mohammed lived in a state of intoxicated ecstasy. Surrounded by visions, he proclaimed the verses and enchanted himself with their supernatural beauty. One might think that this teaching was as fantastic and as exalted as the visions around him. But the Arabian prophet incorporated the primitive conditions of the land from which he sprang. Here, the weird *fata Morgana* of the desert was paired with the clear, dry air. Strange visions created a dry, clear, sober product which is called Islam.

Islam knows nothing of fantasy; it is logically constructed, and as legible as the ledger of a merchant. It has but few principles, but these rule the whole relationship between man and God and between man and man. Islam is not only religion, it is a social teaching as well. In his visions, Mohammed received a sober, rational and, in its exact simplicity, an overpowering teaching. "One must believe in one God, govern one's passions, fight the foes of the faith, and believe in the reward for one's deeds after death." The whole of its dogma is contained in this one sentence.

For Mohammed, God, the Only One and the Omnipresent One, was a being who could not be described. It is a sin to try to explain or describe God. Eternally damned are those who dare to represent God in picture, stone, or in words. God is like the light, like the flame, like the sea, eternal, immutable, incomprehensible. Whoever tries to comprehend God or to describe Him, manifests his lack of faith. Even the slightest attempt to show God in any form must be opposed. All the prophets forbade the representation of God, but the desire to understand Him is strong in man. Man draws the picture of another man or of an animal. Others will pray to the drawing, thinking it is God. That is why Islam was for all times forbidden the representation of a living being in picture or stone, so that man will not succumb to the temptation of praying to images and idols. "Say, 'He is God alone! God the Eternal! He begets not and is not begotten! Nor is there like unto Him any one!'" This is the principle with which Mohammed deliberately separated his teaching from that of Christianity. Jesus is a prophet endowed with divine grace; perhaps He is even a prophet without sin. But damned be they who speak of him as the Son of God, who would give to "God alone" a son. Jesus is a prophet, and Islamic legends relate that this prophet, who was less sinful than Mohammed himself, was not crucified, but rescued from the cross and ascended into heaven. It was a phantom who was crucified. Yet Jesus was a man like the others, like Mohammed, like Moses, a man who preached the divine, but whose words were forgotten, twisted and misinterpreted by helpless men. Mohammed wished to recall these words to mankind.

Mohammed's teaching has but few ritual decrees, and these few merely serve to maintain discipline among the faithful. Nor does Islam recognize a hierarchy, monks or a priesthood. Man needs no intermediary when speaking to God. Temples and assemblies for prayer are unnecessary. Everywhere, at home or abroad, alone or in company with others, can man pray to his God. When many pray together, anyone may be the leader or *imam*. In Islam there is no consecration, no division into layman and priest. Each man is his own priest. To give evidence of the unity, of the community of the faithful, only the prayers are prescribed. The community of the Moslems is not a religious community. In this it differs from all other religions, for it is essentially the core of a state. The membership in the community is a social duty. "Pray to God, be good to the captive and the poor and the orphan, and give alms," says the seventy-sixth *Sura* of the Koran. "Do you wish to walk the narrow path of faith?" says another portion of the Koran, "then ransom the captives, feed the hungry, be compassionate and helpful. Damned be the pious who do not give alms, the benefactors who secretly malign those whom they help, or those who give away money and distribute alms so that others may envy them. They are like hard rock on which nothing can grow."

Islam raised charity to an article of faith and carefully defined it. Every Moslem who owns more than twenty camels must annually distribute two and a half per cent of his income to the poor, or contribute such a sum to the proper officials of the community, who in turn see to its distribution. The beneficiaries of these taxes were carefully enumerated. They were the poor, the suffering, slaves who wished to purchase their freedom, debtors who could not pay their debts, as well as travellers and foreigners who were strangers in the city. In looking back, it would indeed be difficult for us to appreciate how important was this social commandment, with its religious inception, for the Oriental world. Basically, it was the first attempt at social relief in a world which was religiously unified.

As a matter of fact, social commands predominate in Islam. In ancient times, being a prophet meant being a social reformer and party leader at one and the same time. Today, Islam is still a social system which, of necessity, is founded on divine law. The social upheaval which Islam foreshadowed was of great importance for Arabia. Islam aspired to break the thousand-year-old community of the tribes. "O ye who believe! be ye steadfast in justice, witnessing before God though it be against yourselves, or your parents, or your kindred, be it rich or poor, for God is nearer akin than either," are the words of the 133rd *verse* of *Sura* IV of the Koran.

Even though the Koran loosens the bonds of blood-relationship, it establishes a new one, that between man and nature. In contrast to many other religious systems, the Koran admits that animals have souls and makes a religious commandment of kindness to all living things. "You will be rewarded if you are good to animals, if you feed them and still their thirst, for there is no animal in the air or on the earth that will not return to God."

In Islam idealism was always paired with a sense of the practical. Mohammed was an exalted, practical person, a rare but, nevertheless, a fruitful apparition. He wished to elevate the moral plane of humanity, and he knew how to do so by the most practical of means. It must be stressed again and again that Islam, the youngest of the universal religions, was founded by a merchant, and an Arabian merchant at that. The natural sobriety of the Arabian race, coupled with the practical thinking of a merchant who sensed actual possibilities and knew how to utilize them, created a religion which, in its objective clarity and complete negation of everything that was mystical, excelled everything else.

It was the ethical importance of Islam which proved to be of vast consequence to the Arabian world. Mohammed was the first to teach the conception of sin, for it was unknown to Arabia before his time. The Arab knew what damage was, and was a past master at demanding reparation. That, in addition, there was a thing called sin, he only learned from Mohammed. The demands which Mohammed made were few. Prayer, fasting and alms were the external marks of Islam. Prayer was primarily a form and an exercise of discipline.

In the first period of Islam, Mohammed still felt himself as one with the Jews and the Christians. For this reason, the faithful were obliged to turn their face in prayer towards the city of Jerusalem, the home of two great religions.

The fast in the month of Ramadan was an additional means of discipline. From dawn to dusk man was not allowed to touch food for a whole month. The desire to eat, to consume huge quantities of food, was only less important than the sexual appetite of primitive man. As evidence of his internal discipline, he was to forego this pleasure once a year.

From a religious point of view, all the other rites of Islam were only of secondary importance. "God will forgive everything," says the Koran, "except placing other gods at His side." Inexorably, Islam demands faith in but one God, in His prophets who preach His word, in life after death, and in retribution for mortal deeds. Out of these few dogmas, Mohammed was able to create a world, an ethical conception which (and history has proved this) satisfied both primitive negros and intelligent philosophers at one and the same time.

The entire Islamic teaching is contained in one, magnificent vision which was revealed on Mount Hirah. All that has been added is nothing but a development of the original, basic idea. But this is also the greatest of Mohammed's miracles. Primitive Islam – and this is its most important feature – was not only a religion, but also a kind of social life. It created hitherto unheard-of social forms, political and judicial theories, which have lost none of their powers of attraction to this day. These replaced the social, religious and political confusion which reigned in the Orient about the year 600, and erected a state of world importance, which became the cultural centre of the world of that time.

"Seek wisdom, even if you must go as far as China," Mohammed once said, for he had the tolerance of the experienced merchant. He knew, too, that the way lay steep before him and he wished to remove everything "which made man stick to the earth." He not only forbade luxury and stimulants, but music and dancing as well, for he, who himself was intoxicated with words, knew the magic power of the dance, of tone, of movement. He knew the pagan, demonic effect they had on man. He, Mohammed, had no need of artificial stimulants, of counterfeit ecstasies, for he knew the narrow path. His teaching was clear and overpowering, sober and yet intoxicating as the sand, as the wind of the desert.

In the fourth year of his mission, Mohammed, the uneducated merchant, appeared before the people of Mecca. Though burning with a feverish ecstasy and carried away by his own words, calmly, collectedly and with deliberation he announced the message which was to revolutionize the world:

"There is no God but Allah, and Mohammed is his Prophet."

THE PROPHET APPEARS

See how poor and miserable he is. The fool
wished to persuade us that God speaks through
his mouth.

Lermontov

What happens when a reputable merchant, who has a good business and
who is known to be a reliable, peaceful person, suddenly becomes ob-
sessed with the strange idea that he is a messenger of God; when he
preaches pious sermons to the assembled multitude and begins to neglect his own
affairs? In normal business circles such a man would first be ridiculed, then pitied
and reasoned with, and finally held to be mad. It was not much different in Mecca.
The Prophet hesitated for a long time before he decided to proclaim openly the new
teaching.

From the time when it had been revealed to him that he was to preach publicly,
a month had passed before Mohammed made his first speech. One day young messengers ran through the streets of Mecca crying, "Mohammed, the son of Abdallah,
the Hashemite, invites every Meccan to come to Mount Safa, for he has important
news to give to the people." There had been much gossip in the city to the effect that
the good husband of Khadijah had come upon evil ways. Much interest was manifest
in the ideas which he had kept secret. Former business partners, old friends and ac-
quaintances who had had many dealings with Mohammed in the courtyard of the
Caaba, hurried to the mount near Mecca to listen to him.

It required a great deal of self-persuasion on Mohammed's part to approach his
numerous business associates with a new idea of salvation. Mohammed disliked publicity, and in the last few years he had but rarely appeared in the Caaba. We already
know that he did not have the gift of speech, and it had taken years of labour to develop such talents as he had in that direction.

When the Quraishites had assembled, Mohammed explained to them simply and
clearly that God had commanded him to preach anew the old, true faith of Abraham
and the prophets. He recited the Koran. Gradually he was filled with enthusiasm and
in vivid colours he pictured the downfall of the mighty people of olden times who
had denied the true faith. He spoke of the raptures of paradise and told them of the
commandments of God: do not kill, do not steal, do not lie. The Quraishites, filled
with pity, listened to him. Was it because of fairy tales like these that Mohammed

neglected his business, called honest merchants together, and wandered through the desert? The few faithful, and young Ali in particular, appeared ridiculous to them. These men and children were not to be taken seriously. Shaking their heads, the Quraishites went their way. Not a single one of them had been converted.

Mohammed was not surprised at his lack of success. Other prophets, too, had met with difficulties. Sin was too deeply and strongly rooted in the souls of his fellow men. Day after day, Mohammed now appeared in the Caaba, leaned against one of the pillars, and began to recite the verses of the Koran in an agreeable, modulated tone of voice. The verses met with approval, and it was soon clear to the connoisseurs that Mohammed had developed into a capable poet.

Poetical merchants were not rare in Mecca, but never had a poet demanded that his verses be accepted as coin of the realm. If one said to Mohammed, "Your verses are very beautiful," or when an expert said, "Your rhythm technique has created a new epoch in our literature," Mohammed's face became clouded and he replied: "I am not a poet and these are not my poems. They are the words of God which come from my mouth." Apparently this put an end to all logic. People shrugged their shoulders and left him. There were not many in Mecca who respected the poet sufficiently to put up with his peculiarities. His constant appearance in the Caaba and his preaching to an empty auditorium soon made Mohammed appear ridiculous in the eyes of the people. Now and again they would point at him with their fingers and say in a tone loud enough for him to hear, "Look, that is the grandchild of Abdal-Muttalib who claims to know what goes on in heaven." When, on these occasions, Mohammed turned around and said, "You are like those who, because they fear thunder and lightning, close their eyes and stop up their ears," his opponents would praise his verses but reply with obscene recitations or with music loud enough to drown the voice of the Prophet. Thereupon, Mohammed would picture the horrible punishments which God could visit upon the sinners. The result of this was that on the following day some young poet would appear with a parody upon the verses of Mohammed and cause the whole city to roar with laughter. Fate decreed that the most clever of the parodists, Amr ibn al-As, was later to be the conqueror of Egypt and one of the greatest generals of Islam.

Undisturbed, Mohammed went his way. When they laughed at him, when the children covered his clothing with filth, Mohammed told them of the people of Ad and Thamud, who had acted in a similar fashion and had perished. However, there were many who held that those who abused the Prophet were unfair. For example, a mighty chieftain of Yathrib said, "A noble person has embraced a new religion. Why do you persecute him?" It was also humiliating to the aristocrats of Mecca that one of their number ran through the streets like a madman, and was laughed at by the crowds. True, his speeches were well formed, but it would never do for Mohammed (in addition to his harmless descriptions of hell and paradise with which they had no fault to find) to pray openly in the courtyard of the Caaba to an unknown, apparently very ancient, God and to slight all the other good gods of Mecca.

In order to put an end to these ridiculous speeches, the gentlemen of the Caaba decided to proceed according to an old formula. They sought out Mohammed and said, "You believe in another god than we. Good! We will be tolerant. Erect a statue of your god in the Caaba in the way the other tribes have done, and pray to him as much as you please. We shall not disturb you, but you must leave our gods in peace." The Quraishites thought this proposal to be both loyal and acceptable. But when Mohammed vigorously declined to accept it, well-meant as it was, the Quraishites began to be uneasy. Either they were dealing with a madman or with a man who might prove to be very dangerous.

Old friends, noble Quraishites, who were sympathetically inclined towards Mohammed, came to him one day and said, "Mohammed, you are known to us as an honest, reliable person. For this reason we are worried about your present condition. We think that perhaps you are ill. Allow us to call the best physicians so that they may cure you of your illness." "I am not ill," replied Mohammed. "Then possibly you hope to achieve money and riches through your conduct. That could be taken care of. If you wish, we will give you a position in the government of the city, which will richly reward you and yours." But when the Quraishites learned that Mohammed refused to accept this as well, their patience was at an end. They could not possibly conceive of a man being in his right mind and still refusing to accept money. Obviously dark things were at work. They determined to undertake drastic measures against the unruly one.

By and large, the Meccans were ready to believe in prophets, angels and gods of all kinds. But all the known prophets had been dead a long time, and though it was quite possible that angels existed they were certainly in some other part of the world. They simply could not believe that one of their own people, a merchant of Mecca, could have anything to do with supernatural things. They knew him too well for that. Was he not just like themselves, did he not go to the bazaars, buy and sell, manage and increase his affairs? Now, suddenly, he claimed to be a prophet! It was laughable. However, in order to be absolutely certain about Mohammed, they decided to demand of him the simplest proof of his divine mission – he was to perform a miracle. "O Mohammed," said the Quraishites, "our valley is barren and narrow, widen it and cause a river to flow through it. Or let your God give you untold riches, or show us some other sort of miracle."

But the Prophet hated miracles. The world around him was full of wonders. One did not know which came from God and which from the evil one. Mohammed had never claimed that he could perform miracles. "God did not send me to work miracles," he replied; "I am merely here to spread the truth among you. I have never said that the treasures of Allah lay in my hands, or that I could practise secret arts or that I was an angel – I, who cannot help myself or believe, if God does not wish it. I am but a man like the others." "If you cannot perform miracles we cannot believe in you." "Jesus did miracles and he was not believed either," replied Mohammed.

At all times, Mohammed was a much-discussed problem among the Quraishites. They knew too much about his former mode of living to accuse him of evil intentions. His appearance and his conduct seemed to justify the belief that he was a madman. But his words, if one listened to him closely, were not at all mad. He spoke of things which were only too well known to the Quraishites, but they did not wish to hear them. He damned the excesses of the rich merchants, and demanded equality for all. He forbade luxury, deceit, the charging of interest, and other things besides. Finally, he fought the old gods of the Caaba and, thereby, not only undermined the foundations of the wealth of the Quraishites, but the very existence of Mecca itself. This was not only a bitter fact, but a dangerous one.

The Quraishites decided to oppose the newly arisen prophet. But Mohammed was equally determined strenuously to propagate his new faith. Since he had been unsuccessful among the Quraishites, he turned to the other people of Arabia. During the month of the feast, he visited the camps of the numerous Bedouin tribes who had come to Mecca. Here he taught the true faith, read the Koran, and now and again secured converts. He much preferred to talk with the Jews and the Christians who came frequently and in great numbers to the Caaba. At that time, there was a difference between his and their faith that was unknown to Mohammed. He often said, "My God is also the God of the Christians and the Jews, the people of the Scriptures."

The Jews and the Christians who visited Mecca were not averse to religious discussions. And in the beginning they also thought that this strange man was one of themselves. Did he not believe in the same God? This indicated progress among the pagan Arabs. The poor Bedouins also listened to the Prophet. With ecstatic attention, they heard the verses of the Koran, and their naive hearts trembled when they heard of the punishments which God could mete out. But more was not to be expected from the simple children of the desert. It happened at times that an entire tribe, while it was in Mecca, would be converted to Islam, but when the people had returned to their steppes, the old gods bobbed up again like corks on the surface of the water.

Mohammed's teaching met with greater success among the step-children of the country, the slaves and the poor city-dwellers. "One may not kill a slave, one must give alms, and one may not accept interest," Mohammed had preached. To the pariahs of the plutocratic Meccan republic these words came as a godsend, especially since they were spoken by a Quraish, a member of the ruling class of the city.

This was far from pleasant for the men of the Quraish. Gradually, the danger which this madman with his lovely songs portended dawned upon them. They sent word to all the tribes that a madman had appeared within their city, and that no attention was to be paid to his words. But the only result was that those tribes which had never heard about Mohammed now began to repeat his name with interest.

Soon open persecution set in. Children ran after the Prophet and threw stones at him. Umm Jamil, the wife of Abu Lahab, Mohammed's uncle, who had always hated the Prophet, put nettles in the places where he was accustomed to pray. When he appeared in the Caaba, he was met with insults. The Quraishites had realized that one of their own had become untrue to his caste.

Other than this, there was nothing that the Meccans could do to Mohammed. There was no public jail in Mecca, nor were there any laws or judges. They could not lock him up. His life, his well-being and his fortune were under the powerful protection of the tribes of Hashim and Muttalib. The leader of the tribe was Abu Talib, the uncle of Mohammed.

In his hands it lay whether or not the Prophet should be placed at the mercy of the Quraishites.

Abu Talib was an old man, and an Arab. He did not believe in the mission of his nephew. Once, when he saw Mohammed at prayer with his forehead pressed to the ground, he said tauntingly, "I do not believe that in order to show one's reverence for God, one should lift the rump and bow the head. But if you insist on bending your head lower than your rump, I will not stop you."

Abu Talib was old. His tribe was not the strongest in Mecca. But he was an Arab, and blood relationship was holy to him. "I and my tribe will protect Mohammed to the last man," he declared to the Quraish when they demanded that the Prophet be given up to them. Uttering dire threats, they left him, and the old man remained deep in thought. He had much to lose. The Quraish were powerful and the welfare of the Hashemites rested upon his shoulders. He ordered Mohammed to appear before him and spoke, "Son of my brother, shall we take upon ourselves more than we can bear? Think of what you do." And Mohammed answered, "If you were to place the sun in my right hand and the moon in my left, I would not turn from the truth. God should teach me something better or give me death." When Abu Talib did not reply, Mohammed thought that his uncle would no longer shield him, that he intended to cast him out of the tribe of the Hashemites. That is the worst that can happen to an Arab. Tears came to the eyes of the Prophet. Crying, he arose and started to leave the room.

But Abu Talib was an Arab, and the blood of the Hashim spoke from him. He could not look at his nephew's sorrow. Before Mohammed had reached the threshold, Abu Talib called out, "O Son of my brother, go where you please and say what you will. I will never deliver you to your enemies." And so the Prophet remained under the protection of the Hashemites.

But the hatred of the Quraishites grew and grew.

THE PROPHET IN THE CAABA

Up to the present, there is no one to be compared with Mohammed.

Olsner

Mohammed went to the Caaba every day. He leaned against one of the holy pillars or stood in the shadow of the sacred edifice, and in an exalted tone of voice recited the verses of the Koran. He was surrounded by a small number of the faithful and a few curious strangers, for Mohammed was constantly a source of wonder. When he began to preach in his melodious voice, a sort of charm went out from him. His followers, who knew full well how hard he had to battle and how pitiful the results were, swore by his name. Even strangers could not withstand the magic of his manner. This was well known and was believed to be due to the magic of his verses.

Many descriptions of the personality of the Prophet at that time have been preserved. He looked poorly, he was thin and it was difficult for him to fight his way. But his pleasant manner never deserted him. His slave, Anas, who had served him for ten years, said later that he had never once been scolded by his master, and that he had never detected any sign of impatience in him. The Prophet rarely spoke disparagingly of anyone and the worst curse he ever employed was, "May his brow be covered with filth." If anyone asked the Prophet to curse an enemy, he would reply, "I have not been sent into the world to curse, but to preach peace and humility to mankind." He visited the slaves and the sick, and was quiet and unpretentious. His entire make-up had something femininely delicate about it, which contrasted strangely with his heroic traits. Full of self-consciousness and yet internally calm, he was an enthusiast who had learned to enflame his fellow men with his own ardour. His exterior was simple, and only the knowing could detect the fire that burned within him. "He was neither too long nor too short but of medium stature; his hair was not too curly nor too flowing; his face was not too full nor too fleshy; it was white mixed with red; he had black eyes, long lashes, a strong head and prominent shoulder blades, a few fine hairs on his chest, and fleshy hands and feet. His step was as light as if he were treading on water, and if he looked to one side, he turned around. The seal of the prophet was between his shoulders, his hands were the most generous of any man's, his breast was the most courageous, his tongue was the most truthful. He was the most faithful to his *protégés*, the softest and most pleasant person in his relationships; whoever saw him for the first time was filled with respect; who knew him better, loved him; who described him, had to say: 'Before him and since his time, I have never seen anyone like him'." Thus he was described by an old Arab.

The Prophet sat surrounded by the faithful, by strangers and by Quraishites in the great courtyard of the Caaba. The verses of the Koran were melodious, and he seemed to pierce the very soul of the people, and to conquer them with the warmth of his eyes and the beauty of his songs. Again and again the people said, "If you are a prophet, then show us a miracle so that we may believe in you." And the answer of the messenger of God was always the same, "Is it not a sufficient and all-satisfying miracle that your ordinary language, O Arab people, has been chosen for the language of the Book, in which each single verse makes you forget your own verses and songs?" It has been told that thereupon the unbelievers decided to call together all the poets of Arabia in the hope that they could compose at least one verse, one syllable, which could compare with the beauty of the Koran. The poets came, proceeded to the Caaba and there began to sweat under the heat of the sun. They worked hard and took a great deal of pains with their poetry. But when they began to recite their verses, even the worst enemies of the Prophet had to admit that not a single one could compare with the verses of the Koran. And since the Arabs are a poetic people, many knelt down in the Caaba and were converted to Islam. The incomparable beauty of the Koran was sufficient proof of its divine origin.

At times, when his verses did not suffice, the Prophet explained at length and in detail the fundamentals of his faith. Since the internal ardour of the Prophet was mixed with the external coolness of his reasoning, he neglected no means by which he might have converted one of the influential Meccans. One day the Prophet stood in the Caaba conversing with a noble Meccan whom he hoped to win over to the true faith. The Meccan was but little religiously inclined, and this served to spur Mohammed on. An old blind Bedouin, having heard of the teachings of the new prophet, appeared in the courtyard of the Caaba to seek his salvation at Mohammed's hands. He approached the Prophet and asked him a question. The Prophet was intent upon his business with the wealthy Meccan and did not wish to be distracted. "Do not disturb me," he said in a tone of annoyance to the blind man, "I am occupied with important business." That same night, the Prophet had a vision. Gabriel appeared and scolded him severely because of his conduct. The Prophet arose early next morning, and ran through the city looking for the blind man. Finally he found him, threw himself about his neck and cried bitterly. "I am a man like the others," he said. "I am not free of sin, but I will make good my sins." He heaped honours upon the blind man and later made him governor of the city of Medina, and whenever mention was made of him, Mohammed said, "Thrice welcome to him on whose account my Lord reproved me." This was the only occasion when the Prophet was led to do anyone an injustice. Arabian sages say that this and other transgressions had occurred because God wanted the Prophet to commit one of each of the human sins, for he was a man like the others.

There is a similar story told of Mohammed's compassion in his later years. When the Prophet had reached the pinnacle of his fame, an ugly old woman appeared before him daily and begged that he might pray to God that a place be kept for her in heaven. One day, when the woman had come with the same request, Mohammed lost his patience and said to her, "Ugly old women like you will never get to heaven." The old woman burst into tears, whereat the Prophet quickly continued, "For at the threshold to heaven, all old, ugly women are changed into beautiful young maidens." The famous Persian poet, Sa'di, wrote a well-known poem around this incident.

The Prophet was compassionate, polite and helpful. His greatest love was for children. He who had endured the hatred of the city of Mecca for years could not allow a child to pass without stroking it or following it with the lovely glance of his eyes. An Islamic proverb says, "All children are born in Islam."

One day Mohammed sat as usual in the Caaba, and a little girl passed by. He called the child to him, stroked her hair and spoke softly to her. The Quraishites, who sat around him, looked at the girl and at the Prophet, and shook their heads. Were not girls lower beings? How could a serious person and, in particular, one who claimed to be especially loved by God, pay any attention to a girl? An old Quraishite, who could stand this shame no longer, arose and said to Mohammed, "Why do you fondle the child? Do you not know that one may kill superfluous girls without fear of punishment?" The Prophet arose, his eyes became serious and large, he lifted up his hands and in a firm voice he revealed a new verse of the Koran: "Do not murder your children for fear you may want, for God will provide you and them with sustenance." And the command of the hour was made into an important law of Islam which put an end to a tradition of the desert which had existed for hundreds of years.

Most of the other laws of Islam ensued from similar, external and trivial causes. Any event, which attracted the attention of the Prophet, might result in a law which governed the destiny of millions for centuries. The prohibition concerning the use of alcohol, which has given a definite stamp to the entire eastern world, was revealed at the time when several of the faithful, in a somewhat intoxicated condition, had come together for prayer and had caused a disturbance.

The law concerning divorce, which brought with it an upheaval of the customs then current, was revealed because of scandal in the Prophet's own household. Mohammed liked to proceed step by step, and to illustrate things with examples. When he had made a decision, he always awaited a suitable opportunity before revealing it.

In the times when Mohammed preached in the courtyard of the Caaba, the divine market-place was often turned into a theological seminary. The priests of the Arabian gods, the Jews, the Christians, and sectarians of all sorts, appeared there to question Mohammed about the nature of his new faith. For hours on end, the Prophet read the Scriptures with Christians and Jews. As a result, the Quraishites spread the rumour that the new belief was copied from the Christians and the Jews. The Prophet had to answer many questions and to enter into many discussions. And it was out of these questions and discussions, out of these numerous quarrels, out of the simple, theological dialectic of the desert, that the edifice called Islam was gradually erected.

But grotesque mishaps and casuistic parables were not lacking, and they were much beloved by the Orient. So, for example, a sceptic appeared one day and asked Mohammed the following: "Allah is supposed to be omnipresent. But I do not see him. Where is he? Why is a man punished for his sins? Allah's will governs sins as well. Why is hell a punishment for the devil? Fire is the devil's nature, then how can fire harm fire?" Mohammed remained silent for a while, as if surprised by so many difficult questions. Suddenly he took up a lump of earth and threw it at his questioner. The seeker after truth became angered at this, and ran through the city to his relations and complained bitterly. "I wished to speak seriously with him, to ask him grave questions, and instead of answering, he threw dirt at me." His relatives surrounded the questioner, and accompanied him to the Caaba to seek redress from the Prophet. "I did not insult the man," replied Mohammed, "I merely answered his questions." When he saw the amazed expression of his opponent, he continued, "You do not believe in God because you do not see Him. The lump of earth caused you pain, but I do not see your pain. You complain of my misdeed and yet you say yourself that everything that man does must come from God. How could the earth hurt you, for earth is your nature, you come from the earth and you will return to earth."

Mohammed did not like things of this kind. Whoever played such jokes could easily go a step further and become a magician or necromancer. Then it would not be at all difficult to hold men in one's power.

From the beginning of time, the Orient has been filled with prophets, who by means of simple artifices which can easily be learned there, acquired the reputation of being holy men. Mohammed had no wish to be that kind of a holy man. He wanted to rule through the power of the word, through the force of conviction. His means for this were example, education and discussion. The religion which he preached to the people was primarily an exaggerated positivism. Everything supernatural, everything that could not be grasped by the senses was hateful to him. The resurrection of man, a dogma which was not accepted by the Arabs for a long time, was not explained by cheap ghostly apparitions as was the case with the other holy men of the Orient, but by the miracle of the death and constant rebirth of nature.

This positive faith of the Prophet necessitated lively examples. All sources agree as to the humble manner of life of the messenger of God. He slept and ate but little, and went so far as to say that over-indulgence in food was a sin. He respected the poor for they were marked by God. Wherever he met them, he invited them to his house and shared his meal, which consisted for the most part of figs and water. Any slave could appear before him and demand justice. Nothing was too trivial to warrant his attention. He comforted all in need of comfort, and he was always conscious of the weakness, as well as the strength, of his own mission. He never looked upon himself as anyone but a person destined to preach the word of God. "Do not ask anything supernatural of me," he said to his followers, "for the angels are supernatural. When God wills, He will send an angel to earth; but I am a man."

And so Mohammed, the messenger of God, lived and preached in Mecca, the city of three hundred and sixty idols. It was the hatred of the Quraishites which altered his mission.

THE FIRST FLIGHT

If I perish, I perish.
Luther

The following story, attributed to Rabi'a of the tribe of the Gamidshi, is an excellent example of the patriotism of the Arabian tribe, of its national consciousness, and its pride. "The best among all people are the Arabs," said Rabi'a. "The best among the Arabs are the tribes of Mudar. The best among the Mudar are the tribes of the Qaisites. The best among the Qaisites is the tribe of Jasir. The best among the Jasirites is the family of the Gamidshi. But I am the best of the Gamidshi. Therefore I, Rabi'a, am the best among all people."

Thus most of the Arabs thought, and still think, as did old Rabi'a, with the one difference that they substituted their own family name and that of their tribe for Gamidshi and Mudar. It is impossible for an Arab to recognize the authority of another family. Under no circumstance will he listen to a man from a strange people, and he will automatically oppose even the slightest of attempts to encroach upon his freedom. In this the Meccans were full-blooded Arabs. Mohammed's intentions aroused violent opposition in them.

Abu Hakim ibn Hashim, of the house of the Mahkzum, was the most conservative among the Meccans. Together with Abu Sufyan of the Ummayah, and Abu Lahab who was related to the Ummayahs, he made up the front of the ancient Arabian school of thought. "We, the Mahkzum and the Ummayah," he said, "have often been in competition with the Hashemites. But our families are like noble Arabian steeds, we have always won the race. Can we now permit the Hashemites to produce a prophet who communicates with God?" These words found much favour among the aristocratic families. But they were really intended for the broad masses. Within the narrow circle of the Quraishites, Abu Hakim's thoughts were quite different.

Abu Hakim was clever, conservative and stubborn. His eyes were constantly turned towards the past and he hated all that was new. He loved the old gods, not because they were gods but because his fathers had prayed to them. He loved the city of Mecca and the noble tribe of the Quraish. He loved the fashionable for its own sake, and hated the common people with their lack of tradition. He was the wisest among the Meccans and the most bitter foe of the Prophet. Mohammed called him "Abu Jahl," "the father of stupidity," but most of the Moslems, who were given to the use of less choice epithets, for a variety of reasons called him "the man with the perfumed behind."

Abu Jahl was small, red-haired, strong, brutal, despotic, cunning and far-sighted. He recognized the importance of Mohammed, even before the Prophet himself had realized it. If the three hundred and sixty gods in the Caaba, so Abu Jahl thought, are to be replaced by a single, omniscient and all-powerful god, it is clear that the man who stands in direct communication with him and receives his commands will be the mightiest man in the world and will demand the power that no Quraishite will ever grant him. If, in addition, the three hundred and sixty gods are retired, the Bedouins will no longer come to Mecca. Other cities will grow and wax rich while Mecca declines. What does this prophet preach anyhow? That all men are equal, that God is just to all, and that one will be punished for one's deeds in another world. This meant that the Quraishites wrongfully ruled over wealth, power and people, that they were no better than the meanest slave, and that they would have to relinquish their exalted position. No wonder that more and more slaves, beggars and servants ran to Mohammed every time he preached. In short, Mohammed's cause was nothing other than a movement of the masses against the long-established rulers of Mecca.

As soon as Abu Jahl had realized this, he was determined to oppose the Prophet to the very end, until the last bit of his false teaching had been uprooted. He decided to dedicate his life to the battle for ancient Arabia, for the noble family of the Quraish, for the three hundred and sixty gods, and for the proud city of Mecca.

Abu Jahl's party was great, mighty and influential. The noblest of the Quraish belonged to it. The struggle between the revolutionary Prophet and the rich merchants soon assumed concrete form. Inasmuch as Mohammed himself was under the protection of the Hashemites, it was planned to persecute his followers. This was not difficult, for most of his adherents were poor slaves, beggars and strangers who had sought safety and protection in the new religion of the rich and elegant prophet. It was permissible in Mecca to persecute one's own slaves or the members of one's own family, and lavish use was made of that privilege. The cellars of the Quraish castles were soon filled with prisoners who had remained faithful to the Prophet. For the unusually stubborn, where ordinary punishments remained ineffective, actual tortures had been provided.

An ardent disciple of the Prophet was the negro Bilal, the first *mu'azzin* in Islam. His owner, an Ummayah, brought him naked and in fetters to the desert, where he threw him face up on the burning sand saying, "You will stay here until you die or give up your allegiance to the Prophet." The negro remained faithful to his master. A few days later, more dead than alive, he was sold to the pious Abu Bakr. In this year, the helpless were completely at the mercy of the Quraish. Mohammed spent the greater part of his fortune in ransoming those of his adherents who were in their power. The persecutions continued. The Hashemites protected Mohammed alone. The fate of the remaining disciples was of little interest to them. It is not surprising that a number of his followers deserted Mohammed at that time. The calvary of Islam was too hard. It is the more astonishing that the very year in which the Prophet suffered so many of his disappointments also saw the coming of the most devoted of his adherents, and that the persecutions in the materialistic city of Mecca brought a reaction which led numerous disciples to the feet of the Prophet.

The Prophet was weak and the houses of his enemies seemed like an armed camp. Blood flowed in the narrow streets of Mecca, and Mohammed's heart was laden with grief. Often he sat for hours on end on the flat roof of his house, looked sadly at the desert, looked at the city of Mecca, and at the eternal blue heavens from which no relief came. The God of Islam is the God of the people of the Book, thought Mohammed, and the people of the Book must aid the messenger of their God. And since Mohammed was weak and could not protect his followers, he decided that the persecuted, who no longer knew how to defend themselves, should emigrate to the court of the Christian ruler, the wise Negus, the Emperor of Abyssinia. He was to give them the peace and protection which was denied them at home.

Huge, intelligent elephants wander through the land of the Negus and white snakes lie between stones and look with large green eyes at sinful mankind. There, black priests pray to the Christian God of Byzantium. Giraffes, dwarfs and spirits live in the land, and over all these, over the priests, snakes, swamps, dwarfs and elephants, rules the King of Kings, the Negus, who is descended from the wise Solomon and the beautiful Queen of Sheba.

The Negus was learned, just and mighty. He was not afraid of the people of the Quraish. When the fugitives from Mecca came to his capital, Aksoum, he received them with friendship and promised them protection. The Negus did not like the tribes of the Quraish, for they were rich and proud, and pagan as well. He recalled the time, long ago, when Abraha, the Abyssinian, had been exiled in shame from Mecca. His heart thirsted to carry the God of Christianity into Mecca and to appropriate unto himself the riches of the city of the desert. That is why he was so friendly to the fugitives from Mecca.

The news of the reception at the court of the Negus spread over swamps, deserts and seas. Soon it reached Mecca, and the faces of the Quraishites clouded over. Mohammed was a danger, but a graver danger still was the Negus. If the enemy at home were to ally himself with the enemy abroad, the good fortune of Mecca would be at an end. The Quraish set up a huge caravan and outfitted it with gold, silver and precious materials. Its leader was the cunning poet Amr, who was sent to heap ridicule upon the Prophet, and to persuade the Negus, with presents, lies and trickery, to hand over the exiles.

At Aksoum, in the great throne room, costly and beautiful presents were spread before the eyes of the Negus. Amr stepped forth and said, "O Ruler, you are sheltering within your walls people who ridicule your and our faith. Deliver them unto us so that we may deal with them accordingly." But the Negus thought of his ancestor, Solomon, of his wisdom and righteousness and said, "I will not hand over the strangers until I am convinced of their heresy." He called the representative of the faithful, Uthman ibn Affan, and commanded him to speak of his faith. "We were ignorant," began Uthman, "we knew nothing about God and committed evil deeds. The strongest fed upon us, the weakest, until God sent us a prophet who taught us to pray to God alone, and to shun evil. He led us to prayer, to giving alms and to doing pious deeds, and he freed us from deceit and wickedness." "What do you think," asked the Negus, "of 'Isa (Jesus) and the Virgin Miriam?" "'Isa is in truth and in spirit the messenger of God born of the Virgin Miriam."

The Negus arose, picked a small piece of wood from the floor and, looking at the ambassadors of the Quraish, he said, "The faith of this people does not differ as much as the size of this little piece of wood from the faith of my people, and not for a mountain of gold would I give them up." And Amr ibn al-As, the future conqueror of Egypt, was forced to leave the country in great shame, for it is a shame for an ambassador if one does not even accept his gifts.

The faces of the Quraish were disfigured with fury when they heard the answer of the Negus. Up till then they had thought that Mohammed might become a danger for them. Now they knew that Mohammed had actually become one, and that he was backed by a still greater one, the Negus. The Negus was mighty. It would have been possible for him to attack the country in order to protect Mohammed, to seize the wealth of Mecca, and all because of the madness which Mohammed preached. The noblest families of the city banded together to defend the Caaba. At their head was the greatest among the Meccans, Abu Sufyan, the leader of the house of the Ummayah. At that time, no one dreamed that it would be the Ummayah who were to derive the greatest benefits from Mohammed's act, and that they were to furnish the first dynasty of caliphs in Islam.

Now that the answer of the Negus had been received, Mohammed had become a dangerous social reformer; what is more, a revolutionary who with the aid of an armed, outside power might possibly overthrow the existing social and political regime and place the slaves in a position of equality with their masters. No wonder that his idea doubled the fear and terror of the Quraish.

And so an abstract idea had been changed into a very concrete danger. Out of the nothingness, the blurred contours of a new world appeared.

But the Prophet of the new world did not go into the land of the Negus. He remained at his post in the city of his mission.

This occurred in the fifth year of the mission, and the Arabian chronologists call the period the first Hidshra, the first flight of the faithful from Mecca.

THE PROPHET IN HIS OWN COUNTRY

Whomsoever God wishes to guide, He opens his heart to Islam.

Koran vi, 125

While the weakest among his followers sought shelter at the court of the Negus, Mohammed, in order to escape from the hatred of his fellow-citizens, withdrew to the well-protected house of his student, Arqam, which lay on Mount Safa near Mecca. Many thousands of years ago, when the Lord of the World in His anger had closed the gates of heaven to Adam and Eve, the first two human beings wandered aimlessly over the face of the earth. The punishment of God lay heavy upon them, and they did not dare to indulge in sinful pleasures. For this reason, they separated at the gates of Paradise and drifted about alone. Their paths led them over mountains and through valleys, until they came to a barren hill in the land of Hejaz. There they met, and their joy was so great at having found each other, that they gave birth to the first people on earth.

The pious Arqam had built his house on this sacred spot, and it was here that Mohammed took refuge from the hatred and contempt of the Quraishites. Since he was a prophet and could not neglect his mission, he went daily to the Caaba, preached Islam and recited the Koran. Abu Jahl, who hated the Prophet more than all the Quraishites put together, decided to persecute him until he would cease his visits to the Caaba. Abu Jahl hated Mohammed as a matter of principle and because of his own love for the free life of the Arabs. This motive lent titanic strength to his hatred. He was actually prepared to sacrifice his own life to the gods and was secretly bent upon persecuting Mohammed until the Prophet, losing his temper, would kill him. Were this to happen, his tribal brothers could safely do away with the Prophet without fear of a resulting blood-feud, and peace would once again be restored in Mecca.

For this reason, Abu Jahl did things to Mohammed which would have transported any Arab into a fury. When he met him on the street, he attacked the Prophet, tore at his beard (the worst insult one can inflict upon an Arab), and heaped all manner of indignities upon him. When he saw that all this was of no avail, he determined upon committing the greatest injury possible to an Arab. He waited until Mohammed again knelt down in prayer in the Caaba, and creeping up upon him he threw the placenta of a sheep at his head. Mohammed arose, looked quietly at the red-headed one, and said, "Forgiveness is greater than vengeance." Calmly he went back to his house and ordered his daughter to clean his garments.

But the shame which Abu Jahl had visited upon the Prophet was too great to remain without consequences, and they followed thick and fast, in the person of his uncle, Hamzah. Hamzah was one of the bravest warriors in Mecca; he was tall, broad-shouldered and feared by all. He had no use for the remarkable teachings of his nephew, nor did he care for religion. He was content with the pleasures of the hunt. One day when he was returning from a hunting expedition, he learned that the Makhzumite, Abu Jahl, had thrown the placenta of a sheep at the head of his nephew. He was furious. He ran to the Caaba and administered a thorough beating to the offender. When he had finished, he shouted, "From now on, the faith of my nephew is my faith, his god is my god. Who will dare to oppose me for it?" Abu Jahl's relatives gathered together in order to slay Hamzah. But Abu Jahl had the wisdom of a statesman. It was true that he wished to destroy the Prophet, but he had no desire to start a blood-feud. He turned to his relatives and said, "Leave Hamzah alone, for he is right. I have done a great injury to his nephew." The blood-feud was nipped in the bud, but Islam won a new, mighty and much-feared follower. Besides Ali, Hamzah was the only Hashemite to confess the faith of the Prophet. Even in our day, Hamzah is the hero of many a romantic Arabian tale.

At that time, Hamzah's conversion was of great importance to Mohammed. The strong muscles of his uncle made more impression upon the enemy than did the threats of eternal damnation on the part of the nephew.

But no one realized that the conversion to Islam of a young, strong though poor lad, named Umar, would be of even greater importance. Up to the time of his conversion, Umar had practised each of the professions open to a Quraishite. He had been, in turn, a commercial traveller, a merchant and a smuggler. And at smuggling he made a great discovery. When he neared the frontier of Byzantium where the customs were stationed, he gave his precious possessions, such as gold and the like, to his camels to swallow. In this way he increased his fortune until the customs officials caught on to his trick. Despite his adventurous nature, Umar was not rich. He remained a poor, striving Quraishite whose talents were wanted by no one. When he had learned that the persecution of Mohammed had become the newest sport in Mecca, he joined the aristocratic party and insulted the Prophet whenever he could. When this also failed to further his ambitions, he decided to commit a great deed and thereby secure both fortune and the gratitude of Mecca.

He planned to murder Mohammed. With drawn sword he set out for the house of the Prophet, and on the way he met an old Arab. "You wish to kill Mohammed?" said the old man. "You had better see to it that there are no Moslems in your own house." He told Umar that his own sister had gone over to Islam. Filled with rage,

Umar hurried to his sister's house and actually found her reading the Koran[1]. He slapped his sister's face, but before slaying her he decided to inform himself as to the contents of the dangerous writings[1] she was reading. Like many others, he apparently had but little knowledge of the object of his hatred, and for this reason he sat down to read. It has been said that he was so greatly and wondrously affected by the verses of the Koran that he ran to the house of the Prophet with the drawn sword still in his hand. His appearance brought fear to the hearts of the inhabitants of the house, but Umar declared that he merely wished to be converted to Islam.

A great future was in store for him, for he was to be the Paul of Islam, the second caliph and successor of the Prophet, the ruler over a huge empire. He built the well-known mosque of Jerusalem, conquered Persia and Egypt, organized the empire, and beat all who came into his way, not even excepting the Prophet's wives, with his big stick, which was more feared than the sword of the mightiest warrior. Until the time of his death, he had great contempt for palaces, soft cushions and civilized life. He lived in a tent and slept on a saddle. His stick erected the world-power of Islam.

As soon as he had been converted, Umar ran to the house of Abu Jahl and said, "I withdraw from your community, for I too am a Moslem." In contrast to most of the faithful, he made no secret of his conversion. He wanted everyone to know about it, to feel the blows of his stick. Umar's field of activity was a great one. Together with the fashionable Abu Bakr and the powerful Hamzah, Umar was the protector of the Prophet in his most difficult years.

The conversion of Umar and Hamzah shook the ranks of the Quraish and it appeared as if the heresy had become widespread. Unpleasant news came from the desert as well. It was learned that a number of the desert tribes had gone over to Mohammed, for word of his miraculous activities had spread, and the Prophet was soon considered to be a figure of political importance. The Quraish were sure of one thing: a social reformer of the most dangerous sort lay hidden behind all the nice sayings and legends of Mohammed. The Quraishite families were now banded together more closely than ever, and they elected the noblest of the Meccans, the chief of the house of the Ummayah, Abu Sufyan Sakhr ibn Harb, to be the official leader of their movement. The situation steadily grew worse in Mecca. Mohammed's enemies gathered together day and night in the government buildings. No one knew what they were plotting. It was only known that their hatred was great and that their determination grew steadily with their hatred. Something was being planned and the fears of the Hashemites grew from day to day.

For weeks Mohammed sat behind the walls of Arqam's house. He too knew that there was something in the wind. Silently, with eyes half closed, he sat upon soft carpets in the house of his friend. Silently his followers sat around him. But the alarmed, hostile city of Mecca surrounded the house, the Prophet and the verses of the Koran.

Mohammed loved the city. He loved the grey valley with its barren rocks, the square buildings, the narrow streets, and the sacred black stone of the Caaba.

Mecca, the Holy Place! When the Prophet had been in the desert, while he had travelled through strange, hostile countries, the hand of the loveliest of cities had protected him. Camels raised their heads when the word Mecca was spoken in the desert. The robber bands of the Bedouins dispersed when they saw a Quraishite in the distance. For Mecca, the plaything of the gods, the city of the birth of the Prophet, was mighty, rich and joyous. The holy well, Zamzam, bubbled in the sand. Its waters were as sweet as the waters of Paradise, and Mecca itself with the Caaba was an image of the palaces of the Almighty. Mohammed loved his city, loved the people of the streets to whom he had first preached the word. Now the city lay before the Prophet and despised him. In the streets, in the squares, in the fashionable houses and in the Caaba, his name was mentioned with contempt. Mohammed knew this and the hatred of the city filled his heart with despair. In the quiet nights, when the Quraish sat at their councils, the Prophet prayed for peace and thought how he could open the hearts of the Quraishites to the new faith. For the Prophet had no desire for the downfall of the city, and he suffered greatly under the reproachful looks of the Hashemites.

One day the messenger of God again went to the Caaba. Hateful glances were directed at him. His followers stood close to him. Not one was sure of his life. In the courtyard of the Caaba stood three female idols, Manat, al-Lat and al-Uzza, moon virgins and daughters of the Almighty. These three were the patronesses of the city and were the favourite goddesses of the Quraishites. The prophet stood next to them. The Quraishites surrounded him, looked at him threateningly, with their hands on the hilts of their daggers, which they kept hidden in the folds of their garments. They awaited a new curse from the heretic.

Because Mohammed was a man like the others and because God wished him to commit one of each of the human sins, the Prophet lifted up his hand, pointed to the moon goddesses and said, "What do you think of Manat, al-Lat and al-Uzza? They are great virgins and we hope that they will protect us before the throne of the Almighty." The eyes of the Quraishites gleamed with joy and the Hashemites breathed more easily. If the Prophet recognized three of the idols, there was no need to worry about the fate of the others. Mecca could continue collecting its treasures in peace. One after the other, the Quraishites approached Mohammed and congratulated him. Not even they had expected so pleasant a revelation.

With his head bowed down, the messenger of God returned to his house, sat down again upon the rugs of his friend and was lost in meditation. Hour after hour passed by and Mohammed did not stir. His friends surrounded him. Each one told of the joy that reigned among the Quraish and of the peace that was to be resumed in

Mecca. Mohammed did not reply. His eyes were tightly closed and his lips softly recited the verses of the Koran. He felt the words of God over him, and the words dealt
with the great sin that the Prophet had committed. The Prophet prayed all through
the night and his face became grave.

Festively attired, the Prophet went to the Caaba on the next morning and again
he was surrounded by the Quraishites. But now their looks were friendly, their hands
were stretched out towards him and greetings came from their lips. Again the Prophet
strode to the idols of the moon goddesses. Again he asked, "What do you think of
Manat, al-Lat and al-Uzza? They are nothing but empty names which you and your
fathers created." Suddenly it grew still in the courtyard of the Caaba, the faces of the
Quraishites clouded over and their hands became fists. They picked up stones and
threw them at the Prophet. Curses came from their lips. But with his head proudly
held high, and surrounded by his pupils, Mohammed al-Amin, the Upright, the messenger of God, strode through their midst.

In this manner the Prophet acknowledged his sin, revealed the truth and sowed
anew the seeds of war, hatred and battle in the rich city of Mecca. For the Prophet
was but a man, a dreamer with a delicate face and soft hands. But the dreamer had
strength enough to confess his sins, to condemn the weakness of a moment, and fear-
lessly to declare bitter truth to the disappointed city.

For God wished his messenger to commit each sin once, repent of each sin once,
and openly confess his repentance.

The disappointment of the Quraish was great. It seemed that Mohammed was
incorrigible and grave measures must be taken against him. But the merchants were
not eager to take decisive steps. They hated bloodshed for they knew that it would
damage trade. As long as Mohammed was under the protection of the Hashemites,
they could unfortunately not touch him. Abu Sufyan, the leader of the Quraishites,
was a merchant and he too hated blood-feuds. He decided to attack the Hashim
along economic lines, in the hope that they might be led to excommunicate the
Prophet from their midst.

A deputation of Quraishites came to Abu Talib and declared: "If the Hashim do
not give up Mohammed to the authorities, they will be excluded from the free community of the city of Mecca. They must leave the confines of the city, they may no
longer offer their wares for sale at the markets, and no Quraishite will do business
with them. Marriage and friendship with the Hashim will be forbidden, and that
forever." This meant ruination and downfall to the Hashemites. None knew this better than Abu Talib, their chief. He did not wish to be the sole arbiter of the fate of
the Hashemites.

He assembled those who were touched by the threatened boycott, all the
Hashemites and the Muttalibs in his house. None of them believed in the prophecy

of Mohammed, they were all tired of the many persecutions, and they were all afraid of the imminent boycott.

It will be difficult for anyone in our day to comprehend that, in the year 616, a great number of normally inclined merchants took upon themselves a fearful fate of their own free will, and that they did this for a faith in which they did not believe, and for a man who was thoroughly unsympathetic to them all. But it was a question of primitive tribal law, and the power of the ancient blood-fellowship proved itself stronger than all the threats of the Quraish. All the hashemites and the Muttalibs, with the exception of Abu Lahab, declared themselves willing to forfeit their lives and their fortunes rather than give over one of their relatives to the enemy.

Abu Talib informed the Quraishites of their intention. On the very next day, a parchment roll was fastened on the door of the sacred Caaba, to remain there for all time, which condemned all the relatives and followers of the Prophet, and banished them from the community of the Quraish.

The same day, with their wives, children and cattle the exiles left Mecca and went to the east of the city where there was an old castle which belonged to Abu Talib. The excommunication of the Prophet had begun.

The Quraishites breathed more easily. Their guards watched at the entrance to the city by day and by night. They need no longer fear the false prophet. The double danger had rested heavily upon the city: the Negus with his huge elephants and his countless soldiers, who could have entered the city at any time from without, had not done so; and from within, the Prophet, the radical revolutionary, had been prohibited and had been banished forever.

Let the Negus come if he wished.

Weeks and months passed. Again the city of Mecca flourished and the caravans passed peacefully through its streets, the merchants and the dealers were contented, counted their money, rejoiced over their wealth, and prayed to the gods of the Caaba.

But the people of the Hashim lived in misery and hunger, and with them, the messenger of God and his small band of followers. The Prophet sat inside the castle. He was surrounded by his people, who hungered in their state of inactivity. But no one, neither Hashemites nor the faithful, dared to reproach him. For the laws of the tribe are like iron. But the Quraishites, too, knew of these laws and they dared not offend against them. When the holy months came, the gates of the city were opened and the Prophet walked at the head of his people to the Caaba, encircled the holy house seven times and preached the truth to the strange Bedouins who had come from the desert. None of the Quraishites dared touch the Prophet during the holy months. But when the feast was ended, the gates were once again shut and the guards watched over the place where the faithful hungered.

The decree of excommunication lasted for three years, for three years the Prophet lived in exile, and for three years the tribe and the faithful endured the curse of the city of Mecca. Soon the Quraishites noticed that merciful ones in their own midst began to take food secretly to the exiles, and they knew that the time for peace had come. At the same time, the mighty emperor, Khosrau, had invaded the land of the Negus and laid it waste. Now there was no further reason to fear the elephants of the Negus, and without the king's warriors the Prophet would be only half as dangerous.

The terms of peace which were offered to the exiles were by no means easy. Mohammed was to promise that he would no longer preach in the Caaba. He did so. Inasmuch as he was a prophet and could not do otherwise than preach, he did not keep his word. But God forgave him. It has already been said that the Prophet was to commit each of the sins once.

However, before the tribe was permitted to return to the city, it was necessary for the Quraishites to maintain their dignity. They had commanded that the decree of exile was to remain at the door of the Caaba for all time, that no human hand was to touch it. To the joy of all concerned, it happened that the parchment disappeared at night while no one was on guard at the Caaba. The gods were held responsible for this, and peace was solemnly celebrated. The Hashemites returned to Mecca, took possession of their houses and resumed their seats in the city's council.

This all happened in the year 619. It was the beginning of a difficult time for Mohammed. Disaster crept round his house, it kept watch at his threshold, descended upon him, and threatened to overpower him.

THE HEAVENLY JOURNEY

> Celebrated be the praises of Him who took His servant a journey by night from the Sacred Mosque to the Remote Mosque, the precinct of which we have blessed, to show him of our signs!
>
> *Koran xvii, 1*

Night lay over Arabia. The holy city of Mecca slept peacefully in the valley. The announcers in the bazaars were silent. A black, hot wind blew from the desert, and dry, heavy air came from the rocks which lay around the city. Exhausted by the night, the heavens and the desert, the Meccans lay in silence on their roofs. They were thinking of their gains and cursing Mohammed. On the following day, as on the day before, the conflict between them would be continued.

The idols stood in the great courtyard of the Caaba, and stared with empty, dead eyes upon the palace of the Ummayah and were silent. But there was no silence in the palace. In a circle made up of the noblest of the Meccans, Abu Jahl thought up new schemes to destroy the Prophet. Mohammed was weakened, deserted and humiliated. It was the tenth year of his mission. Night lay over Arabia, black, impenetrable night.

In his house, to the north of the Caaba, Mohammed lay awake. The night surrounded him. He was alone. He worried over the prophets of old, over the stones that were thrown at them, and at the glory of their sacrifices.

Mohammed's bed was lonely and dreary thoughts filled his heart. He had suffered three blows and the future filled with dangers lay black before him. Abu Talib, Mohammed's uncle, had died in his big palace, surrounded by all the Hashemites. For years his firm hand had protected Mohammed and for years Mohammed had lived in peace and security. Now the Quraishites could do as they pleased. Khadijah had died three days after the death of Abu Talib. She had been the first to recognize his mission and for fifteen years she had been faithful and loyal to Mohammed. This blow was the hardest. Mohammed no longer had a wife nor had he any sons. Now that he and the faithful were at the mercy of the Quraishites, life had become unbearable for him. So he decided to seek help and shelter in the city of Ta'if. With his slave, Zaid, he had ridden through the desert and arrived in Ta'if at night, where he encountered nothing but contemptuous laughter, hatred and suspicion. His own relatives in Ta'if turned from him, and with insults and in disgrace he was chased from the city. Children and slaves threw stones at him. It was only through the courage of Zaid that he was saved. The Quraish had made their preparations carefully. With his face covered with blood, Mohammed returned to Mecca. But the gates of his native city were not open to him, and it was only after lengthy and humble pleading that he was permitted to return.

With his eyes wide open, he lay upon his solitary bed and looked out into the night, and the agony in his soul was great. Suddenly he saw a man, dressed in robes embroidered with gold, enter the room. Mohammed recognized him, for he always knew him no matter what his dress was. It was Gabriel. This time he did not bring a new revelation. A much greater honour was in store for the Prophet. Gabriel led al-Buraq ("Lightning"), the heavenly steed. The creature had a human head, the torso of a horse, the gleaming tail of a peacock and white wings. "Ride with me," said Gabriel, "and great things will be shown to your eyes."

Al-Buraq flew over deserts, valleys and mountains and landed, as God had commanded him, at the great wall of Jerusalem. On that night, the guardians of the temple were unable to close its gates. They had to remain open for the messenger of God. They were held open by a divine force. Mohammed entered the temple. He was approached by the spirits of Abraham, Moses and Christ, who greeted him, and Mohammed prayed together with them.

Suddenly he saw a stream of light descend from heaven and shine upon Jacob's rock. Mohammed approached the light and saw a ladder which he ascended together with Gabriel. They went up and knocked on the silver doors of the first heaven. Adam opened the doors and greeted the greatest of the prophets. Mohammed saw many wondrous things in the first heaven, including a rooster whose comb reached to the second heaven. The distance from heaven to heaven, as everyone knows, is five hundred years.

The Prophet prayed and then wandered to the second heaven, which was made of gleaming steel. There he was greeted by the saintly Noah. In the third heaven, made of precious stones, the Messenger of God met an angel whose eyes were so far apart that it took seventy thousand days to go from one eye to the other. In the fourth heaven the Prophet saw an angel whose size was the length of five hundred days. In the golden fifth heaven, the Prophet was greeted by the pious Aaron, the brother of Moses. In the same heaven he met the Angel of Revenge, whose face was of red brass. In his hand he carried a fiery lance and lightning came from his eyes. He sat on a throne surrounded by a wreath of fire, and a mountain of glowing chains lay before him.

An angel whose body was made of fire and ice lived in the sixth heaven, which was made of gleaming stones. Moses also lived in this heaven, and his face became sad when he saw the Prophet, for he knew that Mohammed would lead more souls to Paradise than he had ever done.

No one knows what the seventh heaven was made of. At its gate he met the patriarch Abraham, the first of the faithful. It was in this heaven that Mohammed saw an angel with seventy thousand heads. Each head had seventy thousand mouths, and in each mouth there were seventy thousand tongues. Each tongue spoke seventy thousand languages and in all these languages the angel sang the praises of the Almighty. Next to the angel stood the Lote-Tree, the branches of which were larger than the distance between heaven and earth. The leaves on each branch were as big as an elephant's ear. Angels sat under the tree, and there were as many as there are grains of sand in the desert; thousands of birds sat on each branch, and every seedling of the tree enclosed a *houri*, a heavenly nymph. In the middle of the seventh heaven stood a house of prayer which was the image of the Caaba. It stood on the spot which lies directly over the Caaba in Mecca. Each day seventy thousand angels visited the Caaba, and Mohammed, fulfilling the old custom, encircled the heavenly edifice seven times.

Not even Gabriel could enter the seventh heaven. The throne of God was erected over it. Seventy veils covered His face so that no one could see Him, so that no one could make a likeness of Him. Nor could Mohammed see the face of the Lord.

The Lord of the World placed His right hand on the shoulder and His left on the breast of the Prophet, and spoke to him at length and in a friendly voice. He taught him the things of life, explained the deeper meaning of prayer, and showed him all honours. Altogether, the Lord of the World spoke ninety-nine thousand words to His Prophet and each word was filled with goodwill.

At the command of the Almighty, the punishments of hell were also shown to Mohammed. He saw Malik, the angel of hell. He saw men who were condemned to swallow fire because they had squandered the treasures of the wise men. He saw men, whose bellies were blown up, tortured by crocodiles, for in their lifetime they had been usurers and cut-throats. Then there were men who had good, fat meat before them and, lying beside it, stinking flesh, and they were forced to eat the bad meat. These were men who but seldom slept with the wives God had given them, who spent themselves on strange women. Next to them, he saw women hanging by their breasts because they had presented their husbands with children that were not theirs. Finally, the messenger of God once again mounted al-Buraq, which brought him back to the earthly city of Mecca.

And so the Prophet's heavenly journey ended. Cosmo-graphically, the journey was open to attack, but it was filled with daring poetry. How long had it lasted? When Mohammed had left his bed, he had upset a cup of water, and when he returned, the edge of the cup had not yet touched the ground.

The next day Mohammed told his story to his old aunt, Umm Hani', who was one of the oldest of the faithful. She listened to him in silence and then asked what he intended to do. "I will go to the Caaba and tell all the faithful and all the disbelievers about the miracle," replied Mohammed. Then the old woman took hold of his garment and begged, "Do not do that, O messenger of God; the disbelievers will have no confidence in you and the faithful will begin to doubt you." Mohammed did not follow her advice. He went to the courtyard of the Caaba, called the faithful and all the disbelievers who would listen to him, and told them about his night's journey.

The people answered the Prophet's vision with howls, laughter and derision. "Do we need any better proof of your madness?" said the Meccans. But the faithful bowed their heads in shame and were ready to leave Islam. For never before had one heard anything similar in Mecca.

Abu Bakr, the noblest of the Meccans, was not in the Caaba when Mohammed related his vision. The Quraishites hurried to his house to tell him of the Prophet's disgrace. "What would you say," they began, "if a man were to tell you that he journeyed from Mecca to Jerusalem in one night, that he had ascended to the seventh heaven, there exchanged ninety-nine thousand words with God, and returned to Mecca in the same night?"

"I would say that the man was a liar or mad," Abu Bakr replied. "Know then," said the Meccans, "that the man who made such a claim is your friend Mohammed, who calls himself the messenger of God." "That can't be true," replied Abu Bakr in anger. "Then go to the Caaba and reassure yourself," said the Meccans, and even the faithful confirmed their words. "Then," said Abu Bakr solemnly, "every word of the journey is true and I believe in it as I believe in day and night." Because Abu Bakr was rich, powerful and influential, none dared to laugh at him. Their belief in the mission was restored to the faithful, but the disbelievers did not cease to ridicule Mohammed. They brought people to him who had been in Jerusalem, and demanded that the Prophet describe the city minutely. They sent messengers to all the tribes in the desert to belittle Mohammed amongst them. They accompanied him with laughter and howling when he walked through the streets, and persecuted his followers.

When the month of the feast came and the tribes of the desert poured into the city, the Quraishites sent messengers to the city limits and to the city gates who said to each tribe: "A dangerous madman lives in our city. He calls himself a prophet and declares that he journeyed to Jerusalem and back in one day, whereas you know that even the speediest caravan requires at least two months. If this madman should speak to you, pay no attention to him."

When the Prophet attempted to preach the true faith to the Bedouins who had come to the city, they turned from him saying, "Your own people, who must know you, have told us that you were a liar; consequently we cannot believe your words."

Mohammed's heart was filled with sadness. Many people fell off from Islam: its protector was dead, and Khadijah as well. The city of Mecca lay around the sacred Caaba, laughing, threatening and ridiculing; it would have nothing to do with the Prophet; it adored dead idols, collected wealth and warned all of the tribes of the desert, "Do not listen to him for he is mad."

And so the Prophet decided to leave the city of his mission, and seek among the simple tribes of the wild Bedouins the protection and faith that he could not find in the courtyard of the Caaba.

THE HIDSHRA[2]

> A martyr is he who gives his life for things other
> than earthly goods.
>
> *Mohammed*

Mohammed again left the city and again he wandered through the desert. The Bedouins journeyed past him, and the camels advanced majestically. The Prophet greeted them, and the simple desert folk returned his greeting. The name of the Prophet was no longer unknown to the nomad tribes and to the wild inhabitants of the desert. "That is Mohammed," they said in respectful tones. "He claims that God speaks through his mouth." The desert liked and honoured everything that was holy, and Mohammed enjoyed a portion of this respect.

There must be something in a man of noble birth who is blessed with a fortune and travels through the desert, speaks of godly things and belongs to the queen of cities, Mecca. At least so the Bedouins thought, and they gave heed to Mohammed's words.

Each desert tribe in Arabia had the secret desire to possess a saint of its own, for it increased its reputation, brought many an advantage and on occasion proved useful. The tribal saint was well-treated, protected against enemies and his advice often asked in important matters. If the saint was intelligent, it was quite possible for him to become the regent of the tribe. At times regular competitions were held in order to secure a real saint and these holy men were often abducted or captured. They were guarded like some precious possession. The highest token of goodwill, however, was when the saint promised to die within the territory of the tribe. There was no greater piece of luck than this for the tribe. When the saint died, a mausoleum was erected over his grave and next to it an annual market was held. If the saint was popular, his grave attracted many visitors and that meant wealth for the tribe. To the people of the desert, Mohammed was a holy man who had fought with his own tribe and now sought refuge. Not all the Bedouins had been in Mecca and so it was that not all of them had heard what was said about the Prophet in the city. But all who saw Mohammed said to themselves, such a holy man can do nothing but bring happiness to the tribe.

The Prophet became aware of his importance in the desert. He was a Meccan and a Quraishite of the noblest race of Arabia. He was clever and had influential followers. Every Bedouin tribe counted itself lucky if they possessed his friendship. A number

of tribes came to Mohammed, kissed the hem of his garment and offered him protection. The Prophet did not accept their offers. He knew that the time of peace had
passed and that the time of battle had come; the proud menace of Mecca lay before
him. He had no means of conquering it peaceably, and for this reason the messenger
of God sought mighty warriors, bellicose tribes and courageous followers who could
level for him the way which led to the truth.

It happened that one day the Prophet of God was passing through the gorge of
Aqabah. It was towards the end of the month of the feast in the year 620. Suddenly
Mohammed saw six or eight Bedouins ranged around a fire. The Prophet approached
them and asked the name of their tribe. "We are Khazrajites and come from Yathrib,"
was the reply. The city of Yathrib was known to the Prophet for he had relatives there.
He knew too that many of its inhabitants were Jews familiar with the Bible, and that
they believed in but one god. "Do you live together with the Jews?" asked Mohammed. And the people of Yathrib answered in the affirmative. "Then know that
the God of the Jews is my God, and I am His messenger on earth." These words
made a strong impression on the strangers. They themselves were heathens, but when
they fought with the mighty Jewish tribes, which happened frequently enough, the
Jews would say, "Take heed, you heathen; when the messenger of our God comes he
will grind you to dust." But even the wisest among the Jews did not know when the
Messiah was to come, so that the heathen lived in peace for the time being. Suddenly
the long-expected Messiah stood before them and made inquiries about the Jews. He
did not seem at all angry.

The Khazraj were a simple, wild people. The Messiah had come, but apparently
the Jews in Yathrib knew nothing about it. It would be wise for them to secure the
goodwill of the new prophet at the outset. They offered Mohammed shelter and protection. But Mohammed was cautious. The time of the conflict was at hand and the
Prophet had to be diplomatic. He promised them nothing and acted as if he were
not at all dependent upon their help. He explained Islam to them and commanded
that they were to return within a year, bringing the best of their people with them.
The wild Khazrajites promised to remain true to Islam and went their way.

A year had passed and the Prophet's situation had become more precarious. When
Mohammed returned to Mecca and shyly walked through the streets, the children
threw stones at him or covered his head with sand. None of the Quraishites would
do business with him, and he was even forbidden entrance to the temple. His followers were impoverished and perishing. Sometimes Mohammed feared that it was
not the renown of a saviour, but the martyr's crown of thorns which awaited him.

When the year was over, and the Bedouins again poured into Mecca, twelve men
came from Yathrib and said that they were the representatives of the Khazraj. They
talked with the Prophet and again offered him their protection. The prophet still

hesitated. He taught them the tenets of Islam at great length, converted them to the true faith and made them swear not to worship other gods, not to steal, not to kill children, not to bear false witness, and to obey the Prophet in all things. But he did not demand the most important pledge of all, that they were to fight for the true faith even if it cost them life and fortune. The oath which they did take was called the oath of the women; when a woman is converted to Islam it suffices that she take this minor oath.

Again the Prophet refused to accept the protection of the people of Yathrib, for the city did not seem safe enough and the people too wild and hostile. However, as a token of his favour, he sent to the faithful in Yathrib Musab ibn Umair, who was to teach them, read the Koran, and arrange the necessary transactions. To the people of Yathrib he said, "Return in one year."

Musab ibn Umair was wise. He had been much beloved in his youth. He knew how to dress well, was a past master in the art of doing nothing and spent his money like no other. All this gave him much experience in life. But his heart had remained empty, had tired of the inane fashionable way of living of that time. He had been converted to Islam and served it with heart and soul. He had been one of the faithful who had emigrated to Abyssinia and had returned clothed in rags. He was not only wise, but cunning as well. He believed in the Prophet and was well adapted to diplomatic affairs. When Mohammed felt that the time was ripe for open conflict, he did not select a preacher to be his representative in Yathrib, but a diplomat. Musab ibn Umair, who had once again become fashionable, proved himself worthy of the trust. He remained in Yathrib for an entire year and recited the verses of the Koran. In addition, he related wondrous things about the wisdom of the Prophet. In that year, he accomplished the conversion of all the tribes in Yathrib. The Jews were converted because they believed that Mohammed was a Jew like themselves, and the heathen because they hoped that Mohammed would defend them against the Jews.

Another year had gone by. In the spring of 622, in the time of the feast, Musab returned to Mecca and brought a stately delegation of seventy men with him from Yathrib. They put up their tents near Mecca, visited the Caaba and performed all the magical ceremonies so as not to attract attention to themselves. Apparently they paid no heed to the mad Hashemite. When night set in, dark covered figures stole their way into the camp of the Yathribites. They were the Prophet and his uncle al-Abbas, who had no faith in his nephew but, being a noble Hashemite, had placed him under his protection.

The Arabs of Yathrib, having been carefully coached by Musab, received the Prophet with all the reverence the simple folk of the desert were capable of. Before any negotiations could take place, a remarkable ceremony had to be performed. It was necessary that Mohammed be officially excommunicated from the tribe of the

Hashim. No one could do this other than his fashionable protector, his uncle al-Abbas, who in all probability was overjoyed at ridding himself of his troublesome nephew in this manner. But al-Abbas was no fool and he took care to retain the goodwill of all sides. He made a long speech, in which he told them how dear his nephew was to him, how secure the Prophet was under his protection even though they did not share the same opinions. But since, for reasons which the uncle could not understand, his dearly beloved nephew wished to join the tribe of the people of Yathrib, he had no desire to stand in his way and acceded to his request most unwillingly. However, he would only do so if the people of Yathrib would swear by all that was holy and dear to them that they would treat his nephew with all conceivable respect. The Yathribites agreed and al-Abbas left the tent. He had won a great battle that night, possibly greater than he himself knew, for later on his family was to furnish the eminent caliphs of Islam.

Now the negotiations started in earnest. The people of Yathrib agreed to take in Mohammed and all his followers and be obedient to him in all good things. At the same time, they humbly asked what these good things were. This time the Prophet went a step further. "You must," he said, "obey me implicitly and must defend me just as you defend your wives and children. You must know that my heart is open to all people and not to you alone. You must sacrifice your blood and your fortune for the true faith, if I command you to do so."

This was a large demand, and again the Yathribites humbly inquired what their reward would be if they were called upon to offer up blood and fortune for the cause. "Paradise," answered the Prophet. The people had learned from the tales of Musab what Paradise was. Of course it would be fine to enter into Paradise, but at the same time one could not afford to neglect mortal things. "If we fight for you and secure wealth and fortune for you, will you not leave us and return to your own people?" asked a wise old man, for he knew how important it was for a city to shelter the grave of a saint. Thereupon Mohammed swore not to leave his adopted home, to look out for its welfare, to love the people and to regard their blood as his blood. This ended the transactions. A rather questionable prophet was turned into an actual statesman and politician.

Mohammed immediately appointed his representative in Medina. He held out his hand to each of the seventy men and left the camp. It had been agreed upon that all the faithful were to depart from Mecca gradually in order to emigrate to Yathrib. The Prophet himself wished to be the last to leave so that none of the faithful need suffer because of him. The emigration was to be carried out as secretly as possible. No one was to know that the Prophet was soon to be called to great things in the city of Yathrib.

When assemblies are held by night, when a large group of people wishes to emigrate, when the seed of a new state is to be planted, it is obvious that it cannot all be accomplished in secret. One day, the Quraishites learned of the plans of the dangerous madman, and the indignation on the part of the bankers of Mecca was great. Had it not sufficed that the Hashemite had disturbed the entire city, that he wished to destroy both trade and the city's gods? And now he even wished to emigrate with all his followers into a strange city where, freed from the jurisdiction of sane people, he might attempt to attack his own city. Truly, this was treason indeed.

The financiers of Mecca at once suggested that stringent measures be taken against the emigrants. But most of the Quraishites would have none of it. On the contrary, they thought the idea an excellent one, for the faithful left the city in secret and were forced to leave their possessions and moneys behind. It would be possible to seize the deserted property or secure it at but small expense. Were immediate action taken against Mohammed, then the emigration would cease and the profits of the Quraishites be curtailed. Since they knew that Mohammed had vowed that he would not leave the city until the last of the faithful had gone, they decided to wait and in the meantime keep an eye on the traitor.

Conditions must have been remarkable in Mecca. Every day one or the other of the faithful disappeared, every day one or the other house was occupied by the Quraishites, and every day young Meccans marched up and down in front of the house of the traitor, sang songs of contempt and derision and swore that they would have their reckoning with Mohammed when the last Moslem had left both city and his possessions behind him.

At last the time had come. Only Mohammed, Abu Bakr and Ali remained in the city. In the great assembly hall of the Caaba, the noblest among the Quraish had come together to decide upon weighty things. All knew that the opportune moment had come to settle matters with the disturber. But not one dared suggest the remedy which would exterminate the movement forever.

The Quraishites were courageous. But at the same time they were merchants and they hated bloodshed. Blood begets blood, and, where blood flows peaceful commerce is at an end, business ceases and capital is decreased. The Quraishites knew this by experience. None of the families wished to take the curse of a blood-feud upon itself. For now Mohammed was under the protection of the Khazraj, who were certainly not to be trifled with. One thing was clear: Mohammed was not to be permitted to leave the city. "We will throw him in fetters into jail," spoke the Quraish, only to become silent again, for they all knew that sooner or later the Prophet would be set free no matter how well he was guarded.

Then the Father of Hell, Abu Jahl, arose, the wisest of all the Quraish. "Mohammed must die," said Abu Jahl, "and, in order to avoid a blood-feud, each family must provide a participant in the murder. Then the blame will fall upon us all, and no hand will dare be raised against all the tribes of the Quraish." Abu Jahl was a wise man. He knew what he was saying. The Yathribites would be powerless against all the families of the Quraish.

Each family selected a youth to aid in ridding the city of the Prophet. However, whenever an entire city comes to a decision, it cannot remain hidden from the individual. Soon the Prophet learned of what had been planned against him and when he was to be the victim of the Quraish daggers, and he determined to flee.

Mohammed was not only a prophet but a man also, and, like other men, he had business affairs in the city. He also had debts and he did not wish to leave before everything had been paid, so that no one could say that the Prophet had fled with the money of others.

Two of the faithful stayed with Mohammed in the city, Abu Bakr and Ali. Ali was the younger and the Prophet decided to leave him behind. When the night had come in which the Meccan youths were to surround his house, Mohammed fled over the wall and took refuge in the house of Abu Bakr. But Ali, wrapped in the mantle of the Prophet and with his green turban on his head, remained on the terrace of the Prophet's house. The Quraish came, surrounded the house, saw the green turban and said, "Now the Prophet can no longer escape." At dawn, they poured into the house from the street, saw Ali quietly sleeping there, and awakened him saying, "Where is Mohammed?" "If I only knew!" answered the sleepy Ali.

Immediately a wild chase after the Prophet set in. Mohammed would simply have to be captured. The Quraishites took their best horses, and with drawn swords and sharp lances they rode into the desert in order to kill the messenger of God.

In the meantime, the messenger of God was crossing the endless, yellow desert. Only his friend Abu Bakr accompanied him. "The Quraish will follow us," said Abu Bakr, "they will slay us with sharp swords, they will cut up our bodies. Wild animals will howl over our graves. Mighty and hateful is this people."

Mohammed remained silent. He looked out into the distance, at the wide world which lay before him, and thought of the city of Mecca, and of the sword which he was now to bring to the people.

It was in 622 that Heraclius vanquished Khosrau. The people in the East and in the West were under the rule of Christendom, the Cross had conquered the world, and no one dreamt that in that year two anxious Arabian riders were carrying the fate of the world in their hands. The reckoning of time in Islam begins with that ride through the desert, with the Hidshra. In the year 622, Mohammed became a statesman, a statesman who carried a sword.

Mohammed rode through the desert. Mecca, in which the faith had been founded, lay behind him. But the Quraishites with drawn swords were riding through the desert as well, and, since their steeds were faster, they soon spied the fugitives in the distance. The fugitives saw their persecutors at the same time, and Abu Bakr said, "O Mohammed, the desert is flat, we are but two, and the Quraishites are behind us."

Then Mohammed replied, "You are wrong, Abu Bakr, we are not two but three, you, I and God." The Quraishites came nearer and nearer and Abu Bakr became more frightened. The fugitives discovered a small cave, hurried up to it and hid in its depths. A miracle happened: a huge spider crawled to the entrance of the cave and rapidly spun its web across it. Soon the Quraishites appeared. "The desert is flat," they said. "The two could not have disappeared. They are in the cave." The wisest of the Quraish looked at the entrance and, finally, said proudly, "They cannot be in the cave for do you not see that an old spider's web covers the entrance? The web would be torn had the two gone in." The Quraish wondered at the wisdom of their leader and rode on.

It was silent about the cave. The two fugitives knelt down to offer a prayer of thanksgiving, but before they had finished they heard footsteps which came to a halt at the entrance to the cave. Three of the Quraishites had remained behind and now stood before the cave. They saw the web, tore it open and entered. Abu Bakr held his breath in terror. And again a miracle happened, for the three men did not search the cave. They rested for a while and then went their way. In such a manner, God protected his messenger, Mohammed.

The Prophet spent a day and a night in the cave in the desert, and Abu Bakr was with him. When the time had come, they left the cave and resumed their flight. Again they rode through the desert. The sun shone unmercifully, the sand was hot and the Prophet was dying of thirst. They met a Jew Naurus, who was bringing water to his children. He saw the Prophet and realized that he was suffering from thirst. "I am the Jew, Naurus," he said, "my children are thirsty; but you must take this water, for we both believe in one God." And so the Prophet's thirst was stilled. To commemorate the event, the Feast of the Saving of the Prophet was called Naurus Bairam.

The messenger of God continued his flight through the desert until in the distance he saw the village of Quba, a suburb of Yathrib. Here the flight was at an end.

Islam had been firmly laid down as a faith and now it was to become an empire. The spirit became power, and the word became deed. The faith was to erect a world, for the nothingness out of which the spirit came had been overcome.

With sword in hand, the Prophet rode towards Yathrib which from now on was to be called Madinat-an-Nabi, "the city of the Prophet." The sword and the Koran were to rule the world.

TO WORK

If Islam means submission to God,
we all live and die in Islam.

Goethe

A pious Islamic legend tells us that on the night when Mohammed was permitted to step before the eyes of Allah, the Almighty had given him the commandment that man must say fifty prayers a day in praise of Allah. Only if he did this could he be sure of Allah's mercy. Mohammed bowed down before the Almighty, promised that he would force man to say fifty prayers each day, and went out of the palace of the Lord of the World.

When he had reached the sixth heaven, the messenger of God met Moses the Prophet. Mohammed's long sojourn in the palace of the Almighty had aroused the curiosity of Moses: which commandments had Mohammed received? Since Moses was a great prophet, he did not have to be ashamed of his curiosity, so he went up to Mohammed and asked what God had commanded him. "Allah has commanded that man must say fifty prayers daily," said Mohammed. Moses shook his head and said, "I am an old prophet, grown honourably grey. I know men too well. They will never say fifty prayers." Mohammed, who respected the words of his predecessor, returned to the throne of the Almighty and said, "O Lord of the World, men will not say fifty prayers a day." In His mercy, the Lord of Mankind remitted twenty-five of the prayers. And again Moses said to the messenger of God, "Nor will men say twenty-five prayers." Again Mohammed returned to the throne of the Almighty and begged for his sinful, weak people, and again he found mercy. Mohammed made the trip from the sixth heaven to the throne of the Compassionate One many times, for Moses was wise and experienced, and the Almighty was merciful. Finally the number of prayers prescribed by God was reduced to five, and even the sceptical Moses had to admit that this was not too much.

This legend is very characteristic of the nature of Islam. It is a religion with a maximum of possibilities and a minimum of responsibilities, a religion which in its commandments, dogma and doctrine has reached a pinnacle of external simplicity. This external simplicity is internally enlivened with a messianic-theocratic trend.

Mohammed demanded but little from his followers, and yet, at the same time, this little was a great deal. "God will make your faith easier, for man is weak," says the Koran, and, in fact, the prayers of the new teaching had been reduced to a minimum. And the minimum had been carefully worked out. No priests and no temples were needed, and even prayer itself was not always obligatory. "You will be forgiven if when travelling you neglect your prayers in foreign lands." Even pilgrimages and fasting could be avoided. Sickness, poverty and the like were sufficient grounds.

On the other hand, the life of the totemistic Arab was full of taboos. A number of foods could not be touched. Here, too, the Koran says, "Forbidden to you is that which dies of itself, and blood, and the flesh of swine, and that which is devoted to other than God." All the external requirements of faith were unimportant in the salvation of man, for God could forgive if they were neglected. "How shall God recognize the faithful?" asks one of the revelations, and the reply reads, "In the love shown for children, members of the family, neighbours and all men. Would you approach God, then love his creatures."

Islam is probably the only world religion which recognizes the belief that the adherents of other religions are not barred from attaining salvation. The famous fifth *Sura* says word for word: "Verily, those who believe and those who are Jews, and the Sabaeans, and the Christians, whosoever believes in God and the last day, and does what is right, there is no fear for them, nor shall they grieve." It was made easy for man to accept Islam. Human frailty was recognized in this religious system, and only now and again, like distant bolts of lightning, verses appeared which illuminated the deep nature of this faith. "Conquer evil through good," says the eleventh *Sura*, and the entire faith can be reduced to one sentence: "Would you approach God, be pure and be just."

The easier, the more comprehensible and tolerant the external interpretations were, the more difficult was the internal way of the faithful which at first had hardly been elucidated. The internal way has best been formulated by a great Islamic mystic: "You will simultaneously have the soul of an animal and the soul of an angel. Cast off the soul of the animal and let the soul of the angel excel."

But the way to perfection is difficult. Not everyone can tread it. Mohammed knew this, and he did not wish for the way to Paradise to be closed to sinful mankind. "The time will come when we shall be forgiven and set free, even if we have fulfilled but one-tenth of that which the Lord has commanded," comforts Mohammed.

The most remarkable thing about Mohammed was that two characters seemed to dwell peaceably within him: the ecstatic prophet and the calm practician. He alone knew the way, and to the others it was to remain hidden for the time being. At first, in the beginnings of Islam, it was only important that mankind, Arabian mankind, should be won over to monotheism. When this had been accomplished, when the primitive assumption of Islam had been accepted, then the rest which still remained closely guarded within Mohammed could be dealt with.

Mohammed did not hurry. His meteoric ascent was basically a step-by-step advance. He began modestly. Year after year he developed Islam into world-embracing importance. Here we meet a deep, internal similarity between Mohammed and Luther. Both trod their ways shyly, slowly and carefully, and they were only half aware where that way led; both developed their teaching gradually, both were masters of caution, vision and discretion, and at the same time they were carried on by a self-conviction from which they never deviated one iota and which they defended courageously. Strangely enough, they were both the creators of a language which made the founding of their faiths possible. In fact, the work of Mohammed recalls that of Luther. Here and there, a revulsion against dead ritual, the intensification of the spiritual life, and the refusing of all middle-men between man and God. Here and there, an internal purity, the capability of the calm reasoning out of a deep inner conviction. "Here I stand! I cannot act otherwise." This confession of Luther's was spoken innumerable times by the Arabian prophet among the stone idols of the Caaba. This was in the year 620, many centuries before the appearance of the northern reformer.

Mohammed's spirit was by no means humble, modest or tolerant. He created a faith and the faith was at the same time a demand. The faith in one god had been proclaimed in Mecca, and only few of the Quraishites recognized the inherent danger of this confession. If there was only one god and Mohammed was his only prophet, then it was logical to assume that sooner or later the Prophet would demand the sole leadership over the entire people, inasmuch as he would be the only revealer of God's will. If the only god spoke through one mouth, then everything which came from that mouth would have to be accepted as divine command. The belief in one god, the belief in his prophet, also brought up the question of world-sovereignty. And since the faith was identical with the Prophet, Mohammed the man would demand this right for himself. This too was the most daring of the precepts of Islam: "I am a man like the others," declared Mohammed; and yet this simple man demanded sovereignty over the entire world.

This demand was the absolute, logical sequel to the tolerant, pliable, basic theses of the Prophet. Never had the Prophet pronounced these dogmas in Mecca, nor had he even hinted at them. But when he founded the State of the faithful, a natural result was the question of sole, unimpaired world-leadership. Islam made demands for world-leadership. The demand was to be realized in Medina.

To Mohammed was given that which had been permitted to but few prophets, thinkers, philosophers and seekers after God, either before or after his time: he was permitted to practise what he preached. Mohammed erected the edifice of a state, a practical *Weltanschauung*, a world-power, out of the abstract words of the Koran. Medina was the incarnation of this work.

The way which led to all this was a spiritual one. In a resplendent world, which actually was split in two internally, there appeared, unaccompanied by any powerful factors, the beginning of all worlds, the word. And the word, the spirit, which was borne by a simple practician, withstood and opposed a host of similar hostile practicians who held all the powerful factors of those times in their hands, with the exception of one: the word.

The victory of Islam is the triumph of the spirit. The right to world-leadership, which the spirit claimed here, must of necessity have contained actual substance, must have possessed a spiritual and at the same time a practical, feasible programme; a goal which made the upheaval of mankind worthwhile.

What was Mohammed's goal? In comparison to the religious systems of ancient times, it is quite possible that this goal contained but little which was new. Yet the old was now carried over with an unheard-of determination into the practical. This practical realization of an abstract, religious teaching for the first time is really the only new note in world-history. The practical theology which Mohammed defended in Medina combined politics, state and religion in an unified whole which was not to be disintegrated in centuries to come.

In contrast to all the states created in the old Orient, the state of God, the state of Islam, was a democratic institution. Its democracy had ensued out of the primitive spirit of the desert. Mohammed destroyed the nature, the particularism of the free tribes. The countless tribes of the Arabs were to be replaced by one large tribe of Islam, which at first was to embrace Arabia and then the world. The internal organization of this great tribe was exactly like the structure of a desert tribe. The members of a tribe are all equal, and equally free are the faithful in Islam.

The form of government in Islam was like the regime known to the tribes. The tribal leader had limited power for he was bound by tradition, and he was merely the first in the council of the elders. It was the same in Islam. Here too there were no monarchs. One knew only the regent of the prophetic office, who was responsible to the wise men of the new faith and who could be removed at any time. But the laws, the traditions which embrace all, go back to the founder of the tribe, in this case, Mohammed. While Mohammed wandered over the steppes, he perceived the primitive system of desert democracy, he tested it, and lent it world-importance. And the system of the poor Bedouins showed itself capable of impressing a characteristic stamp upon the world of the Orient, and has influenced its fate even down to our day.

Mohammed and Islam deserve credit for having been the first to give democracy (that is, the thesis of absolute equality of mankind) development on a broad scale. The equality of mankind remained a fundamental axiom until the downfall of the caliphate. For hundreds of years races, classes and castes disappeared in this world-embracing system.

Equality of mankind was theologically founded in Islam, for the democracy of

Islam was a theocratic democracy. Men were slaves of God and as slaves they were equal. Each one was strictly ruled by the laws of God. Equality in Islam was not tantamount to freedom, just as the pre-Islamic Arab was anything but free. The ideal of Islam was like the ideal of all Oriental conquerors and leaders: the dependence of man upon a simple law, yet firm as iron, before which everything called man was equal.

The empires of the Orient were practically all built on this law. Genghis Khan, Tamerlane, none of them wanted anything else. Their empires rose and fell. Nothing could impede their decline. But Islam remained. Its democracy, its laws, its social conceptions endured. For behind Islam stood the free, untrammelled, creative spirit. This spirit could not perish.

Mohammed had appointed the warrior Mu'adh to be governor of the province of Yemen. "How will you decide in questions of government?" asked the Prophet. "According to the laws of the Koran," replied Mu'adh. "And if you find no answer there?" "Then I will follow your example." "But if that does not suffice?" "Then I will follow the dictates of my own spirit." The Prophet praised the warrior and held him up as an example to others. For the Prophet knew that one could rule men with weapons, laws and punishments, but that they can only be led through the free spirit.

This spirit of the boundless, free, eternal desert gave to the Prophet the leadership over the world of the Orient.

The beginning of this leadership was Medina.

III.

THE STATE OF GOD

Here ends the life history of the Prophet Mohammed,

    and his career as a statesman begins.

The sword prepares the way for the spirit.

Through the power of the word, a State is born in the desert.

The way of this State is the way of Islam.

The State was Mohammed.

THE CITY OF THE PROPHET

> The Faith fled to Medina like the snake fleeing
> into its hole.
>
> *Bukhari*

A city, a country accustomed to the free life of the desert, suddenly and without making any conditions submits to a strange fanatic who had been driven from his own home. It sacrifices its independent existence, takes up with the enemies of yesterday and capitulates to the despotic will of the stranger.

How is that possible?

By marching eleven days to the north of Mecca, one comes to the city of Yathrib, which lies in the middle of a small oasis. Once upon a time, so long ago that no legends concerning it have come down to us, the region was volcanic. At that time the earth quaked, streams of lava poured over the land, flames arose from the craters and the entire country burned to the shores of the great sea. All this happened in the grey past when there were no human beings to create legends in order to record the past.

Legends tell us that the Amalekites came from the North, and that their chief, Yathrib, discovered a few water sources there and built a number of clay huts to which he gave his name. The legendary Amalekites were followed by the Jews, who settled in the country in order to carry on trade in the wild, bare desert. In ancient days, three Jewish tribes ruled over Yathrib, the Banu Nadir, the Banu Qainuqa and the Banu Quraizah. The tribes waged war, rivalled one another and did not differ much from the heathen tribes of the country.

Yathrib was but a small, unprotected city. Trade did not seem to prosper there. Its inhabitants spent half their time in war with their neighbours, rivals and the professional robbers in the desert.

It happened that in the 4th century after Christ a dam suddenly burst in Yemen in the south of Arabia and turned a fertile piece of land into barren desert. A number of tribes were plunged into misery; they left the land and wandered northwards to seek their fortune anew. Among the emigrants were two Yemenite tribes, the Khazraj and the Aus. The Jews, the ancient rulers of the city, were capable merchants but they had no talent for politics. They permitted the two tribes to enter their city and a sort of contract was made to govern their relations with one another. The immigrants were to till the soil and fight the enemy, while the Jews were to carry on trade and remain at peace. Actually, both races were nothing but desert people who had never submitted to any restraint. Trade, pillage and war were one and the same thing to them, and tribal ties meant more than religion, contracts and political wisdom.

The five tribes paid but scant attention to their treaty. They warred with one another regardless of religion. Jews fought Jews; Arabs fought Arabs. Jews allied themselves with Arabs to fight other Jews. A general state of anarchy reigned in Yathrib. But the five tribes which were constantly fighting one another were dependent upon a common factor, the green fertile oasis. Therefore, the war of all against all never broke the feudal laws; the palm trees, fields and wells remained sacred.

The oasis was rich, productive and famous. Tall palms grew there, the air was heavy-laden with the perfume of flowers, and the dates of Yathrib were known in all the deserts, while the Jewish goldsmiths were famous throughout Arabia. Five tribes shared the rule over Yathrib, pursued agriculture or trade, fought with one another and had no idea that there was any form of community life other than the continuous feuds of the tribal republic of Yathrib.

Actually, the possession of the city was a source of weakness to the five tribes. Both city and oasis were unprotected. No one in all Yathrib knew how to erect fortifications around the city. The cultivating of fields and palm trees bound the inhabitants to the earth which they were forced to defend. Having renounced the free existence of the nomads, they had become sedentary.

The entire Arabian world is divided into two, the nomads and the city-dwellers. Strangely enough, the nomads always remain nomads even though they become sedentary, and it is equally true that the city-dwellers are always regarded as such no matter how much they may wander about. It is not their present condition which counts, but their past. In every walk of life and under all circumstances, the city-dwellers and the nomads are taught to hate and fight each other. The history of Arabia and the history of the caliphate down to our own time is filled with this hatred.

The fashionable merchants of Mecca, who had lived in the city for generations, were regarded as nomads. They were descendants of pure and noble Bedouins, and even though they were merchants they remained pure Bedouins in character and manner. The people of Yathrib who had wandered in from Yemen, the Aus and the Khazraj, were looked upon as sedentary, although they were less firmly bound to their city than were the fashionable Meccans to the capital. A fierce hatred was deeply rooted in both cities. The Meccans despised the inhabitants of Yathrib who were dependent upon the soil, and these in turn looked with jealousy upon the gentlemen of the Caaba, protected by their three hundred and sixty gods, who set the fashion throughout the desert.

Despite its fourteen thousand inhabitants, Yathrib remained a helpless city. It had no government. By means of a treaty which had never been taken seriously and because of their common interests, the tribes were but loosely connected. As in Mecca, there was no ruling power, no common religion, no laws, no gaol and no monarchs. Instead there were blood-feuds, primitive desert laws, and the melancholic, never-ceasing envy of Mecca, the queen of cities.

To this republic, to this city which was not a city, came Musab ibn Umair, the envoy of Mohammed, whose object it was to win over these remarkable people to the faith of the Prophet.

How did he succeed?

Musab ibn Umair was an intelligent man, familiar with the principles of Oriental diplomacy: to observe, to promise and to remain silent. This brought him success.

At that time, the rivalry between the tribes of Yathrib had assumed a definite form. The Jewish tribes, formerly the rulers of the city, had lost their position to the two Yemenite tribes. The result was that the victors fought one another while the Jews peacefully (a peace actually filled with feuds) awaited the coming of better times. But all the tribes were filled with the same fear, the fear that a mighty enemy might come and drive them out of the rich oasis. They were equally afraid because they were well aware that they could never be as wealthy, as mighty and as united as their proud neighbours of Mecca.

The people of Yathrib knew but little about the new prophet nor did religion mean much in their life. The Jews had their rabbis, the heathen had their idols, and that sufficed for their metaphysical needs. They knew that prophets existed and that a prophet, alive or in a mausoleum, could benefit a city. Mohammed demanded but little: he merely asked for asylum, something which an Arab would never deny a stranger. Obviously, the inhabitants of Yathrib never suspected that the domination over the city was connected with this asylum. At first they had merely pledged themselves to give hospitality and, in accordance with the law, to defend the guest. There had been other decisive factors in the invitation extended to the Prophet. The Aus and the Khazraj knew that the Jews were awaiting the coming of a great prophet. They thought it a wise move to have an Arabian prophet in their midst who did not ask much and promised a great deal. In recognizing him they were not obliged to make any sacrifices. The sober men of Yathrib cared but little for their heathen idols. They had no Caaba, no annual market and no way of utilizing their gods to advantage. On the contrary, there was good reason to doubt their power. On the other hand, the new religion seemed quite promising and one could afford to try it out. Then, too, it would greatly annoy the hated Quraish and harm the prestige of the Caaba and its gods. That was a joyous prospect. Musab had considered all this and explained it to everyone who would listen to him, with the result that the number of converts visibly increased.

The Jewish tribes as well, although they had no thought of relinquishing their own religion, were quite sympathetic to the Prophet. They knew that Mohammed believed in one God and that his God was also that of the Jews. They had heard that the Prophet spoke with great respect of the people of the Scriptures and that he even placed them above the heathen Arabs. It was safe to assume that, in the case of war, Mohammed and his followers would take the side of the Jews. They thought that he was a *hanif*, qualified to bring about reconciliation between the participants in blood-feuds, to restore peace and order and likewise give a new lease of life to commerce. *Hanifs*, God-fearing men and the enemies of idols, were known to them and often were under their protection. For this reason they had no objection to taking in another holy man into their community.

Both the Jews and the heathen were sorely mistaken.

But the Prophet too was mistaken, for he had thought that the Jews would recognize the true faith and go over to Islam. He was much in error. A difficult conflict lay before him, a conflict with the people of the Scriptures, who would have nothing to do with the teachings of the new sage.

Nevertheless, Musab proved himself to be an able diplomat. His promises, his praises and his insinuations made considerable impression upon the simple sons of the desert. The influence of the important, fashionable Moslem who had come from Mecca was not unimportant. Wholesale were the conversions to the new religion and the new adherents were ready to destroy their old gods.

When Mohammed together with Abu Bakr, exhausted by their flight, arrived in Quba, the majority of the tribes of the Aus and Khazraj had embraced the new faith. Pieces of the shattered wooden and stone idols lay in the dust of the narrow streets.

From that time on, Yathrib was called Madinat-n-Nabi – the city of the Prophet – Medina. This occurred on Friday, the second of July, in the year 622.

THE CREATION OF THE STATE

L'état, c'est moi.
Louis XIV.

Covered with dust and dirt, their clothing torn, their camels exhausted, the Prophet and Abu Bakr reached the hill and village of Quba, the vacation spot of Yathrib. The Prophet's tired camel knelt down under a spreading fruit tree. The news of Mohammed's arrival had spread fast. All the inhabitants of the little village ran up to greet the new prophet. Mohammed sat in the shade of the tree next to a well. To mark the turning point in his career, he took from his finger a large seal ring, which he had brought with him from Mecca, and threw it into the well.

The people of Qub'a did not know which of the new arrivals was the Prophet. Some bowed before Abu Bakr and others before Mohammed. Then Abu Bakr arose, stood behind the Prophet and began to wave a cloth over Mohammed's head; this was the first royal honour shown to the Prophet.

The messenger of God spent four days in the village of Quba. The faithful came to him to pay their respects; unbelievers came, listened to his words and were converted. The mighty sheikh, Buraidah ibn al-Hasib, together with seventy of his followers, fell at the feet of the Prophet and swore to die for the true faith. Heathens, festively attired, came from Medina, damned their gods and greeted the Prophet. None in Medina knew of his humble origin; none could say they had known him when he herded the sheep of the Hashim.

On the second day following his arrival, a poor slave named Salman al-Farsi came to the house of the Prophet. He was a Persian by birth who for decades had sought the true prophet throughout the world and had now found him in the oasis of Medina. Salman was born in Isfahan, had been a fire-worshipper and then had left both faith and the home of his fathers. He had wandered all over from convent to convent, from one holy man to another, taking up in himself the wisdom of all gods, until an old monk had told him of the new prophet who was to restore the faith of Abraham. Salman came to Medina, awaited the Prophet and became converted to Islam. And since all men are equal in Islam, he became more important than many of the nobles of the Quraish. He became Mohammed's councillor and Islam's first engineer. "Salman, the Persian, created the teaching of Mohammed," the Meccans later said derisively.

On Friday the sixteenth, in the month of Rabi', the Prophet, dressed in festive garments, entered Medina accompanied by seventy riders and all the Meccans who had emigrated. The newly converted sheikh carried the banner of the Prophet before him, a green turban fixed to the end of a lance. The inhabitants of Medina stood in front of their houses, astonished that a poor, banished, peaceful seeker after God entered the city like a triumphant conqueror.

Mohammed had relations in Medina. This made his task so much easier. His grandmother belonged to the Khazraj tribe. Family ties are so strong in Arabia that this fact sufficed to convert many to the new faith. Abu Ayyub, a distant relative of Mohammed, placed his house at the Prophet's disposal. Although Mohammed moved into his house, the first thing he did was to buy a piece of ground in the middle of the city, which was to be the centre of the new faith. And it was there that Mohammed decided to build the house of God.

Weeks went by, and gradually Mohammed began to take stock of conditions in Medina, to recognize friends and to judge his enemies. He was still a private person, still without power, and merely the leader of a spiritual movement. But his goal was sure: the domination of the city of Medina.

He was no longer alone. He was surrounded by the numerous emigrants from Mecca who were more closely allied to him than ever in the strange city. These emigrants, called *muhajirun*, had been tried in suffering and conflict; they had lost their all in Mecca and most of them had been banished by their relatives from their own tribes. They were now entirely dependent upon themselves and the Prophet.

The Arab cannot bear solitude, and so the *muhajirun* formed an association amongst themselves, a sort of family. The Prophet was naturally its leader. The emigrants who had come to Medina had nothing to lose. In order not to go under among the strange tribes, they had to stick together. The first necessity was to care for their material existence. They had been uprooted, could expect aid from no one and had brought nothing but their bare lives with them into exile.

But this was the least worry of the Prophet. The Meccans were the most thorough among the Arabs. There is a well-known story concerning a pious *muhajir* who, clothed in rags and entirely without means, met a rich friend of his in Medina. "O poorest among the poor, how can I help you? My house and my money are at your disposal," said the native inhabitant. "O best among my friends," answered the exile, "merely show me the way to the local market. The rest will take care of itself." As a matter of fact, he hurried to the market, started some sort of business and was soon wealthy again. Only a few individuals found it necessary to look for support to the rich, native followers. The emigrants, moreover, brought valiant determination with them and were entirely free of family relationships and blood-feuds. Inasmuch as they were the oldest among the Moslems, they looked upon themselves as the pride of the new faith, and instead of obeying their former family-head they now heeded Mohammed alone. They were not hindered by moral obligations of any sort. One day the Prophet discovered that, as leader of the well-disciplined *muhajirun*, he played a far from unimportant role in the Medinite anarchy.

The plight of the natives who had gone over to Islam was much more difficult. They had not yet realized that the Prophet claimed universal sovereignty. Although they prayed to God, they believed that the temporal power belonged to one of their own. Up to that time, Medina had no visible leader in the city. The noblest among the Khazraj, Abdallah ibn Ubayy, was also of the opinion that the crown of the city of Medina belonged to him. It was now a matter of the Prophet acting more and more as a diplomat and a determined ruler. Slowly he succeeded in making the newly acquired converts absolutely submissive to his will. These, for the most part adventurous and young people, received the name of *ansar* – supporters of the Prophet. The *ansar* were a mighty prop in Mohammed's politics. The others believed no more firmly in Islam than they did in their old gods; they merely believed because the new religion was easily understood. The messenger of God called them *munafiqun*, which means hypocrites. Their leader was Abdallah, who had accepted Islam as a matter of form because he hoped to exert influence. But Abdallah was rich and stupid. There was no cause for the Prophet to fear him. With the other *munafiqun* he cheered the Prophet when he was successful and threatened to desert him when he was less fortunate.

Aided by the *muhajirun* and the *ansar*, the Prophet soon assumed a power in Medina second to none, and achieved this without anyone being aware of the fact. The exiles, the supporters and the hypocrites, the three groups which surrounded the Prophet, came from heathen stock, from the Arabian people. But the Prophet had come to Medina because he had heard that Jews and Christians, the people of the Scriptures, lived there.

The few Christian sectarians living in Medina soon went over to Islam. Mohammed recognized the holiness of Christ. This sufficed for the modest Christians, lost in the desert. But it was another matter with the Jews. They made up the majority of the inhabitants of Medina and they were proud of the faith which they had received from God. They knew that Mohammed had great respect for the people of the Scriptures, and at first they looked upon him as a half-Jew, as a sort of Jewish sectarian, for there were many people of that kind in the desert. None among the Jews thought of accepting the leader of Meccan immigrants and native heathens as a prophet, or of embracing his religion. In addition, they began to feel the active competition of the Meccans in business, and they decided to inspect the pious leader rather more closely.

Mohammed desired peace with the Jews. He believed in the unity of Islam and

Judaism. From his very arrival in Medina he had made advances to them. He now wore his hair unbraided, in the Jewish fashion, and avoided all that which stressed the difference between himself and the Jews. In order to point out the internal relationship between Judaism and Islam, he had commanded the faithful to turn their faces while in prayer towards Jerusalem – the holy city of the people of the Scriptures. This was the first *qibla* in Islam. It was meant to announce the relationship with the people of the Scriptures.

But none of this was proof to the Jews that Mohammed's was a divine mission. Such proof could only be furnished in wise discussions with the rabbis. The wisest authorities on the Scriptures were assembled to judge the holiness of the Prophet. To the rabbis, holiness was identical with a knowledge of the *Torah*. They came, spoke with the Prophet and determined that they knew the *Torah* better than he did. This finished him with the Jews. Apparently the Prophet could only impress the heathen.

But the political importance of the Prophet still remained, and the Jews had not overlooked it. They hoped that his influence upon the heathen would restore peace and order so that trade could automatically gain. For this reason they tolerated the Prophet and looked on indifferently, while the armed *ansar* and *muhajirun* constantly grew more influential, while the political importance of the Prophet grew from day to day. As the future was to show, they had made a grievous error.

Surrounded by the faithful in Medina who were ready to fight at a moment's notice, Mohammed felt that he was the bearer of a great power, and he was determined to organize that power. He needed unity among his followers, and to bring this about was one of his most difficult tasks. The emigrants and the supporters of Mohammed belonged to different tribes, to the two hostile categories of the Arab people, to the sedentary and to the nomads. From the beginning of time, hatred had existed between them, and only hatred could exist. The arrival of the Prophet changed but little of that condition. Both parties rivalled each other, and when an *ansari* was praised it displeased the *muhajirun*, and vice versa. Under the external covering of a common faith, lay the inherited hatred of the tribes.

It was Mohammed's task to conquer these hostilities. Hatred was the bequest of the family, therefore the power of the family must be crushed. At first the Prophet tried to get the native followers to take the emigrants into their own families. When this attempt failed, he cautiously, laboriously and diplomatically began to adjust the differences. But this promised little security for the future. Finally, Mohammed remembered that in religious matters his word was law. The relationship of both groups of his followers was made into dogma. In the eighth *Sura* of the Koran God commands through the mouth of Mohammed: "Verily, those who believe and have fled and fought strenuously with their wealth and persons in God's way, and those who have given refuge and help, these shall be next-of-kin to each other."

A remarkable influence must have emanated from Mohammed and the Koran. The verse of the eighth *Sura* did not obliterate the hatred between the castes. But it did disappear from the surface of life; it became unnoticeable and unseen. The tribes obeyed as far as they were able. Through this, an external unity in Islam was achieved and that had to suffice for the moment. A verse of the Koran brought about the unification of the community, the kernel of a new state, and, furthermore, the visible expression of the power of the Prophet.

This community, this armed force, needed a focal point, and so one of the Prophet's first acts was the building of a meeting house, a house of prayer – the first mosque of Islam. In the central place of the city, there where his camel had knelt down, the Prophet began to build. Daily he appeared accompanied by numerous followers. With his own hands he helped in the building, dried bricks in the sun, carried clay and helped erect the walls. This was the first house of God, the *masjid an-nabi*. Mohammed's hands helped to build it. Since Mohammed was a man and did not possess the power of looking into the future, he did not know that he had erected his grave with his own hands. The mortal remains of Mohammed were interred in the *masjid an-nabi*.

The mosque was simple and without ornament; externally it suited the sober faith which was preached within it. A piece of ground one hundred ells square was surrounded with walls made of dried bricks. Palm trees were planted in the square and one-third of the building was covered with palm leaves. Three doors were placed in the walls, one in the direction of prayer, one in the name of Gabriel and one in the name of mercy. The "door of mercy" led to the house of the Prophet. The courtyard was used for prayer, for assemblies and for sheltering the homeless. This was the first mosque, the mother of the most beautiful buildings of the Orient, a poem of the Arab people turned into stone.

The Prophet built a few huts for himself and his followers next to the mosque, and their poverty gave evidence of the consistent modesty of the Prophet. Low walls of clay, leather mattresses which rested on the ground, two roughly constructed seats, a water bottle and some flour bins made up the entire equipment. Mohammed refused to have expensive furniture. His life like his faith was extreme simplicity. The Prophet mended his own clothes, swept the courtyard, milked the goats and worked in front of the oven. He did not change his method of living, even at a time when he exercised autocratic power over all Arabia. His income, the tribute received from the vanquished, the spoils of war were all distributed among the poor. He believed that the giving of alms was the most precious deed in the eyes of God. Much to the dislike of his followers, the courtyard which surrounded the huts was constantly filled with beggars of all kinds. When he was advised that, being a prophet, he should avoid the populace, he replied with the following fable.

"When God Almighty created the earth, it shivered and shook in its unrestrained freedom. No man was able to stand upright on the ground. To quiet the earth, Allah took high mountains and secured them upon the surface. Since that time the earth has remained quiet. When the angels in Paradise heard of this, they were astonished and thought that there could be no greater creation on the part of God. 'O Allah,' they said, 'is there anything in your creation stronger than mountains?' And Allah replied, 'Iron is stronger, for iron can break the mountains.' 'Is iron then the strongest thing created?' 'No, fire is stronger, for it can melt iron.' 'And what is mightier than fire?' 'The water, for it can quench fire.' 'Is there anything in creation mightier than water?' 'Yes, the wind, for it can overpower the water.' 'O merciful God,' said the angels, 'which is the mightiest thing on earth?' And Allah replied, 'The best and most beautiful of my creations is a compassionate man who gives alms. If he does so with his right hand and hides it from his left, he is more powerful than all things.'"

In the courtyard of the mosque, leaning against a palm tree, Mohammed preached the life which he himself led in his hut. He was surrounded by Moslems, Jews, Christians and pagans. He chose Friday intentionally as the day of the great sermon, of the great prayers, for on this day both the Jews and the Christians were free from saying their own prayers and so could listen to his sermons. One of his first talks was not about the strife which he brought nor the power which he claimed, but about the love of one's neighbour. "When a man dies," so he said, "his heirs will ask what fortune he left behind him. But the angels will ask what good deeds did he do? What is a good deed? Anything that will bring a smile upon the face of others is a good deed, is the love of one's neighbour."

In Medina, the Prophet liked to explain the essentials of his faith in short, clear phrases to the people who surrounded him. These sentences gave a faithful picture of Islam, which in its political formation was also based on moral principles. "Tell me the main rules for a pious life," a new convert asked of the Prophet. "Speak evil of no one," answered the Prophet. "How can I honour the memory of my dead mother?" asked another. "Through water," said the Prophet. "Dig a well for her and give water to the thirsty."

It was in the demi-obscurity of the courtyard of the mosque that the Prophet and his pupils discussed the questions of life. Islam, which was to rule practical life, was both clear and all-embracing. For example, the Prophet disliked excessive eating and drinking, and singing as well, and he categorically forbade dancing, music, sculpture and painting. It is said that he was once asked, "Why, O Prophet, are you against the arts?" And Mohammed replied, "Because I pity the artists who make pictures of persons and bodies. On the Day of Judgment, Allah will command the artists to give life to the figures which they have made. And the artists will be in great distress."

But all the pious talks, commands and laws were now of secondary importance to the Prophet. It was much more important for him to ascertain through conversations, questions and answers, how much he could rely upon the faithful in time of need. Soon the Prophet saw that the Moslems would do anything which he would command them to do. He could confront the families of Medina who were divided in rivalry, with a united, disciplined and determined army of the *ansar* and *muhajirun*. This made him master, made him absolute sovereign, and he began to expand his power, to build the edifice of the faithful, the State of God.

One day, the Prophet assembled all the representatives of the families of Medina and the best of his followers around him. "We, the people of Medina, live in feuds and bloodshed. I came to this city to bring peace. That peace I now announce to you." And he read to them a constitution which he had prepared, the law which was now to govern existence in Medina.

With this first piece of legislation in Islam, Mohammed showed himself from an entirely different side. He disclosed the statesman, with clear views and determined precision; in short, a politician quite different from the man the Arabs had heretofore known. The statesman who had existed within him had now come to life.

These laws are summed up as follows: all the faithful make up a State which takes over the rights formerly held by the family, such as blood-feuds, warfare, etc. Mohammed is the leader of the State. Jews who live in Medina become members of the State and are to be protected and defended by the faithful. The Prophet decides as to war and peace. In case of need, all the inhabitants of Medina must pay taxes. Whoever violates the laws of the Prophet or transgresses against religion loses all protection, even that of his own family. Only misdemeanours of a private nature are subject to the justice of the family. Blood-enmity among the Moslems may no longer extend to an entire family. Blood-vengeance because of the murder of a heretic no longer exists for the Moslem. All the faithful are sworn to vengeance if one of them is harmed because of his faith. An agitator against the Prophet may not receive protection from anyone, not even from his own family. In face of all other people, the Moslems make up a community in which each member is equal. Jews and Christians who enjoy the protection of the faithful are subject to the laws of the Prophet in all public affairs. They are only subject to military duty when war is waged in defence of the city. In all other matters, they are the equals of the Moslems. The Moslems must aid one another, they must ransom their own when in captivity and see to it that there are no needy among themselves. Neither Jew nor Christian can be forced to accept Islam. The inhabitants of Medina must always be loyal to Islam and its laws under pain of punishment. All differences which occur in the future in the city of Medina are subject to God alone and His Prophet.

These laws constituted a *coup d'état* such as Arabia had never before experienced. Although at first in a somewhat restricted fashion, the bands of blood-relationship were broken and replaced with new, unheard-of judicial categories, the rights of the tribes were subject to the will of the individual. At the close of this declaration, the representatives of the various families looked at one another in consternation. They saw themselves surrounded in the courtyard of the mosque by the determined faces of the Moslems whose profession was religion and whose leader was the Prophet. The Moslems had strong muscles, their expressions were menacing and they rattled their weapons. Apparently most of them no longer felt any tribal ties whatever. They were the praetorian guard of the new prophet, the storm troops of Islam. Medina had nothing with which to oppose them.

The representatives of the families, the Jews, the *munafiqun*, the hypocrites and sceptics submitted to the ultimatum proclaimed by force of arms. They accepted the law.

Thus, as a private person, Mohammed began to dictate laws.

Thus the State arose from nothing.

Thus the theocracy began, the prototype of all Islamic States, whose influence has been felt until our day.

THE WAY TO POWER

The sword is the key to Heaven and Hell.
Mohammed

Medina, the refuge of the pious, lay in the desert surrounded by fields and palms. The word of the Prophet, the word of Islam ruled in the city. But Medina was only a single city, and not a large one at that. A time was to come when the words of the Koran were to ring out over all countries and continents, over all the deserts, cities and villages, and be heard by all the peoples of the earth. These peoples were distributed over the whole world, they had their own gods and their own rulers. They were not willing to lend their ear to the Prophet. The world did not wish to come to Mohammed of its own accord and so it was that he decided to use force. It seemed to him that the world was living in misery, heresy and sin. To save the world from sin, to make the word of God known to all, to destroy the false gods, to protect mosques, synagogues and churches was Mohammed's aim; and for this reason the messenger of God decided to tread the way which led to earthly power. A huge swamp barred his way: the swamp of politics.

Mohammed was forced to cross that swamp. Murder, treachery and deception filled it, and whoever wished to cross it had to shed strange blood, take filth and sin upon himself, and be as sly and brutal as he was firm and wise. For a time at least, such a one had to forget both love and mildness. Many prophets, sages and holy men of the world sank deep into the mire and remained there eternally; ceased to be prophets and holy, for the filth of the great swamp lay heavy on their shoulders. Wisdom, indulgence and power disappeared in the slime. Covered with the filth of sin, the holy men reached the other shore of the swamp and were turned into despots, rulers, demons and servants of the underworld. The poisonous swamp is treacherous and alluring, and it lies before all those who wish to better the world. Many men had lost in the swamp the treasures they wished to transport across it, and but few reached the other side pure and untainted. The way to power leads through the swamp of sin.

Mohammed too had to cross the swamp of sin; he too had to pass through blood, filth and deception, but the words of God gleamed bright on the other shore: "Recite in the name of the Lord." The messenger of God took many a sin upon himself, he spilled blood, ruled brutally and heartlessly, dealt craftily and slyly. But no one in the world ever left the swamp of sin with as pure a heart as did Mohammed.

Unexpectedly, Mohammed came into power, and his might rose visibly. Adventurers and warriors of strange tribes who had been unsuccessful at home came to him from the desert and the steppes. They had heard of the power of the new prophet, were converted and, in the courtyard of the mosque, in the houses and in the streets of Medina awaited the moment when their swords could be put to use. They had fled from their homes and Islam had become their profession.

The Prophet knew that the time of conflict had come. In the distance lay the proud city of Mecca which still ruled the desert. The mighty city had cast out the Prophet, and since he had fled he had been forgotten. There was no room for him in the great square of the Caaba. In Mecca, the Prophet and his teaching had been forgotten, despised and ignored. The battle had ended victoriously for the Meccans. They did not begrudge Medina to him and returned to their own affairs. But the Prophet wanted to remind them of himself, he wished to awaken their memory, and, as in the years of his banishment in the desert, he wished to be again the topic of the day. It would be necessary for him to challenge Mecca so as not to be forever forgotten in the distant provincial city of Medina. The only way by which he could do this was by means of conflict. One day he assembled a group of the faithful around him, and, leaning against the trunk of a palm as was his custom when preaching, he told them of his intention in the form of an Oriental fairy tale. For he knew full well that in the desert nothing is mightier than a fairy tale told by a wise man.

"Many prophets," Mohammed related, "were sent to earth by God and each of them was given the task of praising one of God's attributes. Moses praised the compassion of the Almighty, King Solomon spoke of His wisdom, His majesty and His splendour, the mild Jesus praised the righteousness, the omniscience and the power of God, and he justified himself through the miracles he was permitted to perform through God's grace. But none of this sufficed to convince sinful mankind. Men remained deep in sin, and all the miracles, from Moses to Jesus, were regarded with the eyes of disbelief. Then God, the righteous One, sent His messenger, Mohammed: and the Lord gave me the mission of the sword."

The faithful listened attentively to the words of the Prophet, but they had no idea that this brief moment was the turning point of their lives, the turning point of Islam. From now on it was to be the sword and not the word which was to decide the fate of their faith. The Prophet went over to the attack. At that time he was fifty-two years of age.

The Moslems who hung about the mosque, who lived by the charity of the Prophet and who had brought nothing with them into exile but their faith in the word of God, were prepared to fight. But they were not the only ones who, with sword in hand, were to defend the word of God. Many of the Moslems had become rich in Medina. Abu Bakr for example sent out rich caravans to Basrah and many others did likewise. They had become acclimatized to Medina, they lived in order to amass wealth and traded just as they had done in the city of Mecca, which they had been forced to leave because of their faith. It was not easy to detach them from their affairs and to entice them into going to war. The same was true of the natives of Medina. They had made a definite pact with the Prophet, which merely obliged them to defend him in case of attack, but not to march into the desert with him, to attack strange tribes and to risk their own precious lives in wars of conquest. The Prophet, who had never been to war and who understood nothing about military matters, knew one thing: discipline and solidarity alone could lead the people to victory. From the very beginning, the new faith had been a faith of discipline. Regular prayers, and the prescribed gymnastic movements of the body which were carried out five times daily in common with all the other faithful, strengthened the soul and aroused discipline and the community spirit. The deeper meaning of prayer was now to bear fruit. The first training field of Islam was the mosque, for the wars which Mohammed was to wage were religious wars. War was the common duty of all people who five times a day moved their bodies in prayer.

It was in this spirit that God, through the mouth of His Prophet, revealed the famous *Sura* of the Koran: "Those who are adherents of my faith need not enter into discussions or arguments about the fundamentals of the faith, but they must destroy all those who refuse obedience to the faith of God. Whoever fights for the true faith, whether he lose or win, will receive glorious reward either here or in eternity."

If this did not suffice, if anyone still hesitated to dedicate his life to Islam, he could learn other things from the mouth of the Prophet. "All who fight for the cause of the faith," said the Prophet, "will obtain rich temporal advantages. Every drop of blood which they spill, every danger and privation which besets them will receive greater reward than fasting and prayer. If they fall in battle, their sins will immediately be forgiven them; they will be carried into Paradise to enjoy perpetual delights in the arms of black-haired *houris.*"

Those who were to do concrete service received concrete promises, and the warlike determination of the Prophet had a theoretic foundation in the doctrine of predestination. Everything that happens to man is predestined from the hour of his birth; nothing happens to man without God's intervention, nor can he ever escape God's will. This teaching, which became one of the corner-stones of Islam, could easily have developed into an inert fatalism. But Mohammed was well aware of the dangers of fatalism, a sort of vegetating in God. For this reason he said, "Entrust your camel to God's grace but tie it to a tree anyway."

And so Islam entered upon the way which led to war, the way to power, to world-sovereignty. In the ten years in which the Prophet ruled in Medina, he conducted seventy-four campaigns and led twenty-four of them in person. These campaigns placed Arabia in his power. There is no counterpart in history to the accomplishments of this fifty-three-year-old merchant who never before had carried a sword in his hand. These wars were called *ghazawat* or *jihad*, which means, sacred wars.

War in the desert is not comparable to any other kind of warfare in the entire world. Properly speaking, it is not war at all but a mixture of pillage and commerce, and no one knows where the one begins and the other ends. Most of the wars of the desert are waged for booty. In the spring, the more powerful tribes attack the weaker ones, rob as much as they can and then disappear as quickly as they came. Wars of conquest were entirely unknown to the Arabs. Mohammed was the first to realize their possibilities.

How does one fight in the desert? Organized and disciplined armies were unknown before Mohammed's time. Whoever was of an adventurous nature or desirous of pillage, simply put on a coat of mail, covered his face with a visor and tied a piece of multi-coloured cloth to his chest, to signify that he was responsible for his own actions. He then sought out a worthy opponent and shouted some sort of an insult at him, such as, "O you son of a whore, do you know that I am the son of a lion?" In a real Arabian fight the entire army never took part. Usually many of the soldiers sat apart and watched their leaders attack one another. The vanquished had recourse to flight and justified their action by saying that they could not possibly fight after their leaders had fallen. However, when one had fled or had been forced to be on the defensive, the procedure was to lock oneself up in a stronghold until such time as the enemy, scenting more profitable prey, retired. Naturally the armies of the desert tribes were not large. A battle in which a thousand people took up arms was looked upon as an historic event.

At first the wars in which Mohammed called out the Moslems were not much different from warfare as had been previously practised in the desert. They were not fought to spread the faith, for the word sufficed for that, but in order to increase the temporal power of the Prophet. In addition, they were to bring in tribute and to extend the sphere of activity of the word. But for the most of the Moslems who participated in them, they were nothing but pillaging expeditions and a means of quickly acquiring wealth. Desert ethics saw nothing dishonourable in this.

Against whom was the Prophet to march? Obviously, against the richest people of the desert, the Quraish. It meant the possibility of becoming rich, of settling old scores, and also of securing the admiration of the inhabitants of the desert. Those who dwelt in Mecca were held in high esteem by the desert, and the Quraish were still the kings who reigned over it.

And so Mohammed commenced his fight with his native village.

The beginning was quite modest. In March of 623 Hamzah, the uncle of the Prophet, started out across the desert in the direction of the sea with thirty warriors and reached the spot where the Meccan caravans passed on their way from Syria. A caravan came but it was escorted by a party of Quraishite horsemen belonging to the Jadhima. For a long time Medina had been on a friendly footing with this tribe and it would have been foolish to shed blood needlessly. But the encounter prepared the way, and in the following month sixty Moslems met a caravan made up of two hundred Meccans. A fight did not ensue because the enemy were in the majority. Even in war, Mohammed preferred wisdom and circumspection. Merely a few arrows were exchanged which was more of a demonstration than it was a battle. Nevertheless, it was a declaration of war. A few similar attempts were equally unsuccessful. The Quraish did not want war. On the contrary, when the men of the Prophet appeared, the caravans took flight and Mohammed was forced to return without having accomplished anything. As a result, feeling in Medina began to grow steadily worse. God did not seem to favour the Moslem arms, and nothing but disaster was visited upon Islam. A handful of Bedouins succeeded in stealing a herd of cattle which had been pastured quite close to Medina, belonging to the Moslems, and in making off with them to the desert. This was not only a material loss to the Prophet, but it brought him dishonour as well and tended to make him appear ridiculous. The success which was to reward the Moslems had not yet come.

Thereupon the messenger of God decided upon a course of action hitherto unheard of. He equipped an expedition of twelve men, and placed at its head a warrior named Abdallah ibn Jahsh and lent him the title of *Amir al-Mu'minin*, which means "the commander of the faithful" and which was later to be the title of the caliphs in Islam. This occurred shortly before the commencement of the sacred month of Rajab during which the Arabs are forbidden to fight or wage war. But the Prophet gave no orders to Abdallah ibn Jahsh. He merely presented him with a sealed message with instructions to open it when he had come to the desert. It read: "Go in the Name of God and with the blessings of God to Nakhlah and there await the Quraish caravans. Force none of your men to accompany you. Fulfil my commands with those who follow you of their own free will."

Ibn Jahsh was a simple warrior and unschooled in the art of thinking. He knew that Nakhlah lay on the caravan route between Ta'if and Mecca and why a warrior should await a caravan in the desert.

Soon he spied a small Quraish caravan accompanied by four merchants. It was the afternoon before the first day of the sacred month. But Ibn Jahsh was merely a soldier of the Prophet, his eyes sparkled greedily when he saw the prey and he knew full well that the Prophet was aware that the sacred month was about to begin. In the middle of the night, as the full moon ushered in the sacred month and the merchants, feeling themselves absolutely secure, sat around their tent, a soldier by the name of Waqqas crept up stealthily, aimed his bow and shot his arrow through the throat of one of the merchants. Immediately the remaining warriors jumped from the rocks behind which they had been hiding and attacked and bound the merchants, for they too were considered booty. Only one of the men attacked managed to escape. The caravan, laden with leather, raisins and wine, fell into the hands of the robbers.

The night attack at Nakhlah was Mohammed's first victory. But it was more than a mere act of pillage; it was a breaking of the century-old tradition of the sacred month and of all the laws of the desert. From now on everything was permitted to the soldiers of God.

The assault made an unpleasant impression upon the faithful in Medina. No one knew what attitude to take up against this scandalous breach of faith. And again God had to speak through the mouth of His Prophet: "They ask you about the sacred month and if it is permitted to wage combat in it. It is a great sin to fight in the sacred month. But in the eyes of God, it is a much greater sin to shut out men from the path of God and from God's house, the Caaba." This revelation accomplished two things. The Prophet acknowledged the tradition, but made it exempt in his fight against Mecca and the disbelievers. This sufficed to quiet the majority of the faithful. The booty was theirs, and God's blessing was apparent.

At the same time, Mohammed dared to take a much more important step. He retained the fifth part of the booty for himself to be used for the future treasury of the new State. The rest was equally divided among the participants in the attack. This was not without consequences. From now on the campaigns attracted not only the needy, but many who had suddenly become most enthusiastic and even those who had not been converted to the new faith. The distribution of the loot among those who had fought for it made the prophet popular in the entire desert. In the future he was in a position to select his own soldiers.

The three merchants who had been captured were permitted to return in peace to their own city, for the Prophet wished to show that in the great swamp of sin he had not forgotten mercy and mildness.

BADR

Here comes a caravan of the Quraish laden with treasure. Approach it and perhaps God will present you with it as booty.

Mohammed

The Meccans placed but little importance upon the incursions of their former fellow-citizens. There had always been many robbers in the desert ready to attack rich caravans. Now, that number of robbers had merely been augmented by a small band, and that their leader claimed to be a prophet was of little consequence. There were many robbers in the desert who liked to be known as prophets. It was pitiful, however, that these bandits were Meccans by birth, that they belonged to the Quraish and that some of them had been reputable citizens. But all this was no cause for sorrow. The refugees, who were now supporting themselves by means of pillage, had been expelled from their relations and families, which according to the Meccans put an end to them both legally and morally. Mohammed's flight seemed to efface the danger which had threatened the three hundred and sixty idols of the Caaba, and business now flourished as never before. There was ample reason for being grateful to the three hundred and sixty idols. What is more, the robbers of Medina had not been any too courageous. They did not attempt any great deeds, and apparently their daring only sufficed to attack treacherously and plunder a few unsuspecting merchants during the time of the sacred month. There was really no cause for fear. In addition, and this was particularly reassuring, the Quraish had concluded pacts of friendship with all the desert tribes through whose lands their caravans passed. Therefore, there was no reason why they should even notice the miserable desert robbers of Mohammed. As a matter of fact, they did not diminish or restrict their trade because of him.

As was the annual custom, a large caravan which was to go to Syria was equipped in November 623. Laden with rich treasure, a thousand camels made their way towards the North. The value of the merchandise was fifty thousand mithqal, or approximately fifty thousand pounds. Two large Meccan banks, the houses of the Makhzum and the Ummayah, and their leaders, Abu Jahl and Abu Sufyan, who were Mohammed's bitterest enemies, each had a share to the value of fifteen thousand pounds, and the rest was divided among almost all the families of Mecca, for the leaders of the caravan accepted even the smallest amount of investment. It sometimes

129

happened that children and slaves contributed as little as half a gold piece, and when the caravan had safely returned they were given a profit of at least fifty per cent. All Mecca was interested in the caravan. As usual, the leader was Abu Sufyan, the head of the Ummayah, which was the tribe that controlled the largest share in the undertaking. Inasmuch as they were to march through the peaceful territory of friendly tribes, they thought it sufficient to take a guard of only seventy horsemen.

The trip to Syria was accomplished without incident. It was true that Moslem robbers lay hidden somewhere behind the hills, but the proud Quraish did not bother about them. The caravan reached Syria in safety, sold its wares and prepared for the return trip which, as always, was to take place in March. Mohammed, too, knew that the caravan would pass through the desert in that month, and he decided that he would not permit it to escape. The weapons of God needed a decisive victory and the treasury required ample replenishing. For months Mohammed travelled through the desert, visited powerful sheikhs, sat with them in their encampments in the desert and distributed presents and promises. Nomads, capable of the most brutal deeds, listened to him with interest. A holy man, who enjoyed great repute among the people, promised them many attractive things and asked nothing in return other than that they close an eye in case it was required of them. Without actually acknowledging his holiness, friendly pacts of neutrality were concluded with the holy man. Mohammed had no desire to accomplish more than that for the moment. He waited until the caravan had started on its return trip. Then he issued a proclamation to all those who wished to serve Allah and his messenger, and ordered them to assemble fully armed at a well near Medina, for great booty awaited the faithful. On 8 March, 623, Mohammed found three hundred men lined up in order at the well. The Prophet was able to hold a small review. First he examined their faith, for this was to be a holy war. Whoever was not a Moslem had to remain behind or be converted to Islam, for this was not an ordinary expedition. All the participants being of the same faith, Mohammed did not have to make them swear allegiance. Children under sixteen had to return to the city as well.

With the rest, Mohammed now set out on the first great war of Islam. The first army of the faithful had little in common with the determined forces of the later Islam. The insignia of this troop were small ribbons. The famed Arabian cavalry which later was to achieve great victories consisted at that time of but a few riders. The entire army had only two horses and seventy camels, so that the soldiers had to take turns at riding. The majority set out on foot. The weapons, too, left much to be desired. Most of the men had nothing but swords or lances, and only a few had coats of mail. These few coats of mail had been borrowed from the Medinese Jews, who were famous weapon-smiths, and the charges were high. But the small army possessed something that no other Arabian troop had ever had: discipline and internal unity.

In the middle of the desert, on the great caravan route between Syria and Mecca, lies the Oasis of Badr. Countless wells, palms and cooling shades await the traveller there. It was here that the caravans camped, that the wanderers recuperated and the merchants rested. The Bedouins who owned the oasis charged high fees and took but little interest in their guests. Led by the Prophet, the army of the Moslems marched to this lonely oasis. Sooner or later the great Meccan caravan would have to pass by.

But the desert is not an empty world. The sand lies dead; silently the heavens hang over the people, but the desert lives. The hot winds chase through the dunes, the sand moves, the cloudless sky looks down threateningly. Solitary riders appear on the horizon, peer at the passers-by and, swinging their lances over their heads, disappear. The desert has a thousand eyes and it speaks to the initiated in a thousand tongues. Abu Sufyan was of the initiated, and he too knew how to read the signs of the desert and how to interpret them. Mohammed's riders had gone into the desert to spy out his route. Abu Sufyan did not see them. He merely saw the dung of their camels. And that sufficed. "These camels come from Medina," he said. "There are date pips in the dung and the dates grew in Medina. Mohammed is surrounding us." Since he was wise and experienced, he sent messengers to Mecca who reported as follows: "Danger threatens our caravan. The robber Mohammed surrounds it. He wants to seize our wealth, to plunder our treasures, for nothing is holy to him who disregards the sacred month." In the meantime, Abu Sufyan changed his route and made a forced march through the desert in order to save his wealth. But Mohammed knew nothing of this. He went to Badr, to the camping place of the caravans.

The news of the danger which threatened the caravan caused an obvious stir in Mecca. Both capital and interest were at stake. The hearts of the Meccans began to beat with warlike beat. The old hatred against Mohammed awakened. Abu Jahl, the seventy-year-old, began to make warlike speeches and to cry out for war. Young sons of the bankers swore to die for the honour of their city. Aged, fashionable merchants dug deep into their purses to equip their servants for war. Over night, an army of nine hundred and fifty soldiers, seven hundred camels and one hundred horses sprang up. The leadership was taken over by Abu Jahl.

The hour of reckoning seemed to be at hand. Even members of the Hashim set out against the Prophet, and his sly uncle Abbas joined up with them. The next day the caravan marched off. It was an army of aristocrats and the whole thing was very fashionable. The more anyone had invested, the more militaristic he was. But those who had only to expect a few pieces of gold had no desire to join up, for they saw but little sense in risking life and limb. Their enthusiasm was not too great. It needed stimulation, and the bankers decided not to be niggardly. Beautiful slaves accompanied the army and entertained the soldiers, drums and singing rejoiced the ears of the brave. The rich ordered cattle to be slaughtered in huge quantities. The whole thing looked more like an excursion of wealthy merchants than it did like an army going to war. None doubted the ultimate victory. A thousand men would suffice to teach the desert robber respect. Mohammed would not dare to approach the caravan. After a bit he was sure to retire.

This assumption seemed to be true. A messenger of Abu Sufyan's met the army in the desert with the joyous news that the caravan was out of danger. Abu Sufyan had taken a safe way along the coast, and the robbers were assembled near Badr and were following a false scent. The aim of the expedition seemed achieved. The fashionable warriors longed for their native markets where they could collect the gains which the caravan had brought them.

But Abu Jahl, the leader of the army and a bitter foe of Mohammed, was of a different opinion. He wished to make an end of the Prophet, to rid the Arabian deserts once and for all of this disturber of the peace, and he thought that a better opportunity would never be given him. He led an army of a thousand men well equipped with arms, horses and camels. How could the horde of the desert robber compare with it? It required much exertion on the part of the old soldier and the few who were of his mind to move the aristocratic army to follow its original plan of proceeding to Badr. If Mohammed accepts the challenge, thought Abu Jahl, he will be defeated, and if he should withdraw he will be covered with shame for all time in the eyes of the Arabs.

It was with great consternation that the army of the faithful learned that they were awaiting not a poorly guarded caravan, but an army of one thousand men. The Moslems now thought that the entire campaign was without sense. The booty had escaped. But now the internal effect of Islam came to the fore. While the Quraish doubted and hesitated, while all claimed that they could not fight against their own relatives, Mohammed assembled the faithful and said to them: "The gates of paradise lie in the shadow of the sword. Whoever falls in battle for the faith, will gain entrance to Paradise, no matter what his sins may have been. God wishes to try the courage of the faithful." So passionate were his words and so impressive their effect that the faithful answered with one voice: "We will follow you even if you lead us into the sand-storms of Southern Arabia or into the waves of the sea." There were no longer any ties of relationship for the Moslems. The Prophet hoisted the large black flag of war, blessed the soldiers and set out with them towards Badr. For the first time in his life the fifty-three-year-old man was to lead in battle. The Quraish awaited the Moslems at Badr and amused themselves with their beautiful slaves.

Two armies, both of which were made up of blood-relations, old friends and former citizens of one city, opposed one another.

Mohammed was not a strategist: he was no army leader, no general. But he was a genius. Like none other, he took in the entire situation. He understood the nature of Arabian fighting, which is disorder and confusion. First the poems of war are recited, then there are demonstrations of daring horsemanship, then the best warriors engage in conflict, the second-class heroes follow, and finally there ensue hand-to-hand fights on the part of all. All this lasts for hours and hours and the hot sun shines down constantly on the heads of the combatants.

In such circumstances, the necessity of having fresh water was of the greatest importance. Mohammed not only grouped his troops masterfully around the wells, but saw to it that all the wells which the enemy were to pass were filled in. Of course this was contrary to the laws of the desert for the wells are sacred. But this time again the messenger of God set himself above the laws of the heathen.

On the morning of 16 March, the Quraish approached the Oasis of Badr. Instead of an unorganized band of wild robbers, they saw for the first time a troop in perfect formation standing at the foot of a small hill. On the hill, surrounded by his bodyguard, sat Mohammed under a roof of palms.

The Quraish approached for battle, and the conflict was to be carried on in the fashion of the desert. First they rode past their opponent, ridiculed him and recited verses; then they withdrew out of shooting range. Now three noble Quraish rode forth to challenge the enemy to duels. Mohammed decided to send out three soldiers of equal birth to the Quraish. The first blood of the battle was sacrificed by a member of his own family. Ali, Hamzah and Ubaidah, three blood-relatives of the Prophet, stormed towards the foe. The faithful called these three "the three lions of God." With swift dispatch, Hamzah and Ali slew their opponents. According to the rules of the desert, the conflict should have ended then and there. But the noblest among the Quraish were spurred on with renewed fury. In small groups they rode up to the Moslems and were wounded when opposed by the firm, united ranks of the faithful. The army of the Moslems knew how to maintain discipline. While the Quraish sat at a safe distance, watching their best warriors fight the enemy without doing anything to aid them, the Moslems obeyed the orders of Mohammed. They did not advance but received the enemy as they came up. The Prophet showed himself to be a military tactician; with inspired assurance he directed his troops.

The entire day was consumed with small conflicts. The military art of the Quraish did not permit them to make one thorough attack. They fought as their fathers and forefathers had fought before them, without plan and without understanding of the simplest rules of warfare. They fought man against man and lost. One by one the best soldiers of Mecca met their death. Abu Jahl, Mohammed's greatest enemy, was slain with one sword-blow, and even in his death agony he did not cease cursing the Prophet. Mohammed stood on the hill looking at a battlefield for the first time in his life. He saw blood flow, heard cries and moaning, and fell into a lethargic spell for a short time. Soon he awoke, prayed and gave commands; then with intuitive speed he produced unexpectedly a new Arabian method of warfare, carried out by the Arabian infantry which was to conquer the world within ten years. His tactics at Badr, which later were to become the basic rules of all Arabian strategy, were quite simple: discipline and the keeping together of the infantry, which was a match for any cavalry attack. It was only at the end of the battle, when the enemy was exhausted, that they in turn went over to the attack at the command of their leader. All the great battles of Islam were won in this manner.

The Day of Badr drew towards its close. Cold storms blew through the valley. Dust covered the battlefield. Then Mohammed arose and cried out: "O believers, only death at the hand of the enemy lies between you and Paradise." Then he bent down, picked up a handful of sand and threw it in the direction of the enemy saying, "May confusion cover their faces." This was the signal for the offensive to begin. The attack of the Moslems began. The conflict was brief. The worn-out Quraish fled into the desert, their camp and a number of their men fell into the hands of the enemy. Seventy Quraish and only fourteen Moslems fell on the field of honour. It was a decisive victory of the three hundred over the one thousand. God had been gracious to Islam.

The booty was collected at once, the bodies of the fallen enemy were thrown into a cistern, and the army returned home. The trophies of war were one hundred and fifty camels, ten horses and seventy prisoners as well as many weapons and clothing. Ali, the Prophet's adopted son, was given Mohammed's daughter, Fatimah, in marriage as a token of his particular bravery.

Only two of the prisoners were executed. Among the living was Abbas, the slyest among the Hashim, the uncle of the Prophet. Mohammed treated him well and demanded a high ransom for him which he received. The uncle returned to Mecca and bore Mohammed no grudge though the ransom sum was large. There were some who said that he acted as a spy in Mecca on behalf of his nephew even though he did not openly belong to Islam. The head of the Hashim, Abu Lahab, Mohammed's arch-enemy, died of spite and envy when he heard in Mecca the news of his triumph. So ended the Day of Badr, the most decisive day of Islam, for on this day the prophet was changed from a desert robber and preacher into a general.

On the evening of the same day, the Prophet said to his faithful: "Not you, but the angels of God fought our victory today." These words were accepted as gospel, and to this day the pious relate how a host of angels borne by the desert winds destroyed the enemy. One of the angels, so the legend says, lost his sword in the sands of Badr, and the Prophet found and kept it. He gave it the name of *dhu-l-fiqar*. The sword was seven metres long, had two blades and was ornamented with verses from the Koran. After the death of the Prophet, it was given to Ali, the Lion of God.

With this sword Islam conquered peoples and empires, seas and continents. It is not for nothing that tradition leads the origin of the sword back to the battle of Badr. Islam was made a world-power at Badr. The three hundred poor desert robbers stood at the turning point in the history of the world.

THE TERROR

The unbelievers deny everything save unbelief.

Koran

Three hundred poor, wild robbers had ridden out into the desert. They returned to Medina as a powerful army led by the most popular man in Arabia, the conqueror of the desert. A battle in which thirteen hundred men participate and eighty-four are killed is neither large nor bloody. In the desert, however, this conflict had been a terrific battle and had the importance of a world-event. Poets dedicated long odes to it, wild Bedouins envied the conquerors of Badr and it is said that all the heretics still remaining in Medina promptly fell on their knees and were converted to Islam at the sight of the rich booty which Mohammed brought back with him. Mohammed was now much sought after and he was the recognized ruler of Medina. Sheikhs of the desert offered to make alliances with him. He personally disposed of a great part of the conquered booty and he and his warriors received enormous sums of ransom for the liberation of the Quraish prisoners.

Sad news greeted the Prophet at the gates of Medina. On the day of his victory, his daughter Ruqaiyah, who had just returned from Abyssinia, had died. The Almighty ordained that the messenger of God was not to grow too haughty.

God had shown him and the faithful the way which led to the victory of faith and to wealth by means of war. They were to continue on that way. Medina was now turned into a military camp. Life was organized along military lines. Armed soldiers patrolled the streets, watched the crowds, listened to suspicious conversations, and anyone suspected of treason was dragged before the high court without delay. New laws were decreed and had to be rigidly obeyed by the faithful. The praetorian guard of the Prophet heard all, saw all and reported all. It was said that a son once, hearing his father make heretical remarks, said to him: "You are closer to me than anyone else on earth, but God is still nearer." Filled with sadness, he denounced his father to the messenger of God, and the Prophet praised him for it. For Islam took precedence over family, tribe or desert law.

The State of Medina became a theocratic despotism in which the will and the mildness of the Prophet alone held sway. His mildness was lavished on the pious. The soldiers who had associated themselves with him, his auxiliaries in the days of dire distress, were now given grandiose titles and honours, and were made aristocrats of the Republic of God. Abu Bakr, who did more for Islam than all the other faithful put together, was given the honourable title of *siddiq*, which means "the pious one," the righteous Umar was called *faruq*, "the saviour," and Hamzah, the oldest among the warriors, was called *asad-ullah*, "the Lion of God". These and many other titles had a better effect than all the words of the pious. The Prophet was aware of one thing: now was not the time to cease his labours. New battles, new victories and successes were to crown the triumph of the faith.

For the time being, the results of his victory had still to be awaited. It was not likely that the Meccans would accept the death of the noblest of their citizens without wishing revenge. As a matter of fact, Mecca's revenge came and it was as grotesque as most of the other military enterprises of the merchants. Three months after the victory at Badr, three months after they had ransomed their tribal brothers with huge sums, Abu Sufyan appeared at the gates of Medina accompanied by two hundred soldiers. He destroyed a date field, burnt two houses and killed two men. However, when Mohammed at the head of his army appeared before the city towards morning, Abu Sufyan did not lag behind his companions. They took to flight so hurriedly that they forgot not only their spoil, but also their own provisions which they had brought from Mecca.

As far as revenge was concerned, nothing more was heard from the Meccans. According to a legend, only on one occasion did they make a murderous attempt upon the life of the Prophet. One day while the Prophet was resting in the shade of a palm near Medina, a warrior of Mecca approached him. The sound of his steps awakened the Prophet from his dreams. He looked up and saw the warrior standing over him with a drawn sword in his hand. But an Arab will not kill his enemy without first telling him of his hatred. "O Mohammed," he called out, "who can now save you from me?" Calmly Mohammed looked at him and replied, "God." Filled with rage, the warrior set upon Mohammed, but in his haste he tripped over a stone and fell to the ground. His sword fell out of his hand, and with lightning-like rapidity the Prophet picked it up and standing over the warrior said, "Who can save you now?" And the warrior answered humbly, "No one." "Then learn how to be merciful from me," said the Prophet and allowed the man to go his way.

It was Mohammed's manner to forgive insults, injuries and even physical attacks made upon him and, if possible, to overlook them. But he was firm as a rock and unspeakably brutal towards all those who dared attack his work, the Koran, or his State. Here he knew no mercy but changed from a peaceful preacher into a merciless judge, into a bloodthirsty despot who utilized every known trick and treachery to punish even the suspicion of ridicule against his faith. In this too, however, he knew how to wait, to deliberate and to choose the right moment. The right moment, after the battle of Badr, had come. Behind the external conversion of the new Moslems to Islam was hidden a good deal of unbelief. The Jews too, who made up nearly half the population of Medina, wished to have nothing to do with the new faith and felt themselves far superior to the Prophet. Jewish youths did not cease making fun of the Prophet by means of vicious poems and verses. Wit was the curse and the strength of the Jews of Medina. The Prophet was more sensitive to verses of ridicule, to loose humour and to disrespect than he was to open revolt and resistance. For private reasons, the Prophet did not persecute or execute many people, and those who were so punished were mostly poets and jokers. "The satire of the poet is more painful than the lance of the enemy," Mohammed once said; for he was without a sense of humour.

The Prophet was now determined to employ an ancient and effective means against the poets and ridiculers, against the Jewish punsters – the terror.

There lived in the city of Medina a Jewish poetess named Asma. Her poems annoyed the Prophet deeply, and his first blow was to be directed at her. Asma belonged to a mighty tribe, and in spite of all his own power Mohammed did not dare bring about a blood-feud. The Prophet decided to do something that had never occurred to any other Arab, to demonstrate publicly that the bonds of Islam were stronger than the bonds of blood. Asma had a single blood-relative who confessed the new faith. He was a blind old man named Umair. The old man, who could neither talk nor fight, was now to do the Prophet a great service. Umair obeyed the Prophet. He went and killed his blood-relative, Asma. But since the murder of a person by a blood-relative does not call for atonement in the Orient, Mohammed had achieved his aim. He had avoided a blood-feud and was also rid of his enemy. When the Prophet learned of the nocturnal murder, he said calmly, "Not even two goats will fight over this."

Medina became the arena of the terror. All blood-ties, all bonds of friendship were broken. Men were murdered without anyone daring to avenge them. No one thought of opposing the terror, for now the Prophet was building the State of God. The Prophet was never unjust in his judgements. His blows were brutal but they only hit the guilty.

Well known is the revenge which the Prophet took upon the Jewish poet, Ka'b ibn al-Ashraf. Ka'b came from a noble family; he was unusually intelligent and very talented. He placed his talents at the disposal of the heretics, travelled to Mecca and there recited verses in honour of the infidels who had fallen at Badr. He then returned to Medina to ridicule the slain Moslems. Mohammed hated a Jew who abetted the cause of the heretics against Islam more than he did any other criminal. "A Jew who fights for the pagans," he said, "is worse than a pagan." So he gave orders to a courageous warrior to kill Ka'b. But Ka'b was cautious and took refuge in a large, strong, Jewish fortress and refused to leave it. His executioner decided to employ a ruse. "From now on I too am an enemy of the Prophet, for he has refused to give me a present," he declared. Under the pretext that he actually wished to murder Mohammed, he came to Ka'b at night in order to discuss the conspiracy with him. He entered the room and asked, "Is it your hair which smells so sweetly?" "Yes," Ka'b replied, "my wife has just perfumed it." "Let me smell it more closely," the soldier said, and as the unsuspecting Ka'b bowed his head he was decapitated by his enemy. This was the first punishment for treason meted out in the State of God.

It was not accidental that the majority of the punishments, murders and acts of terror were directed against the Jews. Slowly but steadily the relationship between Mohammed and the three Jewish tribes of Medina grew worse. It became more and more apparent that there was no place in God's republic for the Jews. The Jews had always belonged to Medina, their names appeared in Mohammed's constitution, they had to pay taxes and in return were protected by the faithful. Mohammed had always hoped that the first nation of the Scriptures which had come into contact with his faith would be converted. Day by day this hope lessened.

The Jews were prepared to submit to the new state of affairs, but their adherence to their own faith was steadfast. Haughtily they looked down upon the wild prophet of the heathen. Versed in Talmudic dialectics, they refuted Mohammed's arguments with ease. Among themselves they ridiculed him, for they, the bearers of the ancient truth, felt that they were far superior to the new faith, the new prophet and the entire wild people of Arabia. But Mohammed could not stand their railing condescension. He realized that in case of war the powerful tribes of the Jews might prove a grave danger to the new State. Even now some of the Jews had made alliances with his political enemies, the Meccans, and they declared openly that at best Mohammed was nothing but a prophet of the heathen.

They were prepared to demonstrate that they could produce from their own ranks as ecstatic a visionary as the Arabs had done. One day they led a Jewish lad named Ibn Sagad into the presence of the Prophet. The boy fell into convulsions, read the Prophet's thoughts accurately and demanded that the Prophet acknowledge that he, Ibn Sagad, was also a messenger of God. Mohammed declared that the boy was possessed, that he was Satan. At the same time, he realized that the Jews spiritually threatened danger to his teaching. He decided, therefore, to replace the acts of terror directed against individuals into a general terror whose aim was to drive the three Jewish tribes out of Medina.

As was his custom, he commenced his task with caution. He had to establish a theoretical foundation to give weight to his future actions. "It is the destiny of the Jews," the Prophet once said, "that they always oppose the prophets sent to them by God." This was the first visible dividing line between the Arabs and the Jews.

Soon other and more decisive steps followed. The Prophet stopped dressing his hair in the Jewish fashion, and he put an end to the discussions with the wise and intelligent rabbis. The fast-days which originally coincided with those of the Jews were changed to other dates. Finally, he revoked one of his most important decrees which had hitherto joined the Moslems with the Jews. He altered the *qibla*, the direction of prayer, which was to unite all the faithful no matter where they might be. Up to that time the holy city of Jerusalem had been the *qibla*: now it was Mecca. Beyond the political and practical importance which it had at the time, this decision considered from a religious and psychological point of view marked a significant phase in the development of Islam. Formerly Islam had been regarded as a Jewish-Christian sect. Now it affirmed its independence and radically detached itself from its forerunners. The changing of the *qibla*, provoked by the momentary political exigencies, proved a symbolic gesture of vast importance. Without knowing it, without realizing it, Mohammed had created a new, independent world-religion.

It was only after careful and lengthy preparation that the Prophet began his open warfare against "the people who opposed all prophets." Three Jewish tribes lived in Medina. All three were rich, proud and, what is more important, inimical to one another. Mohammed knew that they would not support each other, and he decided to begin with the weakest and least important of the tribes, the Banu Qainuqa.

The Banu Qainuqa were not numerous. They could not furnish more than seven hundred soldiers. For the most part they were weapon-smiths, and they owned no fields and no date palms, but they were rich in arms, gold and other metals. They lived in a number of fortresses which surrounded the market place in the centre of the city.

It was easy to find a pretext for the conflict. One day, a Moslem dairymaid visited the market to sell her milk there. A Jewish jeweller approached her and, in a spirit of fun, fastened her dress to the bench on which she sat. A few young men surrounded her and praised her beauty, but she paid no attention to them. She sat there quietly and offered her milk for sale. When she finally wished to get up, much to the amusement of the entire bazaar, her dress fell from her body. As a matter of fact, jokes of this sort were not uncommon in rude Arabia. It happened that at the same time a young Moslem was passing through the bazaar, and, seeing the shame which had been visited upon one of his own faith, he drew his sword and slew the Jewish jeweller. A violent tumult ensued in which the young Moslem also was killed.

When the news of the bloody fray had spread through the city, the Prophet did not order the Qainuqa to pay blood-money as he had previously ordained in such cases, but called all of the faithful to arms. The Banu Qainuqa did the same, but, since they were better weapon-smiths than weapon-bearers, they saw fit to entrench themselves within the walls of their fortresses. So it happened that a siege commenced in the centre of the city of Medina. Mohammed demanded that the Qainuqa be converted to Islam, which they refused to do. The siege lasted for fifteen days and the Qainuqa, who had run out of provisions, were forced to surrender unconditionally. Mohammed was determined to make the Qainuqa feel God's wrath, and they were to be dealt with according to the laws of war. According to these, the men were to die and the women and children to become slaves. It was only with difficulty that Ibn Ubayy, the mighty leader of the *munafiqun*, and Ubadah, who belonged to the Quraish and was friendly with the Quainuqa, moved Mohammed to be merciful. The Quainuqa were given their freedom, but their property, their gold and their precious weapons were forfeit to the victor. The booty was distributed among the faithful. This was the end of the Banu Qainuqa, for none of their tribal brothers had come to their assistance even though the Jews made up one half of the population of Medina.

The spoils which had been divided among the Moslems enriched them greatly and opened up to them unsuspected sources of wealth. There were more Jews in Medina besides the Banu Qainuqa. Many *munafiqun* were now more closely attached to Mohammed than ever before.

Mohammed took his time. The riches which he promised the faithful were to be the reward for valiant deeds of war: The State of God was to be tried in battle. Again and again Mohammed sent his warriors into the desert. The time was filled with minor encounters with the Bedouins, with friendly pacts and sermons. But all the attacks had nothing but booty in view, and for this reason they preferred plundering the wealthy caravans. Since the richest caravans were still those of the Quraish, renewed conflicts between Mecca and the State of the Prophet were inevitable.

In November 624, Mohammed sent his adopted son, Zaid, into the desert together with one hundred soldiers, in order that they might attack a caravan and secure its wealth. Zaid was singularly successful, and at Qaradah, not far from Mecca, he attacked the autumn caravan of the Quraish. The merchants fled and the entire caravan fell into the hands of the Moslems. Gold and silver to the amount of forty thousand pounds was secured by the pious, and the sum, after one-fifth had been given to the Prophet, was divided among the faithful.

Mohammed's prestige among the tribes of the desert was unlimited. At first it had been feared that all Mecca would appear at the gates of Medina to seek vengeance. Month after month passed and nothing stirred from the direction of the Caaba. Apparently one could plunder the Meccan caravans without fear of retribution.

At the end of five months after this robbery had occurred, a stranger rode through the streets of Medina and requested to be brought before the Prophet. It was a messenger from his Uncle Abbas, the leader of the Hashim. The sly banker, who was fully informed as to all which took place in Mecca, wished to assure his own future and had sent an important message to his nephew who had gradually risen to power, to the effect that Abu Sufyan, accompanied by three thousand warriors, was on his way to Medina.

The great robbery was to be followed by a great revenge.

THE VENGEANCE OF THE QURAISH

> Whoever wishes to be born, must destroy a world.
>
> *Hermann Hesse*

What had happened in Mecca since the affair at Badr? The news of the battle had caused great consternation. Although the caravan had been saved, honour had been irretrievably lost. The noblest Quraishites had fallen in the fray, nearly every banker had lost some member of his family, and all feared that trade would decline. But the Quraish did not lose courage; they beat their breasts, dug deeply into their money-bags, and financed the punitive expedition which had been sent to Medina. Upon the death of Abu Jahl, Abu Sufyan had become the sole leader of the tribe. He was a fashionable, noble and wealthy merchant though he had no military qualifications. He had been accustomed to rule with money and thought that he could break the power of the Prophet by the same means. He engaged poets and sent them into the desert in order to inflame the Bedouin tribes by means of verses for his attack against Medina. He paid money to the desert sheikhs so that they would attack the Prophet. As for the rest, he continued to carry on his business affairs. Under such conditions, the vengeance of the Quraish could well have taken many years, had not two factors intervened, the one private and the other public. The private factor was Hind, the wife of Abu Sufyan. Hind was energetic, distinguished and sure of her aims. She hated Mohammed more than all the other Meccans put together. She had reason to hate him, for her father and two of her brothers had fallen at Badr. Incessantly, Hind agitated for war against Medina. Had it not been for the energy of his wife, it is doubtful if Abu Sufyan would have undertaken his campaign. The other factor was the pillage of the caravan at Qaradah. Not only the honour but the wealth of the Quraish had been affected by it. Trade towards the North had been practically annihilated by that one blow. No one dared to send caravans into the desert, and without the caravan trade the existence of Mecca was inconceivable. The time was ripe for energetic and forceful action, for the wealth and the existence of the city was at stake. Abu Sufyan acted slowly as usual but with all precaution. On 21 March 625 an army of three thousand men appeared at the gates of Medina. It was no longer the joyous expedition of Badr. Three thousand camels equipped for war and two thousand horses accompanied the army. Seven hundred men had coats of mail and helmets. It was evident that the Quraish had prepared for a war of annihilation.

Mohammed knew that this was to be a decisive battle and he knew too how to prepare himself for it. He assembled the best of his warriors in the courtyard of the mosque and began to explain to them the plans for the battle. He recited his plan in the form of a dream. "I saw myself," he told them, "clad in an invulnerable coat of mail. My sword was broken at the hilt, but nevertheless I was able to kill a ram." "What does this dream signify?" asked the faithful. "We must remain in the city," replied the Prophet. "She is our coat of mail, and though poorly armed we can defeat the enemy." He described his plan of defence in the fortresses, the narrow streets and the houses to his soldiers. The plan was convincing. Carefully prepared sieges were usually favourable to the besieged in Arabia.

But the faithful, who were accustomed to success and victory, were not at all pleased with the plan. "Why should we allow our fields to be destroyed?" they asked. "Why should we not confront the enemy as is worthy of men? Does not God safeguard our weapons?" The enthusiasm of his men was so great that the Prophet was forced to accede to their demands. Having prayed, he put on his coat of mail and reviewed his army in the great square of Medina. There he noticed that the Jews had also prepared to defend the city. "The Jews are to leave the army," he said. "We do not need their assistance."

With those who remained, there were about a thousand men, and with but few camels and two horses Mohammed set out at night for Mt. Uhud to meet the Quraish. When the faithful saw the superior forces of the Quraish, they said, "The messenger of God was right; we would do better to defend ourselves within the city." Then Mohammed arose and declared, "When the messenger of God has put on his coat of mail, he will not take it off." He took the three standards and divided them among the three divisions of his army. When the morning dawned, Abdallah ibn Ubayy, the leader of the *munafiqun*, and three hundred of his hypocrites arose. Ibn Ubayy said: "The Prophet has acted upon the advice of children; we cannot follow him." And they left the army and returned to Medina. Now only seven hundred faithful remained to withstand the attack. But the Prophet called after the hypocrites, "Fear saves no one from death."

On the morning of the next day, three thousand Meccans confronted the seven hundred faithful. On this occasion the army of Mecca was again unorganized and without discipline. For this reason it had brought Hind and many other fashionable Quraish ladies, to encourage their warriors. The women called out for revenge and were more bloodthirsty than the men. The Meccans did not wish to be shamed in the eyes of their women. On the way, at Uhud and all during the day, the women had sung songs which they had improvised according to custom. Their songs were to the effect that if the soldiers were this time to take refuge again in flight they would not be permitted to rest at the sides of their wives. But it was not this threat, dire as it was, which decided the battle.

Quite accidentally, without having given it any particular thought, Abu Sufyan had appointed a young aristocratic Meccan, Khalid ibn al-Walid, a commander of the cavalry. It turned out that Khalid was a good general, a fact which no one had expected. Uhud was his first battle, but later his troops were to conquer Syria, Persia and Asia Minor for Islam. Khalid was to become the Murat of Islam and Mohammed knew how to appreciate him, for at Uhud he had opportunity to learn of the young man's military prowess much to his own sorrow.

The battle began according to custom, with a brief skirmish. Then the attack of the faithful began and the Meccans, unorganized and undisciplined as they were, fell back despite the encouraging shouts of their women. The Moslems had already invaded the camp of the enemy and thought the battle had ended. They fell upon their prey and began to pillage. Suddenly the unexpected occurred. Khalid ibn al-Walid showed that he was a born soldier. He collected the rest of the cavalry, threw himself upon the plunderers and with one blow decided the battle. They began fighting hand to hand and the Moslems were driven back. Soon the battle was raging on the hill in front of the tent of the Prophet. The battle was lost to the Moslems. But it was then that their military training came to their aid. They did not disperse as all other Arabs had done when they knew a battle was lost. They stubbornly held their ground, and a heroic defence set in before the tent of the Prophet. The standard-bearer of the Prophet was the famous Musab ibn Umair. He was fighting in the first ranks of the faithful. When a Meccan cut off his right hand, he held the flag with his left. When this too was cut off, he pressed the flag to his bosom with the bloody stumps of his arms until a lance of one of the enemy pinned him to the ground. Hamzah, the uncle of the Prophet, was slain by an arrow. A Moslem woman, who had witnessed the death of her sons, threw herself into the fray. The Prophet himself shed some of his blood in this battle for the faith. An arrow wounded his lip and knocked out one of his front teeth. A well-directed stone injured his face. It was an unquestionable victory for the Meccans, and Mohammed withdrew with the remains of his army. The cause of Islam was manifestly lost.

A miracle happened. Instead of following the enemy with his victorious army, instead of pressing on to Medina and destroying Islam forever, Abu Sufyan remained on Mt. Uhud. Apparently he thought his task completed. The dead of Badr had been avenged. It had not occurred to the fashionable Meccan to add political victory to that of his sword. Following Arabian tradition, he rode after his enemy with bloody lance in hand to boast of his victory. In the fields he met Umar, his former friend. They insulted one another, but since the battle was at an end neither drew his weapon. Finally, Abu Sufyan declared that he would return in a year to complete his victory.

And so the bloody day of Uhud came to an end. The Meccan women fell upon the bodies of the fallen Moslems like a horde of wild hyenas. The Oriental intoxication of victory began. Lips, ears, noses and private parts were cut off from the bodies. Hind, the wife of Abu Sufyan, even tore the liver out of the corpse of Hamzah and ate it before the eyes of the astonished Meccans. Then she climbed on top of Mt. Uhud and cried out into the darkness: "We have paid you back for the day of Badr. I could no longer endure the pain caused by the loss of my father, my brother and my son. My heart has been lightened. Hamzah healed my heart when I tore the liver out of his body."

According to Arab theory, the victory of the Meccans had been complete and there was no longer cause for vengeance. Nevertheless, Mohammed's astonishment was great when he saw the army of the Quraish begin its march homewards. Islam, the State of God, was out of danger. As a matter of fact, he had practically held the field. Exhausted, the soldiers turned towards Medina.

On the following day, disregarding his wounds, the Prophet mounted his horse and accompanied by a few friends rode into the desert. It was a demonstration and he wished to show that he had not given up the battle.

But Uhud had been, and remained, a defeat, and the usual consequences of defeat were not lacking. The neighbouring tribes, who had strongly adhered to Mohammed, began to rebel. The representatives of the Prophet were slain in the oases of the desert. A general revolution seemed imminent. It was only among the *muhajirun* and the *ansar* that faith in the Prophet remained unshaken. It was more than obvious that the battle had taken place at Uhud contrary to the wishes of the Prophet. Had they followed the plan of the Prophet, had they not left the city, the defeat would have been spared to them. Even on the battlefield defeat could have been avoided if they had not set upon the enemy like a horde of heathen. There was no reason to reproach either God or His prophet.

But feeling was different in the camp of the Jews and the *munafiqun*. They thought that the hour of retribution had come. Secretly negotiations were begun between the powerful tribe of the Banu Nadir and Abdallah ibn Ubayy. A conspiracy was being hatched. Its aim was the murder of Mohammed and the driving out of the *muhajirun*. To accomplish this, Abdallah promised to furnish the Jews with two thousand men to oppose the Faithful.

The plan came to nothing. Mohammed heard of the conspiracy and determined to make an example. As leader of the new State he ordered the Banu Nadir to leave the country without delay. Naturally the Jews refused to comply and, like the Banu Qainuqa, they shut themselves up in their fortress, the Castle of Sahra. At the same time, they sent messengers to Abdallah and to the other Jewish tribe in Medina, the Banu Quraizah, and asked for aid and protection. Again both of these failed in the hour of need and showed that they were unable to unite in opposition to the Prophet. The Quraizah and the *munafiqun* could come to no decision and did not accede to the request of the Nadir. Before Abdallah could assemble his two thousand men, Mohammed besieged the Jewish fortress. A new victory was accorded to him. The Nadir were unable to fight and were quickly forced to capitulate. The siege lasted but eight days and not an arrow was shot off. In order to retain their lives and the faith of their fathers, the Jews left Medina and remained forever in the desert. Their property, the great date groves, the tilled fields, the entire wealth of a mighty tribe, fell to the victors. The Banu Nadir were permitted to take only their naked bodies and the ancient faith of their fathers into banishment. But the Prophet gave them one chance. Whoever was prepared to accept the faith of the Prophet would be permitted to retain his wealth and to remain in the city in all honour. The Jews bowed to their destiny and did not avail themselves of the Prophet's offer.

It is worthy of mention that only two members were converted of the entire numerous tribe of the Banu Nadir. They were richly rewarded by the Prophet. The property and the wealth of the exiles was distributed among the most pious and poorest of the *muhajirun*.

In this manner, Mohammed recompensed himself for the bloody defeat of Uhud; in a similar fashion he rewarded his associates and drove out of the city all those who would not believe in the power of God and in His Messenger.

Filled with fear and anguish, frightened lest they should lose both wealth and faith, only one tribe out of the three large and mighty Jewish tribes remained in Medina, the Banu Quraizah.

But their hour, too, was soon to come.

THE PROPHET RULES

The best thing in the world is the command.

Burte

In time, life in Medina assumed strange forms. Almost overnight a small anarchic tribal republic was changed into a despotically ruled, united State. The duration of the damage done by the defeat at Uhud was not long. Mohammed held the reins of power firmly in his hands. The number of internal enemies constantly diminished and the power of the faithful constantly grew.

Armed soldiers filled the streets of Medina. They told of the great victories they had won over the nomadic tribes of the wild Bedouins, of the rich booty which they brought back with them from their campaigns, of the terror which they had spread in the desert, of the infinite power of Allah which lent them honour and renown. Piety and a hunger for booty now dominated the city of the Prophet. Medina, encircled by palms and wide fields, belonged to them and the wealth of Islam grew daily. Where once the wild Khazraj and the Aus and a few Jewish tribes had fought countless feuds, there now reigned iron-clad discipline, peace and comfort under the unbending will of the Prophet.

The Prophet did not permit the city to rest upon its laurels. Again and again he assembled his warriors, and again and again he sent them into the desert. Now and then he himself put on his coat of mail, hoisted the standard of the Prophet, and rode into the steppes, to spread the true faith by means of sword and word, and to hunt rich booty for himself and the faithful.

Mohammed's power was great. He was first among the Arabs, he had accomplished a great deed in that with the power of his word he had torn asunder the ties of blood-relationship. Only a few years before, Mohammed had owed his life to the indomitable family-feeling of the Hashim, who would have made any sacrifice before giving up a relation of their own free will. Now he had thrown off the fetters of blood-relationship. As long as the tribe counted more than the word of God, Islam could not rise to power. Individual followers of the Prophet lived scattered over the desert oases among strange, warlike tribes. Many did not disclose their faith and the Prophet permitted them to keep silent. Whoever began to believe in the Prophet did not submit to the power of the sheikh, but merely smiled ironically when the elders of the tribe conferred about the fate of its people, for he now served a much greater truth than the ancient truth of the tribes.

Mohammed knew the art of attracting and holding men. Whoever believed in him had to serve him, and whoever served him had to abandon the laws of his fathers, the laws of the tribes. In this fashion, Mohammed gradually created a secret organization which spread itself over all the deserts of Arabia. But this was as nothing compared to the great power he was later to wield among the tribes. He learned of everything that happened in the desert from the members of his secret organizations who lived all over the desert. He learned of the intentions of the enemy, of the dispositions of the Bedouins, which routes the caravans would take and at which place in the great country God would reward his arms with victory and booty. He would then set out with a troop of his soldiers, vanquish the enemy with lightning-like rapidity, and return to Medina. Every successful campaign secured new adherents to the faith, and the booty which was distributed among the warriors assured him the fidelity of the *ansar* and the *muhajirun*. His power was boundless since he had been the first to set up a truth which was greater than the truth of the tribes.

In the whole of Medina the old laws of the tribes were no longer observed. In desperation Abdallah ibn Ubayy sought to maintain the bonds of relationship. But the influence of the Prophet was stronger than that of any other man. Young men who went forth to war returned with loot and divided it among themselves, and no longer paid heed to the elders. They obeyed the Prophet; Abdallah and the *munafiqun* could no longer oppose the word of the Prophet nor his all-embracing truth. Wherever the Prophet ruled, the old law gradually died out. For this reason the Prophet did not fight the *munafiqun*, for he knew that time and his victories were working for him in Medina.

The conquests of the Prophet, the rich treasures which he brought back with him, the property of the exiled Jews which he distributed among the pious changed the face of the city. The persecuted, ragged, hungry and homeless fugitives who had lived off the bounty of the few rich had completely disappeared from the picture. Pillaging expeditions and the treasures of the exiled Jews had enriched the former beggars. Now they owned date palms, fields and gold. No one could guess the value of their wealth, for the power of the Prophet grew steadily and the power of the Prophet was the wealth of the pious. For years the faithful had endured persecution and deprivation. They had been hunted and exiled, they had lost their wealth if they possessed any, and were never certain of their own lives. Now the blessings of God shone upon them. The Prophet led them to wealth and power, and they were actively engaged in compensating themselves richly for the suffering they had once endured. The pious city of the Prophet slowly began to change into a minor Babylon. The Moslems gave themselves over to pleasures, wine flowed through the streets of Medina, music could be heard coming from every house, and the pious warriors feasted upon the beauty of strange slaves. Huge sums were lost at dice. The victorious *muhajirun* began to enjoy their lives.

The Prophet permitted the faithful to enjoy the good things of life. He knew the suffering they had borne for him, and he knew that everyone could not be a prophet, that everyone could not love prayer more than anything else in the world. Islam was not Christianity, and the Prophet did not preach asceticism. But he knew, too, that the joys of life permit the power of life to become lame. "Pleasant scents, women and above all else prayer" were best loved by the Prophet. For this reason he was willing to permit the faithful to enjoy these three also. But excesses might lead the State of God into danger, and so Mohammed decided to tame the *joie de vivre* of the faithful gradually. Thus it came about that a series of precepts which were born of the need of the hour were established and were destined to place this minor Babylon under the yoke of stricter morals. These laws were always revealed at a propitious moment. This method assured to Mohammed the consent of sensible people.

When, for example, one of the faithful was carried away by a suddenly awakened lust for gambling and lost his entire fortune, which he had earned on the battlefields, to some infidel, Mohammed assembled the faithful, told them of the sad incident and then forbade all gambling for the future. On another occasion, when one of the faithful appeared at prayer completely intoxicated and disturbed the Prophet in his sermon, Mohammed forbade the use of alcohol. In this manner, Mohammed arranged the life of his city. These laws remained for all time and ruled the life of the Moslems. Later they formed the entire spiritual picture of Islam.

So the laws against alcohol, gambling, dancing, singing too loudly, and many more were called to life. On the other hand, the Prophet always tried to protect the faithful. He did not wish his city to resemble a cloister. Any one was permitted to follow the example of the Prophet and, like him, to live the life of an ascetic so that he could enter the portals of Paradise. But the Prophet did not make this into a command. The Prophet knew one thing and he constantly repeated it: "The nature of man is weak, and the time will come when the fulfilment of one-tenth of the commandments will suffice to enter into the portals of Paradise."

Neither power nor wealth changed the Prophet. True, each campaign and each battle brought him in one-fifth of the booty, for it was his prayers and not the courage of the soldiers which brought about victories; but even that one-fifth was distributed among the poor or used to reward the particularly pious and courageous.

He did not change his own manner of living. As in the earlier times of his poverty, deprivations and persecution, the Prophet arose at the break of day, cleaned the courtyard, mended his own clothes and said his morning prayers. When pious students arrived, he spoke to them about the faith, alms were distributed and future campaigns discussed. Daily the Prophet, in his well-worn clothes, held court in the yard of the mosque and gave his decisions as the highest authority in matters both worldly and spiritual.

Pious associates collected his decisions and sayings, which later became the foundations of Islamic law. The verses of the Koran were also assiduously noted down. In accordance with the primitive circumstances of the desert, they were at first written on the shoulder-blades of dead animals, later on rough, raw leather and finally on parchment. The individual verses were placed in boxes and stored in the huts of the wives of the Prophet. But most of the *ansar* and the *muhajirun* knew the verses by heart, and if they did not there was no dearth of poorer Moslems who were glad to recite them without end for a small fee. The day of the Prophet was spent in giving judgements, making battle plans, reciting pious prayers, sermons and revelations. He also enjoyed simple handiwork. He often appeared at public works and, in spite of his advanced years, took up a spade, sang pious songs and enlivened the lazy. The puritanical side of his life, his sober, unimaginative piety was not noticed by his followers. His life in Medina was too dynamic, his career too eventful.

The Prophet accepted power, wealth and the sudden change in his own destiny as a matter of course. God had promised him power over the desert, God had sent him as the last prophet into the world; consequently there was no need for him to wonder at the development of events, nor was there need for him to burst into praise merely because the word of God had been fulfilled. This would only have shown a lack of faith. It was only when the army and the State of God were in danger, as at the time of Uhud, when the entire edifice of Islam threatened to collapse; it was only at such times that the Prophet folded his hands, raised them to heaven and reminded Allah of His promises. "Almighty," he would say, "help us or else there will be no one to pray to you." As had been the case in Mecca, the house of the Prophet was open to all in Medina. Heathen, Christians, Moslems and Jews could enter his house at any time; they could ask him questions and enter into learned discussions with him. The Prophet did not surround himself with a halo either as messenger of God or as head of the State. He mixed with the people and the people were permitted to ask him anything. Islam was a theocratic democracy. It was only with great care and by the issuing of special decrees that the over-faithful were restrained from appearing in front of the Prophet's house at night to see with which of his wives he was and what was going on. For the majority of the people the Prophet, the messenger of God, was merely a man who differed from the others in that from time to time he was permitted to hear the words of God.

But the word of God had changed. In Mecca the word had revealed the faith in God. In Medina the word of God erected the State of God. The style of the Koran had been changed as well. It no longer contained flaming threats and avowals; now it merely revealed laws. The word of the law was clear and objective. The power of expression and the force of the iron sentences was unchanged, unchanged the visits of the Archangel who brought the words of God to Mohammed in short, terse verses.

In time the Archangel became a daily manifestation for Mohammed. He appeared, visible to the Prophet alone, in assemblies, in the house or on a ride through the desert. Sometimes the angel assumed the form of a man, that of a friend of the Prophet's, Dihyah al-Kalbi. The Prophet recognized the Archangel in every form: he spoke with him, received his commands and revealed the laws in glowing verses to the pious faithful.

And so, surrounded by the pious, Mohammed, the messenger of God, the ruler of the new State, lived in the city of Medina. It was only rarely that the Prophet had time to spend in pious meditations. The State of God was in danger. Victorious and threatening lay the resplendent city of Mecca on the other side of the desert. Daily, while at prayer, the Prophet turned his face to that city, which had remained invincible and full of danger.

Abu Sufyan had called out at Uhud, "In one year I will return and destroy the false prophet." The year of the forced peace was nearly over. Filled with sorrow, the Prophet looked at the bare sand dunes behind which the army of the Quraish would soon appear. Again he would have to fight against the city of his fathers, and now more than ever the destiny of the Republic of God, the destiny of Islam, would depend on the outcome of a battle.

A DITCH AND VERY MANY JEWS

> For whom the Lord loveth he chasteneth.
> *Hebrews xii, 6*

When the Prophet had expelled them from the city of which he was master, the Banu Nadir sought asylum and protection among distant tribes in the desert. Not very far from Medina there is a group of oases which make up the prosperous colony of Khaibar. Khaibar was rich and feared in the desert. The noble and courageous warriors who lived there in the shade of the palms were Jews, but they were not as noble as the Banu Nadir. Among the Jews of Arabia, the Nadir were considered the flower of humanity, for, according to legend, they were direct descendants of the prophet Aaron, the high priest of the Jews. For this reason the Nadir were received in all honour by the people of Khaibar. They were given land and palms, houses were built for them and they were promised protection. The pious Jews of Khaibar honoured the seed of Aaron, and the more honour they paid his memory, the more they hated the false prophet who had humiliated the noblest tribe of the desert.

The inhabitants of Khaibar sent out messengers in all directions, to all the Jewish tribes as well as to others with whom they were friendly. They spread the news of the treacherous master of Medina, who had come to the city as a guest, had begged shelter and protection and had then exiled his hosts, robbing them of their possessions, and breaking the pacts which he himself had made with them. The Arabs, Bedouins and Jews listened attentively, nodded their heads and blamed the Prophet for his conduct. But when the messengers began to speak of revenge and war, they shrugged their shoulders and said: "We are poor, simple Bedouins. Why should we be concerned with your troubles? If we are to risk our lives, our camels and our horses, then promise us a portion of the booty and pay us a part of that portion in advance." The hatred of the pious people of Khaibar was so great that they pledged their date crops and sacrificed their money, in order to secure the aid of the people of the desert.

The tribes of the desert are numerous and their sheikhs are greedy. The gold of Khaibar did not suffice them. So it was that a holy Jew, Huyayy, and with him Kinanah ibn Khakayk, Hanzalah ibn Qais and the *hanif* Abu Amir mounted their horses and rode to Mecca. There was gold in Mecca, and the Meccans hated Mohammed more fiercely than they did anyone else. Upon their arrival, they went to Abu Sufyan and said, "O Abu Sufyan, your faith is better than the faith of Mohammed, and your sword is stronger than his. Let us fight together against Mohammed, for we hate him as much as you do." And Abu Sufyan concluded an alliance with the Jews.

From that moment on gold poured into the desert. The tribes arose and swore by all their old gods that they would destroy Mohammed. Abu Sufyan and the people of the Jews were certain of victory. But Abu Sufyan was a merchant, and his business was more important to him than war. He waited for the end of the Month of the Pilgrimage, for the end of the great fair. It was only then that he collected the tribes for the attack.

It was an enormous army that set forth for Medina. Abu Sufyan led ten thousand men. In a land where an army of thirteen hundred was considered a great event, one of ten thousand had never been seen. Singing songs of victory, the army marched through the desert. Every sheikh, every leader, whether he were an Arab or a Jew, began to count in advance how much his share would be. At the head of the army rode the noblest of all the Arabs, Abu Sufyan, and at his side the mightiest of the Meccan warriors, Khalid ibn al-Walid and Amr ibn al-As. The three leaders of the vast army were going to Medina to destroy the Prophet. None of the three dreamed how closely their names would one day be connected with that of Mohammed. The son of Abu Sufyan and the son of Hind, who ate Hamzah's liver, was Mu'awiyah, the fifth caliph of Islam, who founded the dynasty of the Ummayah, the brilliant dynasty of the caliphate. Islam owed its great victories over Asia and Africa, over Byzantium and Persia, to Khalid ibn al-Walid and to Amr ibn al-As, the son of a courtesan, a diplomat and a poet. These were the victories which gave world-power to the Prophet and world-power to the caliphate. Now all three were riding at the head of an army of ten thousand in order to destroy the Prophet and the city of Medina.

Mohammed heard of the approach of the large army through his followers, who were secretly distributed throughout the desert. The news struck terror into the hearts of the people of Medina. They forgot the beautiful slaves and thought no longer of the forbidden or permitted pleasures of life. They thought only of the great army which was larger than all of the previous Arabian armies put together. Experienced warriors, great bandits, even Mohammed himself, were frightened. Mohammed knew that the city of God could not be vanquished but at the same time he thought of his own words: "First entrust your camel to God's care but tie it to a tree anyway." But where the tree was to which the camel was to be tied Mohammed did not know. All the means of war, all the methods of defence which were known to the Arabs, would be powerless against the gigantic army. It would be impossible to confront the enemy in open battle. They could fight in the narrow streets or seek shelter in the fortresses, but none of these means seemed to indicate salvation. Looking down from the fortresses, the city of Medina was entirely unprotected. There were no walls of fortification and they could only depend upon the natural protection of the hillsides, rocks and precipices. Three sides of the city were protected in this fashion, but on the fourth side Medina lay wide open and exposed to the enemy's attack. Clearly the army could approach the city from the fourth side, and no one knew how the city could defend itself. Fear, anguish and desperation reigned in Medina. The soldiers of the Prophet were accustomed to primitive methods of warfare; they were without experience of large battles, and none of the Arabs had ever seen an army of ten thousand men before.

But Islam was not only the faith of the Arabs. It was open to all the peoples of the world, and many races were represented in the city of the Prophet. When, after his great flight, the exhausted Prophet had arrived at Quba, an alien slave, the Persian Salman, had come to him. He had been converted to Islam and had been accepted as a free and equal member of the faithful. It was this Persian who was to save God's state. Salman had travelled much and gained experience. His way had led him through Persia and Byzantium and through all the militaristic states of the old world. He had not only visited convents and preachers, but he had seen the army of the Emperor of Byzantium march through the fields of Iran and the warriors of the Sacred Fire besiege the ramparts of the Roman Empire. He had heard much about great campaigns and of the craft of war, and he had retained all this in his wise Persian head, so that now he was able to make use of it. He went to the Prophet and gave him valuable advice. His suggestion was that a wide ditch be dug from hill to hill across the road which opened up the way to Medina, and it was behind the ditch that the army of the Prophet was to await the enemy. He was confident that the ditch would prevent the conquest of Medina. It was a primitive idea and any of the generals of Byzantium or Iran would have laughed at it; but it appealed to the Prophet. The work was begun at once, and night and day the digging was carried on with enthusiasm. Salman, the engineer of the Prophet, directed the work and Mohammed himself helped. Finally the huge ditch, which separated Medina from the world of deserts and tribes, was completed. The small army was entrenched behind it and nervously awaited the foe.

Slowly and confidently the army of ten thousand made its approach. Soon it saw the fortresses of Medina and trembled with delight at the thought of victory and plunder. Abu Sufyan rode ahead and examined the ground, when suddenly, from a distance, he saw something strange and confusing. When he had come closer he saw a wide ditch. Although Abu Sufyan was a wise merchant, he was neither intelligent nor versed in military tactics. The unexpected filled him with consternation. He had never before seen anything like it.

As if petrified he stood in front of the ditch. He was obviously shaken by the enemy's move. Behind its leader, the army of ten thousand stared also, and was equally puzzled. How was the ditch to be crossed? It was too much for the minds of the simple sons of the desert. The soldiers looked at one another, shook their heads and were speechless. A ditch had never before been provided for in Arabian warfare. The army was hypnotized by the ditch like a chicken by a chalk line. The whole thing required careful reflection. They would come to more practical decisions later.

The grotesque situation in which the Bedouins found themselves was characteristic of their simplicity. The victorious march of the ten thousand was actually halted by the ditch. Still undecided, the tents were put up and, having nothing else to do, they began the siege. As a matter of fact, what were ten thousand to do against a ditch? For them war meant fighting in an open field. Anything else was incomprehensible. The army of the Prophet kept watch behind the ditch. Overjoyed at their unexpected success, they bided their time.

That which followed is but little reminiscent of the glorious deeds of the ancient Arabs. Day after day, Jews, Meccans and Bedouins appeared at the edge of the ditch. They hurled insults at the army of the pious with all their might. "What sort of warriors are you," they thundered, "if you hide behind a ditch? Is this a war worthy of the Arabs? Did our fathers or our grandfathers fight like this? You are cowardly dogs and no Arabs! Come over here and show us what you can do!"

But the brave warriors of the Prophet were not to be disturbed. They sat safely and securely behind the wide ditch, untouched by the cries of the heathen. Now and again, a daring pagan attempted to climb over the ditch. They permitted him to cross only to kill him with much pride and ceremony. The days passed by with insults and the exchange of an occasional arrow. It was soon obvious that the huge army was filled with discontent, and there were good reasons for this. Confident of a swift and certain victory, Abu Sufyan had not hurried his campaign. He had waited until the pilgrims had left Mecca at the expiration of the Month of the Pilgrimage and until the harvest had been gathered in the fields of Medina. Now, when the siege had begun, he soon realized that the harvest was out of his reach and safely stored in Medina. The army of the ten thousand which had counted on the crops was without provisions. The Bedouins, who had gone to war at considerable expense in the hope of quick and rich reward, were forced to see their camels grow thin and themselves wasting their time. Their previous enthusiasm began to cool considerably.

It was while facing this predicament that Abu Sufyan decided upon a general attack. Since his hope of victory was not great, he determined to ally himself with the last of the Jewish tribes in Medina, the Banu Quraizah who lived in a large fortress outside the city. The Quraizah, who were subjects of Mohammed, readily agreed to break their oath since the Prophet had broken his against the two other Jewish tribes of Medina, and they promised to attack Mohammed's army from the rear. Thereupon Abu Sufyan gave orders to prepare for the attack. The preparations lasted for days.

When they had been completed, it happened that the day of the attack was a Saturday. The Banu Quraizah and all the other Jewish tribes of the army declared that they could not possibly break the century-old laws of their fathers and take upon themselves the sin of fighting on a sabbath. When Abu Sufyan tried to move the Jews to participate in the attack, the Jews of Khaibar announced that, in their opinion, the whole campaign was a failure and that they at least had no desire to call down the wrath of the Prophet upon their brothers in Medina by participating in the attack. Other tribes, who apparently had been influenced by Mohammed's secret agents, became equally disinterested. Conditions continued as they were for a few more days, a few skirmishes took place, and then the patience of the Bedouins was exhausted.

One day, heavy clouds covered the heavens, rain began to fall in torrents and a violent hurricane from the desert upset the tents of the nomads. The Bedouins attributed this to Mohammed's magical power. They had no desire to, nor could they, fight against magic, particularly the magic of a coward. There was nothing for Abu Sufyan to do but withdraw with honour. He wrote a letter to Mohammed, accused him of cowardice and treachery against the old-established traditions of war, and swore that at the proper time he would return to take bloody vengeance. Then he got on his camel and gave orders for the return march.

The coalition which had been organized against Mohammed was irreparably split. The Prophet and the State of God had been saved, and, unconquered, the army of the *ansar* and the *muhajirun* returned to Medina. This occurred on 15 April 627.

Now the hour had come for the last Jewish tribe in Medina, the Banu Quraizah. Mohammed had learned of their negotiations with the army of the Quraish and he was determined to settle with them. On the day on which Abu Sufyan gave up the siege of Medina, Mohammed and his soldiers marched to the fortress of the Quraizah. Another siege began.

The Jews were unable to make any armed resistance. They had retreated to their stronghold and waited for what was to come. At the end of twenty-five days they surrendered unconditionally to the Prophet. They had hoped that they would be permitted to leave the city, as the other tribes had been. But the Prophet was not at all inclined to be merciful. It was only upon the request of the Aus, who had long been friendly with the Quraizah, that he decided to place the decision in the hands of an arbiter. The role was entrusted to a pious member of the Aus tribe, Sa'd ibn Mu'adh.

Sa'd ibn Mu'adh was a fat, full-blooded man given to choleric outbursts. He passed for a friend of the Jews. He had been injured in a skirmish which had taken place behind the ditch and now lay gravely wounded. The wound pained him and Sa'd knew that his days were numbered. Because of their alliance with the Quraish, he felt that the Jews alone were responsible for his death. With great care, the heavy, mortally wounded Sa'd was carried out of his tent, placed upon a donkey and surrounded with pillows. In this fashion he was led to the place where the decision was to be given. When he arrived, he demanded that the parties concerned agree unconditionally to his terms. The Jews were the first to swear and they did so gladly. Sa'd was an old friend upon whom they could count.

The dying man propped himself up in his saddle and delivered his judgment: "All the men of the Banu Quraizah are to be executed and the women and children sold into slavery." Mohammed did not protest against the verdict. It was exactly in accordance with his wishes. On the other hand, he promised mercy to those who would become converted to Islam.

On the morning of the next day a deep grave was dug in the market place. The old, cruel Orient was to intoxicate itself with blood in the centre of the city of Medina. Islam showed its claws. One by one, the Jews were brought to the market place in chains, made to stand at the edge of the grave, and decapitated. Although the Jews of Medina had not known how to live courageously, they did know how to die bravely. Not a single one of the Banu Quraizah betrayed his faith in order to save his life. They died silently and courageously. They saw their brothers being slain before their eyes and knew that their own heads were soon to follow.

Soon the grave was full. Blood ran over the market place. The Prophet and the leaders of Islam stood at one side. They watched the executions and said nothing. Worlds are born in blood. The day drew to a close, and still Jews were brought to the place in chains. Soon it was night, and the Prophet gave orders for torches to be brought, so that the faithful could see the blood of the enemy being shed on the market place. In the middle of the blood-covered city, his face strangely lit up by the burning torches, stood Mohammed, the master, the messenger of God.

Among the Quraizah there was a Jew named Zubair, who had once saved the life of the great Moslem warrior, Thabit. Thabit recognized him among those condemned to death. "You were good to me and saved my life, O Zubair," Thabit said to the Jew. "I will now reward the good which you did to me." He went to the Prophet and begged for Zubair's life, and asked that his family be permitted to retain their possessions. Since Thabit belonged to the tribe of the Aus and was a mighty warrior as well as a pious Moslem, Mohammed granted his request. Overjoyed, the warrior ran to Zubair and brought him the good news. But the Jew said, "Lead me to the place of execution, for I would like to follow my brothers who died there and those who are about to die. I do not wish to have my life spared by the bloodthirsty man who has slain all around me. The pail of my life has run empty and I am impatient to be reunited with my friends." Having spoken, the old Jew went to the place of execution, where he was decapitated by Ali, for the cousin and the son-in-law of the Prophet acted as executioners on that bloody day. Zubair the Jew was not forgotten by later generations. His actions were considered as an example of martyrdom by the Arab people and all the faithful. Among the people of the desert his memory is honoured to this day, for Islam was the first faith in which theologians and the church fathers were permitted to praise and admire the heroism of people not of their own faith.

This was the end of the Jews of Medina. Their faults had not been numerous. They protected themselves as well as they could, sought peace and were afraid of the power of the enemy. They had invented cruel jokes at the expense of the Prophet, sung impudent songs about him, listened to him only to contradict, and adhered rigidly to the primitive faith which they brought with them from their old home. It was that which brought about their destruction. The Prophet could no longer tolerate their presence in the city where the word of Allah and his prophet reigned supreme. The Banu Quraizah knew how to die courageously. Much of their cowardice in life was compensated by their death.

Medina, the city of the Prophet, was now the unified city of the faith where, no longer touched by the rude ridicule of the unbelievers, Mohammed could govern the great community of the Moslems.

THE MOTHERS OF THE FAITHFUL

> The greatest treasure of man is a virtuous wife.
> *Mohammed*

At the eastern entrance to the mosque in Medina there were nine lowly clay huts arranged in a semicircle. The doors of the huts consisted of dark curtains. Some of the huts were enclosed with small verandas. The curtains protected the life and activities in the huts from the gaze of the curious.

It was in these huts that the "mothers of the faithful," the numerous wives of the Prophet, lived. Mohammed had more wives than were allowed by the laws of Islam, for only four wives were permitted to each of the faithful. The Prophet, whose life was filled with work and prayer, was allowed to have as many wives as his strength permitted inasmuch as he was a favourite of Allah. Other prophets like Solomon, David and Abraham had enjoyed a similar privilege. Solomon had a hundred wives. God allowed him to have them, for superhuman virility is the sign of the prophet. Mohammed was the seal of the prophecy. His strength was immeasurable. But Mohammed was an ascetic, and although his strength was greater than that of Solomon, he had only fourteen wives.

Mohammed was married to fourteen wives. Fourteen women had the title, "mother of the faithful." But countless were the number of women who came to Mohammed and asked for his love. To all of them Mohammed gave his love, for his heart was filled with sympathy. "Put off whomsoever thou wilt of them and take to thyself whomsoever thou wilt, or whomsoever thou cravest of those whom thou hast deposed," God said to Mohammed (Koran, *Sura* 33, *verse* 51). And in *Sura* 66, *verse* 1, when it appeared that fourteen wives were not sufficient for the Prophet, Allah revealed to Mohammed: "O thou prophet! wherefore dost thou prohibit what God has made lawful to thee, craving to please thy wives?"

Great was the number of women to whom Mohammed had given his love. Till the end of his life, the Prophet did not cease to give his favours to beautiful women, to admire them, to pet them and to place his arms around them. One desire burned in Mohammed's heart, and drove him from one woman to another, from one slave to the next. Mohammed wished for a son who would be worthy of his father's inheritance, a son who could take over God's state and complete Mohammed's work. But his wish was never fulfilled and until he was an old man Mohammed wandered through the flower-garden of his harem, sought out beautiful slaves, embraced countless women and prayed to Allah, the Creator of man. But no son was given to him. The last of the prophets was not to have any heirs.

Nine huts surrounded the mosque and in them lived the wives of the Prophet. Almost every wife had a hut of her own, which assured marital peace. It was only now and again, when the Prophet brought a beautiful slave with him from one of his marches, that a wife would share her house for a time with the new arrival. The best – that is to say the least lowly of the huts – belonged to the favourite wife of the Prophet, the beautiful Aisha, daughter of Abu Bakr, the friend and well-wisher of Mohammed. Aisha was six years old when Mohammed had first seen her in Mecca, and he could not take his eyes off her. This was shortly after the death of Khadijah, who at that time was Mohammed's only wife. Abu Bakr, who had understood the enraptured look on the face of his friend, promised to give his daughter to him when she should be old enough for marriage and love. But Mohammed's rapture was so great that after three years, he married the nine-year-old Aisha in Medina. He himself was fifty years old at that time.

"I sat," recounted Aisha, "on a rocking-chair and was playing with other girls. My mother called me, took me by the hand and led me to the door of the house. My heart began to beat but gradually I again became quiet. I washed my face and hair, and my mother dressed me up and led me into the house, where there were many women. They received me with good wishes and they also decorated me. When they were finished, they gave me over to the Prophet."

Aisha was the favourite wife of the Prophet, and of the many who were his she was the only one who had come to him as a virgin. Following the ancient Arabian custom, he had paid her father, Abu Bakr, twelve ounces of gold. Later on this was also the price Mohammed was willing to pay for a wife. He never paid more. During the first year of the great flight it was impossible for Mohammed to raise twelve ounces of gold. But since tradition had to be maintained, the father of the bride, Abu Bakr, lent the gold to his friend Mohammed, who in turn solemnly offered it as the purchase price for Aisha. Memories of the first hard years in Medina were connected with Aisha in Mohammed's mind. In spite of his power, Mohammed had still been poor at that time and he had never even thought of amassing a fortune. For this reason his wedding was a poor one. The marriage feast consisted of milk, the marriage bed was a sheep's stall, and the nine-year-old bride's dowry, two shirts, two simple silver bracelets and a little silver money. For poverty was the virtue of the Prophet. "In the first years of our marriage," said Aisha, "it happened that for months we never lit a fire, for our food was water and dates. Now and again someone would send us some meat. Wheat bread was never seen two days in succession in the house of the Prophet."

But fate presented Aisha with richer gifts at a later time. When Aisha married she was still a child, and she had brought her toys with her to the house of her husband. She played with dolls and amazed the faithful, for dolls are representations of human beings. They are strictly forbidden in Islam. But Aisha was permitted to do much that was forbidden to others of the faithful. She was very pretty, witty and playful, liked to wear gold rings and anointed her hair so much that the ointment often ran down her forehead. But her playful, childish face covered an energetic, wise character. As the favourite wife of the Prophet and as daughter of the first Caliph, she later played an important role in Islamic politics. She was familiar with literature and was a past mistress at intrigue. She could read, and collected many of the Prophet's sayings; and after Mohammed's death she was considered the supreme authority in matters of law and religion. Her influence upon the Prophet was of untold value to Abu Bakr and his party. For Aisha, the small, tender maiden, had definite sympathies and antipathies which she expressed in definite terms. The present division of Islam into Sunni and Shiites was largely due to her antipathy for Ali. Aisha died at the age of sixty-seven, forty-seven years after the death of the Prophet.

If Aisha was the favourite wife of the Prophet, then Saudah was certainly the least beloved. She was a widow of Mecca and Mohammed had married her two months after Khadijah's death, merely because an Arab cannot remain unmarried without damaging his reputation. He never loved Saudah and it is possible that he would have divorced her, had it not been for the fact that she was very intelligent. One night a week was spent by Mohammed in Saudah's hut. He did not enjoy it and merely did so because he thought it was his duty. When Saudah learned of Mohammed's love for Aisha, she did an amazing thing and probably something which had never been done before. She officially gave over her night to Aisha. She gained a good deal through this. She remained in her hut until the end of her life, regularly received presents from the Prophet and was looked upon as a 'mother of the faithful.' Mohammed knew how to be grateful. "Even on the day of the resurrection she will be my wife," Mohammed said of Saudah.

Hafsah bint Umar, the daughter of Umar, was also not among the favourite wives of Mohammed. She had been married to a Moslem warrior. After the death of her husband, Umar was on the look-out for a suitable marriage for his daughter. Despite his great power, he could not force anyone to marry his daughter, for she was both old and ugly. Umar felt humiliated and did not know what to do. When Mohammed heard of this, he had pity on his friend and did what but few men would have done; he married the daughter because of his friendship with her father. He was also a good husband to her, visited her regularly, gave her presents and did not neglect the nights which were allotted to her.

On the other hand, his love for Zainab was both gentle and genuine. She had had a very romantic past. Zainab had been the wife of Zaid, the former slave and adopted son of Mohammed. Mohammed had seen her and was pleased by her appearance, her seriousness and her piety. He visited her a number of times and talked with her. One day Zaid came to Mohammed and said, "O Prophet, I am but a simple Moslem and you are the messenger of God. Your deeds are greater than mine and your wish is stronger than mine. Take my wife for you need her more than I do." And the slave Zaid divorced his wife and gave her to the Prophet. Zainab was pious and very beautiful. She loved the Prophet because he was a prophet, and did not wish to accept any money or presents from him. Before she had married Zaid, she had been a shoemaker and had sold her wares in the bazaars. Even as 'mother of the faithful' she did not stop her work. The money she made was divided among the poor of the city. After Mohammed's death, when all the wives of the Prophet were presented with gold by the Caliphs, she alone remained poor and without demands. The Caliph Umar gave her a huge fortune, which she distributed among the poor. Each of the wives of the Prophet was entitled to choose something from the treasury of Islam, but Zainab took nothing but a lovely dress in which she wished to be buried. When she died she was carried on Mohammed's bier to her grave, for next to Aisha she was Mohammed's favourite wife.

Mohammed's wives were numerous, and he loved them ardently. He devoted much of his time to his harem, and there are many provisions in the Koran concerning the wives of the Prophet. For example, they had to hide their faces modestly behind veils in the presence of strange men. At first this fashion was copied by the upper classes and then came into general usage. The wives of the Prophet were also forbidden to remarry after his death.

The harem was made up of the nine huts around the mosque. Mohammed himself did not possess a hut. Even in the days of his grandeur, when he ruled over all Arabia, he did not have a house of his own. His nights were regularly and systematically planned. Each wife knew which night the Prophet would spend with her. Only a new wife had the right to receive Mohammed three nights in succession.

Mohammed knew how to maintain peace in his harem, and it probably took more diplomacy than did his various campaigns on behalf of Islam. Whenever he brought a present to one of his wives, a similar gift was given to all the members of the harem. On the other hand, he did not spoil his wives, and it was considered a great event when, returning from a successful battle, he gave each of them eighty measures of figs, corn and wheat. He did not permit gossip or jealousy among his wives and they were severely punished when guilty of either. If one of his wives disobeyed him, the punishment might be that he would refuse to visit her for so many months. Aisha was not exempt from these punitive measures, for Mohammed was just to both his subjects and his wives. He was also quick to defend and protect any woman who had been dealt with unjustly.

On one occasion Mohammed set out against a rebellious Jewish tribe. He destroyed the tribe and brought back with him a pretty Jewish maiden. The girl, whose name was Safiyyah, became his eleventh wife. The harem was annoyed at the arrival of each of Mohammed's new wives, and Aisha, the most temperamental of them all, did not cease insulting the Jewess Safiyyah because of her faith. One day Mohammed heard them quarrel and said to Safiyyah: "Safiyyah, say to this woman, 'My father's name was Aaron, my uncle was Moses, and who were your fathers? Heathen!'" Thereupon he banished Aisha for two months.

Not all of Mohammed's marriages were love matches. An Oriental conqueror battles against the world with his sword, but he assures his possession of it by means of the tender ties of marriage. If an eastern people is to obey its ruler, then it wishes to be related to him. Even in our day, the harem of an Oriental ruler contains women from all the provinces of his country. The people feel themselves related by blood with the children of the ruler, and this assures unity within the country. A similar fate was not spared Mohammed. The noblest families and tribes sent their prettiest women to him so that he might marry them.

Once Mohammed received the news that the head of the royal tribe Kindah wished to send him his daughter for a wife. The nobler an Arab is the longer his name. One can have some idea of the nobility of this particular bride from her father's name which was: Mu'man ibn Abi al-Jun ibn al-Aswaa ibn al-Harith ibn Sharahil ibn al-Jun ibn Akal al Marar. The daughter of this famous man was considered one of the most beautiful of all the Arab women. Asma was brought to Medina with much pomp, the marriage was celebrated with all due ceremony, and Asma moved into one of the nine huts. Although Asma was very beautiful she was stupid, and the inhabitants of the harem, who were jealous of each new competitor, knew how to benefit by it. Shortly before the bridal night, one of Mohammed's wives came to Asma, admired her beauty and, being very friendly, gave her some advice. Among other things she said: "If you wish to find approval in the eyes of the messenger of God, say to him when he enters your hut: 'God protect me from you.' Only in this manner can you be sure of his love." Asma followed the advice and when Mohammed entered her hut she said: "God protect me from you." She then lifted her veil and looked at the Prophet. "May God protect me from you as well," replied the Prophet, and leaving the hut, he sent her a letter of divorcement. In spite of her fashionable parents, he remained steadfast and refused to forgive Asma. It has been said that Mohammed often sent back his brides on their bridal nights because of similar tricks perpetrated by his wives.

At the height of his power, when he ruled over all Arabia, Mohammed was subjected to a veritable assault by women.

His last marriage was celebrated two months before his death. If a general conquered a distant province, or if some ruler wished to show Mohammed his respect, he would send him a number of beautiful slaves in addition to other treasures. Mohammed would either present them to his friends or keep them for himself. In the year 7 of the Hidshra, when the Christian governor of Egypt had heard of the Prophet, because he was afraid and also as a precautionary measure, he sent him a thousand bars of gold, twenty pieces of Egyptian linen, a white donkey, some honey, a eunuch with whom the Prophet could do nothing, and two beautiful Egyptian slaves who were immediately converted to Islam.

The Prophet took one of them but did not marry her. She was a light-skinned, curly-haired Copt, Mariyah. Mohammed loved her passionately. She became his favourite concubine and he visited her frequently despite the objections of his wives. Mariyah was the only one among all the women who fulfilled his dearest wish; she bore him a son, Ibrahim, the heir of his empire. But his happiness was short-lived for the boy died when he was one year old.

Years passed by. The youthful prowess of the Prophet began to wane. When he was sixty the Prophet found it difficult to maintain the schedule of visits to his wives. But the wives lived in their huts and were young and strong. Mohammed was a wise man and he had pity upon his wives. He knew that women ranging from seventeen to twenty years of age could not love a sixty-year-old man whole-heartedly, even if he were a prophet. In his wisdom and mildness, he decided to extend freedom to his wives. He assembled them about him and revealed the words of God in the 28th verse of *Sura* 33: "O thou Prophet, say to thy wives, 'If ye be desirous of the life of this world and its adornments, come, I will give you them to enjoy and I will let you range handsomely at large! But if ye be desirous of God and His Apostle and of the abode of the hereafter, verily, God has prepared for those of you who do good a mighty hire.' Reflect upon the words of God," said the Prophet, "and answer according to your conscience." All the women replied: "We love God, His messenger, and that which comes after death." Only one of the women, Fatimah of the tribe of Kilab, preferred the joys of her youth. The Prophet gave her many presents and dismissed her. Later on she became so poor that she was forced to collect camel dung to be used for fuel. She died in dire poverty and was called ash-Shaqiyyah, the miserable one.

The 'mothers of the faithful,' the first wives of the Prophet, lived modestly and in retirement. Little provision was made for their personal requirements and nearly every comfort was lacking in their huts. There was not even a place where they could satisfy their needs, so that they were often forced to retire to the desert at night for this purpose. It was only during the last years of his life that the Prophet caused conveniences to be erected, for he suspected that their nocturnal excursions were also for other purposes.

The wives of the Prophet owned nothing and they were overjoyed at the smallest gift. Their entire fortune consisted of twelve ounces of gold which the Prophet had paid for them.

Later, when the Prophet was dead and Islam had already encircled an entire world, the women were richly provided with gold. The treasuries of the Caliphs were constantly at their disposal. The widows' pensions were small fortunes, and more money was offered for the lowly huts than had ever been possessed by all Arabia. So, for example, the caliph Walid paid fifty thousand gold *dirhams* to the heirs of Zainab for her hut, a huge fortune in the eyes of the old world. The Jewess Safiyyah left a fortune of one hundred thousand gold *dirhams*.

All the treasures of the Orient were now at the disposal of the Prophet's wives. Their relatives were given the highest positions in Islam. Umm Salamah, who at first did not wish to marry the Prophet because she had children for whom Mohammed would have had to provide, lived to see Ali appoint her sons as governors of entire provinces. For generations, the blood-relations of the wives of the Prophet, together with his own relations, made up the aristocracy of Islam. The wives themselves were given all honours up to the time of their death, and not a single caliph dared deny them any wish.

In this fashion posterity honoured the women who had loved God and His messenger more than all the joys of existence, the women who lived in narrow huts in which the Prophet spent his nights, and who never had wheaten bread to eat on two successive days.

AISHA AND THE HISTORY OF THE WORLD

Bella gerant alii, tu, felix Austria, nube!

In the fourth year of the Hidshra, the Prophet of God and his warriors set out into the desert to give battle to the rebellious tribe of Mustaliq. The desert was vast and the ride monotonous. The enemy was far away and could not be seen, and the army suffered under the burning sun of the desert. The days spent in the campaigns were tiresome and monotonous. It was therefore the Prophet's custom to take one of his wives with him. This practice did not stop him from sometimes returning with two wives. On this occasion his choice had been the beautiful Aisha.

During the march of the caravan, Aisha was carried in a covered litter. When the time had come for rest, Mohammed entertained himself with her. When they had arrived at their destination, a brief skirmish ensued with the enemy tribe and it was soon subdued. Slaves were distributed and the loot collected. Much to Aisha's displeasure, Mohammed took a woman home with him. The return march had begun and, since the campaign had seemed to be without danger and had promised much booty, a number of the hypocrites, the *munafiqun*, had participated in it. They were headed by Abdallah ibn Ubayy, who still hoped to be King of Medina. When the loot had been divided, quarrels broke out among the hypocrites, for they had fought merely for the gain to be derived and not for the faith. The Prophet, in his wisdom, realized that the *munafiqun* and Abdallah were not fighting for justice but rather to harm him. For this reason he caused the camp to break up at dawn and to march all day, for he knew that tired persons do not seek quarrels.

Since Mohammed's mind was occupied with deciding the quarrel which had broken out, and because of the new wife he had with him, he could devote but little time to Aisha. She was being carried on a litter. She was so light that the bearers could hardly feel her weight. Because of the scarcity of food on the campaign, she had become thinner and lighter than she had been.

When they were in the vicinity of Medina and the day had begun to break, the Prophet gave the command to the army to continue its march. The camels were awakened in the darkness and their loads placed upon their backs. The warriors then said their morning prayers, in which Aisha joined. Thereupon she went into the desert to satisfy a natural need. When she had returned and was about to enter the litter she noticed that she had lost her necklace made of shells.

Aisha was a beautiful woman and a vain one. Shell necklaces were not common in the household of the Prophet. She hurried into the desert to look for the missing piece of jewellery. The men whose duty it was to lift the litter on the back of the camel had seen Aisha return to the camp. According to their orders, they had turned their eyes away so as not to violate her modesty. After a time they approached the litter and lifted it up, thinking that Aisha had long since taken her place in it. They did not notice a difference in weight for, as we have already said, the favourite wife of the Prophet was slender and light. The caravan went on its way. When Aisha, who in the darkness had not noticed the breaking of the camp, returned, she found an empty place and no litter, no camels and no Prophet. She was alone, deserted and helpless in the desert.

And so began for Aisha and for the history of the world the adventure of the necklace, which was to have unforeseen consequences for the Prophet and the men around him.

What happened in the desert, what experiences Aisha had in the solitude are only known from her own account. According to her story she remained seated in the deserted camp, awaiting the return of the caravan when it should discover her absence. Hours passed by and Aisha began to tire in the monotony of the desert. Her eyelids became heavy and she fell asleep. Suddenly she was aroused by a strange voice. She opened her eyes and saw before her a young, handsome warrior, Safwan ibn al-Mu'attal. He too had remained behind in the desert and was following the caravan. He had seen a woman in the desert, had come up to her and, to his amazement, had recognized the favourite wife of the Prophet. Aisha had been awakened by Safwan's respectful cry, and she immediately covered her face. Safwan offered Aisha his camel and both reached the caravan of the Prophet without having exchanged a single word.

So much for the story told by Aisha. The army, the Prophet and all who were with him merely saw how Aisha, after she had been missing for an entire day, had reached the caravan, beaming with joy and in the company of a handsome youth. This caused a great stir. Aisha told everyone who crossed her path how she had lost her necklace and how respectfully she had been treated by the warrior Safwan. But the more she told her tale, the more incredulous were the eyes of the listeners, the more supercilious were their smiles, and the more friendly their bows.

When the army had reached Medina, the story of Aisha's necklace had already become the main topic of conversation. The soldiers, and the *munafiqun* with Abdallah ibn Ubayy at their head, ran through the city, spreading the tale of how Aisha had remained behind and alone in the desert, and how she had rejoined the caravan with a handsome youth. What could it all mean? Soon all Medina knew how the fifteen-year-old Aisha had pulled the wool over the eyes of the sixty-year-old Prophet despite all his wisdom.

The Prophet, too, heard about it, and the first result was that he ceased his nightly visits to Aisha. Only now and again he entered her hut by day, petted her casually, inquired as to her health, and then left after a brief interval. Obviously, the spoilt daughter of Abu Bakr, the mightiest man in Islam, had no desire to tolerate such treatment. She quickly decided to say that she was ill and requested the Prophet to permit her to move into the house of her parents so that she might have better care. The Prophet agreed.[3]

Aisha learned from her parents that she was the topic of conversation of all Medina. The Prophet did not visit her in the house of her parents. Daily Aisha awaited the letter of divorcement. She also expected the death penalty, for that was the punishment which the Prophet had ordained for adultery at that time.

The affair soon assumed political importance. An avalanche had been set rolling and none knew whom it would bury.

It is difficult to separate politics and women in the Orient. The unity of an entire state may sometimes depend upon the marital policy of a wise ruler. Adultery might bring one party into power and cause the downfall of another. A province might rebel if a woman who belonged to it was banished from the harem of its ruler. Hostile parties might become ardent partisans if the wife of their enemy was forced to leave the harem. The woman in the harem is the representative of her tribe. She incorporates the party of her father, and a definite political ideology may stand or fall with her. The harem is in fact nothing other than a strange Oriental parliament, in which all the various parties of the country are represented and opposed to one another. The disputes of political parties converge in the harem, and the power of the ruler is supervised and limited by the parliament of women. This is the importance of the harem, and for this reason a simple love affair can often have significant consequences in world history.

The harem of the Prophet was no exception. Love, calculation and politics are inseparable in the Orient. This manifestation cannot be judged by European standards even though the difference between the Oriental and the European harem is but slight. An Oriental love-affair must be judged as a political act. It has political consequences, and each party and its representatives know how to defend themselves vigorously.

Aisha was not only the favourite wife of the Prophet, she was also the representative of a definite, mighty and influential party which had no desire to be deposed. She was the incarnation of the party of the oldest and ablest companions of the Prophet, the party of Abu Bakr and Umar, the pillars of the new faith. They were the defenders of the ideas of the theocratic, Islamic democracy, the democratic State of God. The party had originated in Mecca and its influence was no based on any blood-relationship with the Prophet. For this reason it was opposed to the degeneration of the theocratic Republic of God into an Oriental hereditary monarchy.

Now that Mohammed was sixty years old, this theory was of vast practical importance. Mohammed had no direct heirs. His closest blood-relative was his cousin Ali, the husband of his favourite daughter, Fatimah. Ali did not doubt but that one day he would be the heir of the Prophet. Was he not the first to embrace Islam, and did he not have two sons, Hassan and Hussain, who were the grandchildren of the Prophet? Nor had Ali forgotten that many, many years before the Prophet had declared before all the tribes of the Hashim, "Here is Ali, my governor."

This suited neither Abu Bakr nor Umar. It was not for this end that they had aided the Prophet during the long and arduous years in creating a state. It was not for this that they had led campaigns, had conquered countries and had preached the words of the Prophet, which said that all were equal in Islam and that precedence was only given to the worthy. They were able and they knew how a state should be governed. Such wisdom was not Ali's. He was merely brave. He knew better than all the others how to attack the enemy at the head of his troops. The foe trembled before the power of his sword and the brutal strength of his youth.

But that was all that Ali did know. When the Prophet declared that his chief delights were his love of women, of perfumes and of prayer, Ali declared with equal frankness that his was sleep. Whereas Mohammed, Abu Bakr and Umar possessed the greatest authority in Islam, that of Ali hardly sufficed to secure the respect of his own wife. His character was weak and his senses impaired. He was lazy, his eyes were expressionless, he had a fat belly and his hands were unusually large. At least that is how his opponents looked upon him. And this sleepy, lazy person, who could only rattle his sword, now claimed the legacy of the Prophet.

But this sleepy hero was well aware of the dangers which the party of the Meccan democrats meant for him. Unskilled and unassisted as he was, he attempted to take some measures against them. He too had a female representative in the entourage of the Prophet, and, as a matter of fact, a very influential one. It was the favourite daughter of the Prophet, Fatimah, who was biding her time in order to bring about a rupture between the democrats and the Prophet. The affair of the necklace was most welcome to Ali. He already saw the enemy destroyed and himself clothed with dignity and office. Already he felt himself the successor of the Prophet.

Although Mohammed was aware of the party differences about him, he took no steps to nominate his successor. Perhaps this was because he still hoped in secret that he might have an heir of his own. Perhaps he had come to the wise decision not to unleash the passions of the contending parties too soon. But now the dispute could no longer be held in check, for neither party was inclined to humble resignation. The Prophet was between two fires.

There was a third party in Medina, the oft-mentioned *munafiqun*, the natives, who hoped to fish out something for themselves from the troubled political waters. Their leader, Abdallah ibn Ubayy, who had never been touched by the Prophet because of his reputation and renown, was now of the opinion that, since the faithful were divided into two parties, it would be comparatively simple for the third party, the natives, to achieve a victory. The dispute over Aisha's faithfulness was grist to the mill of the *munafiqun*. Abdallah still hoped to come into power. Thanks to the Prophet, Medina had now become the central point of Arabia. Wealth kept pouring into the city in great quantities, and as far as Abdallah was concerned the benefits received by the old inhabitants of the city belonged to the city. It was natural that he, the most fashionable man of Medina, wished to profit by them. He felt that he was the obvious successor and heir to the Prophet, and, since he did not take religion too seriously, he could easily speculate on some *coup d'etat* which would bring control into his hands. After all, Medina was his city and not that of this alien prophet. The dispute among the immigrants proved opportune for the *munafiqun*. Apparently the structure of the new State had begun to shake. The loss of a necklace in the desert resulted in these unexpected developments.

While Aisha sat inconsolably crying in the house of her parents and awaited the letter of divorcement and the death penalty, the battle raged between the parties in Medina. The split of the faithful into two parties became more and more obvious. For or against Aisha, for Ali or for Abu Bakr, were the war cries of the day. The *munafiqun* were in between and inflamed one side against the other while they prepared themselves for the decisive blow. The entire hatred which had existed between the tribes, between the Hashim, the Quraish, the Khazraj and the Aus, and which had been so carefully extinguished, threatened to break out anew. Hassan, the Prophet's own poet, wrote satiric verses about Aisha and sought favour in the eyes of Abdallah. The house of Abdallah was constantly filled with friends and warriors. They felt themselves to be the future rulers of Medina and merely awaited the outbreak of the conflict between the immigrants, in order to engage decisively on their own behalf.

Mohammed stood in the midst of this sudden conflagration. His manly vanity had been hurt; he loved little Aisha, and the carefully erected state had begun to collapse.

The Prophet turned to Ali, for Ali's blood was his blood. "What should happen to Aisha?" the Prophet asked. And Ali replied, "Let the law take its course. Send her the letter of divorcement." Ali talked with Mohammed at such length and so passionately that the latter became confused, for God did not speak to His prophet.

Not Ali and those around him alone accused Aisha, but the *munafiqun* as well raged against the wife of the Prophet, for they did not dare insult Mohammed. Mohammed realized that the time had come to break the power of the *munafiqun* once and for all. A necklace which had been lost in the desert was now to do that which sermons, campaigns and victories had failed to do. But his first task was to bring about peace in his own camp between the *ansar* and the *muhajirun*.

One day, early in the morning, the Prophet appeared at the house of Abu Bakr and ordered that Aisha be brought before him. "Are you innocent or guilty?" asked the Prophet. And Aisha replied, "You have heard too many evil slanders about me. If I now say that I am innocent you will not believe me, but if I confess my supposed fault you will not question the truth of my words. Therefore I will have patience." Having spoken, she turned her back upon the Prophet. Before she could leave the room, a loud cry came from the mouth of the Prophet. He fell to the ground. His body began to tremble and beads of perspiration appeared upon his forehead.

Abu Bakr, his wife and Aisha surrounded the Prophet respectfully. They knew that now Allah himself was speaking with the Prophet. Perhaps they had an inkling of what was to come. Slowly his body became calm, slowly the Prophet opened his eyes, a smile appeared upon his face and he said, "Aisha, God has recognized your innocence." Then the Prophet arose and revealed the words of God, verse 11, *Sura* 24: "Verily, those who bring forward a lie, a band of you – reckon it not as an evil for you, it is good for you; every man of them shall have what he has earned of sin; and he of them who managed to aggravate it, for him is mighty woe."

With this, peace was pronounced. No one had dreamed that the supreme authority would interfere in this love affair. Mohammed alone realized the political importance of the event. The immigrants and the auxiliaries, whether they were adherents of Ali or of Abu Bakr, had to submit to the words of God, for God's words were the foundation of the State. To question that was to question the entire State of God. Peace between the two parties had been precariously restored.

But it was quite different with the *munafiqun*. They cared but little for the power of God's words, for at heart they believed neither in Allah nor in His Prophet. They wished to assume power, to profit by the riches which were pouring into the city of Medina. They did not cease to make use of the necklace affair nor did they stop their intriguing among the two parties. But now these tactics were welcome to Mohammed. God had revealed, and Mohammed prepared for a terrific blow. He read the words of God to the public and made mention of those against whom they were directed. It concerned only the *munafiqun* and Abdallah ibn Ubayy who stood at the head of the sinners. "Fearful punishments await those who slander a woman without having any proof," the Prophet revealed, "and only those who have four witnesses to the adultery may announce it."

When these words had been spoken, the Prophet called the leaders of the *mu-*

nafiqun, who were in chains, into the square of the mosque. Abu Bakr's men threw them to the ground and beat them unmercifully. No pity was shown them, for together with Aisha's honour the Prophet also defended that of the State.

Legends say that, as a result of the punishment, two leaders of the *munafiqun* were blinded and two lamed. Only Abdallah ibn Ubayy was spared. Hatred without purpose was alien to the Prophet, and he did not wish to dishonour the most fashionable of all the Medinese. In front of the mosque he asked: "Who will protect me if I take vengeance upon him who has injured my honour?" Naturally, all the warriors who were present arose and swore, with their hands on their swords, to protect the Prophet against all harm. This public comedy sufficed. Abdallah understood the warning and knew that it was now a matter of life and death. The party of the *munafiqun* had been completely destroyed by the words of God. Abdallah was alone and forced to resign. Now he knew that he would never wear the crown of Medina.

And so ends the story of the necklace – the most piquant story in Islam. The energy of the Prophet saved the State. Again he sublimated his feeling of personal vanity to protect the State. The necklace was the way which led to the destruction of the *munafiqun*.

The story of the necklace had another important consequence, even though it was not apparent at first. In it lay the origin of the countless wars, conflicts and slaughters which shook the Orient for hundreds of years. It was Aisha who started the upheaval. She was only a woman and but fifteen years of age when the disaster occurred. Until her death she did not stop hating Ali, who had sought to separate her from her husband. This hatred finally brought about the momentous division of Islam: the split into the Shiites, the adherents of Ali, and the Sunni, who followed Abu Bakr and Umar in the path of the Prophet.

So ended the adventure of a fifteen-year-old girl who let her necklace fall into the sand.

THE POET OF THE PROPHET

I take a piece of grey, miserable life and make a
legend of it because I am a poet.

Sollogub

In the city of the Prophet there lived a man of horrible appearance whose name was Hassan. His hair was combed to the front, he wore a black beard and dyed his moustache red. When he was asked why he disfigured himself in this fashion, he replied modestly: "So that my face may look like the blood-covered jaws of a lion." By profession Hassan was a poet; but his talent was mediocre, his conceit was great, and his ambition never satisfied. For all these reasons Hassan abused everyone, and the worse his verses were, the more insults they contained.

One day the Prophet commanded that Hassan be given a beating because of his evil tongue. Hassan was extremely sensitive to corporal punishment. He preferred a quiet life, never went to war and even stayed at home when his native city was being besieged by the enemy. He was greatly annoyed by the beating given him by the Prophet's orders. He was much too much of a coward to confront the Prophet openly, and so he secretly wrote a scurrilous pamphlet about him. When he learned that news of this had reached the ears of the Prophet, he fled in terror to the city of Fadak, but he was soon overtaken by some of Mohammed's followers and slightly injured. Hereupon the gentle poet broke out into such wailing that all his relatives hurried to the spot thinking that the poet lay in the throes of death. Naturally he was soon healed, and he plagued the inhabitants of Medina with his complaints and with his demands for reparation.

Gradually Hassan began to understand that the power of the Prophet was great and he became a partisan of the messenger of God. On a number of occasions he appeared, accompanied by influential relations, before Mohammed's house and sought entrance. But he was never admitted.

Mohammed did not like poets. They talked too much for him and their words rarely contained the truth. "They speak that which they do not do," says the Koran. Once Mohammed said, "The poets write satires which are more painful than wounds. Among all mortals, the poet has the best opportunity of going to hell." Therefore, Mohammed did not wish to have anything to do with the cowardly Hassan. However, since many wicked and derogatory songs had been composed about the Prophet by Quraishite poets, he decided to receive Hassan. Proudly Hassan appeared before Mohammed and said, "I am a great poet. My name, my honour and my songs will best protect the Prophet, for I honour the messenger of God."

As Mohammed was familiar with the ways of poets, he did not attach much importance to Hassan's words. He presented him with a young slave and a piece of property, thinking that this would be the best method of securing his allegiance. Thereupon the poet went to Abu Bakr and informed himself about the weaknesses of the enemies of the Prophet. Then he went home and began producing many satirical poems. This amused the Prophet and the faithful very much. And so it was that the battle between Mecca and Medina became a conflict of poets. But the poets of Mecca were more talented and their poems were much more bitter than those of the simple Hassan.

The faithful came to the Prophet and asked him to command the noble Ali to write a defamatory poem about Mecca. "No," the Prophet answered, "Ali is not to occupy himself with such lowly deeds; he is destined for greater things." He then turned to Hassan and asked: "Can you write a poem ridiculing the Quraish tribe without harming me, for I myself am a Quraishite?" "That is very simple," replied Hassan, "I will draw you out of the numbers of the Quraish just as one pulls a hair out of a piece of dough." "Good," said the Prophet. "If you promise to do that, then put out your tongue." When Hassan obeyed, the Prophet touched the tip of Hassan's tongue with his staff and blessed it. This worked wonders. From that time on Hassan was sharp and bitter, his poems affected the Meccans like pointed arrows, and the Prophet often spent nights in listening to him.

The travelling Bedouin spread these songs among all the tribes and they were more efficacious than the sayings of the pious. Once a tribe came to Mohammed and said: "Our poet has written many malicious poems about you in which he shows that you are an impostor. If one of your people can prove the contrary in a well-written verse, we are prepared to be converted to Islam." At first Mohammed did not wish to entrust the task of converting the tribe to so menial a person as a poet, but finally he empowered Hassan to do so. Although the enemy took great pains, the truth out of the mouth of Hassan conquered. The great tribe acknowledged that Hassan's poems were better than those of their own poet, and they were converted to Islam.

Thanks to the blessings of the Prophet, Hassan, the miserable poet, received many honours. When the war between the Arabs had come to an end and Mecca had embraced Islam, the Prophet forbade all verses which might arouse enmity among the faithful. When peace had been declared, Hassan met the poets of Mecca for the first time. Quite among themselves, they decided to recite their verses to each other in secret and without witnesses. Since Hassan was wise, he wished to be the last one to recite his verses and he therefore asked the Meccans to begin. One after another the poets read the verses which they had written about Hassan. Hassan sat there and was so annoyed that perspiration ran down his cheeks. But he waited patiently until his turn would come to recite his satires. When the Meccans had finished, they mounted their horses and rode away without giving Hassan an opportunity of reading his verses.

Filled with rage, Hassan went to Umar, who at that time was already a Caliph, and told him of the shameful manner in which he had been insulted. Umar knew the hearts of poets, and he decided to do Hassan a great favour. He assembled the people of Mecca, called in the poets and permitted Hassan to recite as many rhymed insults as came to his mind. In this manner, Hassan eased his heart.

In order to be just, the Caliph ordered that all the poems which Hassan had written, as well as those which had been written against him, be collected in a book. Whoever read the one had to read the other and from that time on none of the poets could complain that they had been unfairly treated.

In this manner the poets were ruled in the land of the messenger of God, the poets whose words made but little sense, whose tongues were sharper than weapons and who, among all mortals, had the greatest chance of crossing the threshold of hell.

In Paradise, where life will be happy, where there will be neither pain nor annoyances, there will be no need for the words of poets. There will be no poets there.

AN IGNOMINIOUS PEACE AND ITS CONSEQUENCES

> Today I gave you a great victory.
> *Koran, Sura 5*

Many years had passed since Mohammed had first revealed the birth of a new world to the people of Mecca. A long time had elapsed since he had begun to tread the path of Islam. On this path, he experienced banishment and persecution, distrust and shame. He had been haunted and exiled, mistreated and slandered. Now he climbed the steep path of action which led to the heights of power.

Sin and murder, robbery and treachery beset the way to power, but the Prophet had surmounted them. He ruled over the rich city of Medina without restraint. The tribes of the desert feared him and a network of the faithful was spread over the entire land. And yet the deed had not been completed; not yet did Islam rule the world of the desert. Something barred the Prophet's way. When he went to battle and conquered various tribes they were converted to Islam. But when the army of the Prophet had returned home, the tribes thought of their old gods, and they made pilgrimages to Mecca to pray to the golden Hubal, the great virgin al-Lat, al-Uzza, Manat, and all the other three hundred and sixty gods.

The Prophet had many faithful adherents, but there, where his hand could not reach, only those obeyed who believed in him or those who hoped to secure renown and reward in campaigns. The number of those who devote themselves to an idea purely for reasons of faith was no greater in the deserts of Arabia than elsewhere in the world. Only a few could decide to throw over their century-old tribal laws and to leave their homes in pursuit of a questionable happiness. These few were the uprooted, the exiles, the professional adventurers and the mercenaries who had nothing to lose. The heart of the people still remained closed to Mohammed.

Even in Medina, where his word and sword ruled, the Prophet could see the cool, calculating glances of the *munafiqun*. He knew that it was not the word but the sword which forced men to obey. But the world of the new faith was not to be created by the sword alone.

Something lay between the hearts of the people and the words of the Prophet. This something was Mecca. Mecca had been conquered, beaten and humbled, but still she remained the queen of the desert, the greatest among all the cities. Again and again the tribes streamed towards Mecca and the ancient gods still ruled in the holy place of the Caaba. The business of the merchants still flourished – as a matter of fact, more than ever. The heart of the desert still throbbed for the holy city of Mecca.

What was Mohammed to Mecca? A despot who, in a treacherous and sly manner, had assumed power in the distant province of Medina. By his astute cowardice, he had succeeded in defying the punitive expeditions of the Meccans and in forcing his erroneous doctrines upon the city by means of brutal terror. Consequently they allowed him to remain in his desert oasis and did not bother with him any more than they did with the other local rulers who had come into power by chance. However, he made himself unpleasantly noticeable by his constant campaigns, which disturbed the peace of the country, harmed trade and endangered the caravans. One had to be doubly careful and increase the price of the wares to cover the risk. This was Mecca's opinion of the ruler of Medina.

But the opinion of the Bedouins, the opinion of the simple people of the desert, was even worse. For them, Mohammed was covered with a dark and irremovable stain. He was a pariah, a man from whom his own tribe, his own city, his family, had turned away. And the city was not an unimportant colony, the tribe was not an unimportant, unknown tribe; the city was Mecca, the queen of cities, and the tribe was the Quraish, the noblest tribe of Arabia. His native city had banished the Prophet, had vomited him out; consequently, thought the Bedouins, there must be something wrong about his teaching, about his person. The respect for the great, holy-city of the Caaba was probably the only spiritual property which was ineradicably planted in the souls of the Bedouins. For centuries it had been the Bedouin's custom to make pilgrimages to the Caaba, and for centuries Mecca had for him been the central point of the world. He was accustomed to do what Mecca did, and to condemn what Mecca condemned. Now a man had come who fought Mecca, and this man wooed the heart of the Bedouins. The Bedouins regarded him with distrust.

The key to the heart of the Bedouin, to his natural, primitive obedience was Mecca, and Mecca would have nothing to do with the Prophet. A latent state of war existed between Mecca and Mohammed. Both damned each other, both had different gods and opposite aims, and the hatred between them was great. In the eyes of the Bedouins, Mecca was morally right because it opposed the apostate who had rebelled against his own flesh and blood.

It was in the month of Dhul-Qa'dah in the year 7 of the Hidshra that Mohammed came to a decision which was as important as it was inspired. It was one of those brilliant inspirations which change the world more radically than bloody wars. Mohammed had resolved to give the wheel of his career a decisive turn.

Mecca, which he had fought and ridiculed, the city which possessed the key to the heart of the world, was suddenly to become the centre of the Islamic world. Mohammed made Mecca and the Caaba, which drew the hearts of the Bedouins like a magnet, the spiritual centre of his anti-Meccan faith. The victory of Islam over Arabia could only be certain when Mecca and Islam should have been fused together, when they should have become one in the minds of the Bedouins.

The method which Mohammed chose gave evidence of a statesman-like vision, of a diplomatic capability possessed by no one else in the desert. Mohammed did not assemble an army with which to subjugate Mecca. He did not attack caravans in order to harm trade nor did he carry on further warfare with the city of the Caaba. He merely declared that the Caaba, the black stone and the courtyard which surrounded it, was the most sacred spot in the world, and that all the traditional ceremonies and rites which had been celebrated in the Caaba for thousands of years were in accordance with the wishes of Allah. The pilgrimages, the processions, the circling of the Caaba, were suddenly approved by the Prophet and were made an integral part of Islam. All that to which the Bedouin was accustomed in Mecca, even the fair, was to remain unchanged, and only the three hundred and sixty gods were to be replaced by the all-embracing figure of Allah. Suddenly, all the old ceremonies were traced back to Abraham, the first prophet; they had merely been defiled by the idolatrous practices of the Quraish. Consequently Mohammed now felt the burning need to praise God in the most sacred place of the land. At the beginning of the month of the pilgrimage in the year 628, he called the faithful together and told them of his decision that, together with them, he would participate in the next pilgrimage to Mecca and assist at all the ceremonies of the Caaba.

As a matter of fact, when the time of the holy month had come, Mohammed, accompanied by fifteen hundred penitents who wore the pilgrims' clothes prescribed in Mecca, set out for the holy city. The faithful were practically unarmed and they took with them the animals destined for the sacrificial altar. It was a master stroke. The heretic, who had violated the sacred months, who had fought the holiest of cities for years, now appeared as a contrite penitent and directed his steps towards the gates of the proud city which had once expelled him.

It was a magnificent demonstration. Everyone could plainly see that the alleged heretic, Mohammed, was actually a pious respecter of the holy city of Mecca. No politician, no demagogue in the world's history could have thought of an abler stroke. The master of Medina, dressed in the garments of a pious pilgrim, crossed the desert. Only the holiest, the most fanatic of his followers, accompanied him. The adventurous, the war-like robbers, remained in Medina, for a holy pilgrimage which gave no promise of booty had no interest for them.

But the fifteen hundred who went with Mohammed were the picked faithful of the community of Islam. Now that Mohammed had determined to pass through the front of the astonished tribes, he was equally determined that his piety was to be sufficiently documented. He was the idol of his followers. The water in which he washed himself became sacred, a hair from his head, the parings of his nails when he cut them were collected and worshipped as relics. His spittle, his beard, his clothes, all were objects of ardent veneration. Such treatment made a deep impression upon the Bedouins of the desert, and upon the Meccans, who had seen evidence of it at the end of the last campaign. "I saw the Shahinshah of Iran and the Emperor of Constantinople surrounded by their courtiers," a Quraishite related, "but never have I seen a ruler who was so honoured by his subjects as is Mohammed by his."

The change which the pilgrimage of the heretic portended was so great that at first neither the desert nor Mecca could take it seriously. The first news of the impending pilgrimage aroused much excitement in Mecca. It was said that the false prophet was on his way to Mecca with a vast army, that it was his intention to wage war against Mecca, to endanger the pilgrimages and the annual fair. An army was immediately collected in Mecca and, led by Khalid ibn al-Walid, it set out to confront the Prophet in the desert. Great was Khalid's astonishment when, instead of an army, he saw a band of holy pilgrims who humbly asked permission to enter the sanctuary. The news was quickly transmitted to Mecca. The eyes of the merchants were filled with pride and joy. Mohammed, the repentant, was humbly knocking at the doors of Mecca. Mohammed called upon the holiness of the Caaba: Mohammed had ceased being a rebel and was now treading the path of righteousness.

It was decided to punish Mohammed with the disdain he merited. Unarmed as he was, he was refused admission to the territory of the holy city. Wondrous to behold, the rebel and heretic obeyed. Contrary to the desire of all the faithful, he remained in the oasis of Hudaibiya which was half within and half without the sacred confines. He contented himself with sending his son-in-law, Uthman, to Mecca with the request that a representative be appointed to negotiate peace with him. Even now the Quraish permitted the enemy who had become so humble to wait a long time. It was only after an agonizing wait that the Quraish sent Suhail ibn Amr to the camp of Mohammed.

Suhail had the reputation of being an able diplomat and a master politician. He took in the situation at a glance. Mohammed lay unarmed before the gates of Mecca, he begged admission to the sanctuary and was, practically speaking, at the mercy of the Quraish. One could dictate terms to him, humiliate him, and Suhail decided not to let so unique an opportunity escape him.

He began to make demands. Without mercy and at great length he discussed terms with the messenger of God, and when they had come to an agreement Mohammed called the pious Ali and began to dictate the peace treaty to him. Now an unusual diplomatic scene occurred. "Write," said Mohammed, "in the name of God

179

the merciful and compassionate." "Stop," Suhail cried, "I do not know that form of address. Write simply, 'In thy name, O God.'" "Begin as Suhail commands," said Mohammed humbly. When Ali had finished, Mohammed dictated: "This is the treaty of peace of Mohammed, the messenger of God, and Suhail ibn Amr, the messenger of the city of Mecca." And again Suhail interrupted: "You are no messenger of God to me or I would never have fought you; merely write your name." To this Mohammed also agreed. But the faithful looked at him with amazement for they were not accustomed to such conduct.

And so the treaty which Suhail regarded as a masterpiece of his diplomacy was made. The treaty read: "These are the conditions under which Mohammed, the son of Abdallah, and Suhail, the son of Amr, the messenger of the Quraish, have made peace. War shall not be waged for ten years between them. During this time the members of both parties are not to be endangered by each other. They may not fight one another. If any member of the Quraish goes over to Mohammed, then Mohammed is bound to return him to the Quraish. On the other hand, if one of Mohammed's followers goes over to the Quraish, then these are not bound to return him. An honest understanding is to exist between both parties which excludes robbery and theft. The tribes of the country are to be permitted to join Mohammed or the Quraish at their own discretion. This year Mohammed may neither enter the sanctuary nor the holy city of Mecca. In the next year, Mohammed and his people may come unarmed to Mecca, and, in the absence of the Quraish, perform their worship."

Suhail ibn Amr had every reason to boast of his diplomatic success. It was clearly an indisputable triumph for the Meccans. The Prophet no longer called himself prophet; he would deliver the refugees who sought his protection, he bound himself to permit the Quraish caravans to travel unmolested, and even now, after his apparent failure, he was returning to Medina. He was merely an ordinary tribal leader who would be permitted to come to Mecca annually, which would serve to increase the activity of the fair. Mecca could not ask for more. It was obvious that the Prophet had been tamed.

The pious followers who had accompanied the Prophet also thought that the treaty meant an ignominious defeat, and, since this defeat had not been brought about by force, they began to doubt the Prophet. His behaviour had been diametrically opposed to his usual course of action and was completely incomprehensible to all his adherents.

The Moslems came together in small groups, discussed matters heatedly, shook their heads, and looked at the Prophet disapprovingly. For the first time in the history of Islam their belief in the master had been gravely shaken. Umar, who was not used to hiding his thoughts, was the first to speak his mind. He stepped up to the Prophet and said, "Are you not the messenger of God?" "Certainly," replied the Prophet. "Are we not believers?" Umar questioned further. "Certainly," was the reply. "Are the Quraish idolaters?" "Without doubt." "Why should we then be humiliated before them?" Umar cried, and his face became grave for he was about to turn from the Prophet. Mohammed looked calmly at the angry face of his friend and spoke: "I am the messenger of God and fulfil the commands of the Almighty just as you fulfil my commands." The Prophet's magic power was so great that Umar gave in. Later, when he was Caliph and ruler of the Islamic world, Umar used to say: "I shall never stop giving alms, fasting, praying and freeing slaves. For I regret the words which I once spoke in anger to the Prophet."

Now the messenger of God gave the command to slaughter the sacrificial animals where they were, shaved his head, and carried out the ceremonies of the pilgrimage. Then he gave orders for the return to Medina. Shortly before their departure, a Meccan by the name of Abu Jandal appeared in the camp, confessed his belief in Islam, and begged for hospitality and protection. In spite of all the laws of honour and hospitality, Mohammed, faithful to the newly-made pact, gave him over to the persecution of the Quraish. It was a hard test for the good faith of Islam.

When the camels had been made ready and the warriors were prepared for the return journey, Mohammed assembled the Moslems about him and said, "Today we fought the greatest victory that God has ever given us."

Despite these words, the Moslems could not forgive Mohammed for the treaty and his humble conduct. Again he was alone. The Moslems eyed him with dissatisfaction, the desert was bare and endless, and in it lay the city of Mecca, which gloatingly celebrated the humiliation of the Prophet. At that time, Mohammed was the only one to realize that the peace of Hudaibiyah was a great and mighty victory for Islam. At Hudaibiyah, Mohammed had unlocked the hearts of the people. With all its humiliating features, the treaty contained one thing, it recognized Mohammed as an equal of the Quraish. No longer was the Prophet a pariah; he had made peace with his native city. One could no longer speak of him as an outcast of the queen of cities. On the contrary, he had publicly demonstrated his love for the holy Caaba. He had taken heavy sacrifices upon himself in order once again to be able to touch the black stone. The peace of Hudaibiyah, the recognition of Mohammed as a friend of Mecca, the "honest understanding" which was in the treaty, black on white, wiped out the stain which had covered the Prophet. He was allowed to enter Mecca again, he could worship in the courtyard of the Caaba like all the rest, and obviously he was no longer a rebel.

It required much courage, a great deal of daring, to throw over the past and to disappoint all his fellow-battlers and friends of ten years' standing in signing the treaty of Hudaibiyah. Mohammed had the courage. He staked everything, for, as Umar said later, "Only a miracle prevented the Moslems from deserting the Prophet on the day of Hudaibiyah."

Mohammed alone knew that the stake which he played meant the rulership over Arabia, that he gambled for the people of the desert which knew but one sanctuary, the black stone of the Caaba. Mohammed risked everything and won. At Hudaibiyah he found the way to the heart of the people.

Neither the faithful nor the nobles of the Quraish who were now celebrating their great victory, the taming of the Prophet, knew this. They were soon to know better.

SOVEREIGNTY IN THE DESERT

Habit suppresses more revolutions than all the
armed forces put together.

Wertheimer

Mohammed knew how to profit by the treaty of Hudaibiyah. On the return journey, he halted at every tribe which was coming from, or going to Mecca. Everyone heard the great news: Mohammed the Prophet had made peace with the people of the Quraish. In the future, like all the Arabs, he would visit the holy stone, for in the eyes of Allah the Caaba was a holy place.

Having arrived in Medina, Mohammed sent messengers in all directions to inform his numerous followers that the Caaba had been declared holy, that Mohammed had adopted all the usages followed by the Arabs in their pilgrimages to Mecca.

Like wild-fire, the news spread from oasis to oasis, from tribe to tribe, that Mohammed, who had violated all the desert laws, who had attacked caravans during the sacred months, who had broken the power of the tribes and had defiled the sanctity of the wells and the palm trees, was prepared to acknowledge the laws of the desert and to make pilgrimages to Mecca like all the others. Only a few knew the terms of the treaty. Only the interpretation which Mohammed gave out was known. This interpretation clearly stated that Mohammed and the Quraish, that Islam and the people of Arabia, were again united.

The consequences of this explanation were soon apparent. Mohammed had again been taken up as an equal in the ranks of the Arabs. Suddenly it appeared with astonishing clarity that the future of Arabia would belong exclusively to Islam. Not a single spiritual factor remained with which to oppose Islam. It had assimilated the few vital elements of the Arabian cult and was now in fact all-embracing. It had accepted the Caaba. What other objections remained?

The idols of the Caaba had actually long been dead and no one believed in them any more. The people merely held to tradition, and the primitive tradition of the sanctity of the Caaba had now been accepted by Islam. Conversion to the new faith no longer meant a breaking with the spirit and the tradition of the people. It was made easier for the Arabs to go over to Islam than for any of the other people of the world. Islam required no sacrifices. As had been the custom for generations, one could make annual pilgrimages to the fair of Mecca, one could kiss the black stone and perform all the ceremonies of the pilgrimage – but a new name had been found for it: Islam. True, one had to renounce the ancient idols of stone and of wood and in their stead recognize the great, invisible Allah.

That was not difficult, for Allah was the old god of past generations, the primitive god of the desert, the god of the ancestral Abraham. Mohammed was tireless in stressing this feature of Allah. He merely demanded the abolition of a later custom, a later degeneration, the removal of the idols in whom the fathers of the Arabs had never really believed. It sounded plausible. It was flattering to the Arabs to see the half-forgotten god of their fathers looked upon as the most important and highest god of all the peoples of all the lands.

In return for their renunciation of the old gods, Mohammed gave the people a social law, an organization which in its thoroughness equalled that to which the Arabian tribes had been accustomed. In addition to this law, Mohammed gave his followers the assurance of the immortality of the soul and of retribution in another world. Both of these teachings had been wholly unknown to the Arabs. Mohammed knew how to hammer them into the minds of the faithful with his astonishing power of suggestion, with the tremendous force of the magic of his words. As a matter of fact, there was no longer any reason for the Bedouin to repulse Islam. And thus it was that Arabian tradition conquered Islam and Islam conquered the Arabian people.

This had been overlooked by the proud Quraishites, and the sly Suhail ibn Amr had no inkling of it. Nor had the Moslems expected this result. Only one man knew the portent of the treaty: Mohammed, who was not only the messenger of God but also the wisest man in the desert.

The consequences of Mohammed's hazardous conduct were soon apparent. His clever propaganda bore the fruit it deserved. The tribes made use of their contractual right, and declared themselves openly for or against Mohammed. One after another they now appeared in long caravans at Medina, made their confession of faith, received the blessing of the Prophet, and swore to uphold the laws of their fathers, to make pilgrimages to Mecca, and to pray to the great Allah, the god of the ancient Arabs.

In the two years which followed the treaty of Hudaibiyah, more men were converted to Islam than since the early days of the Prophet's mission. The old gods were destroyed. Islam grew like an avalanche and soon assumed vast proportions. The tribes vied with one another to be converted, for they too sensed the beginning of a new era. It was no longer necessary for Mohammed to persuade his warriors. They knew that where Mohammed fought there was holy loot and God's benediction. The campaigns grew larger and larger, the booty grew richer, and more ardent became the enthusiasm of the Bedouin who went to war.

Unexpected success did not confuse the Prophet. He remained patient and careful, for he no longer wished to take any risks. He had to advance surely and could only achieve his goal by means of careful preparation.

With painstaking carefulness and loyalty, just like a serious merchant, Mohammed fulfilled the shameful treaty he had concluded with Mecca. Here, too, he showed that he was far superior to all the other inhabitants of the desert, not only in piety but in the great art of politics as well, for he carried out the terms of the treaty of Hudaibiyah so accurately and so honestly that it was finally the Meccans themselves who begged him not to take it too literally.

This happened in the following manner. Abu Basir of the tribe of the Thaqif, who lived in Mecca, one day discovered the desire for adventure and the love of God within himself, and fled to Medina. The Meccans learned of this and sent two warriors to Medina with the request that Abu Basir be returned to them in accordance with the terms of the treaty. Without hesitation, Mohammed granted their request and surrendered the fugitive. On the way, however, the captive managed to slay one of his guards and to escape into the desert. By means of begging and robbing, he lived in the desert, where he was joined by others who, like him, had fled from Mecca and had been surrendered by the Prophet.

The slaves and the poor of the city of Mecca now fled in greater numbers to Medina, where there was no poverty or slavery for the faithful. Under the leadership of Abu Basir they made up a dangerous company of about seventy men. This band now sought out the great caravan route between Mecca and Syria as its arena, and, since its members were poor and had nothing to lose, they fell upon the great caravans in the name of Allah, robbed the property of the Meccans and spread fear and terror about them. The Meccans saw that they were being robbed of the fruits of their treaty. Once again the trade of Mecca was endangered. Abu Basir was both brave and sly; he knew how to hide in the rugged mountains and defied his pursuers. Mohammed merely shrugged his shoulders, shook his head and declared that he could do nothing against the free Moslems, who, according to the treaty, were not permitted to belong to his community. Finally, in order to restore peace in the desert, the Meccans were forced to ask Mohammed to revise the treaty of Hudaibiyah and to take the refugees officially into his community. To this Mohammed agreed, and from that day on the attacks and pillage ceased.

This caused the prestige of the Prophet to grow. For Mohammed himself there was no longer any doubt that he would soon be the sole ruler over Arabia. This would have been a source of great satisfaction to the once poverty-stricken Meccan merchant, but for the Prophet Mohammed, for the last messenger of God on earth, it was only the beginning, the prelude to a much greater career.

Since the day of his mission, since his first sermon, Mohammed had thought of Islam as having an universal appeal. God had sent His Prophet to all the peoples of the world as the last one to reveal the truth. If God had given the rulership over Arabia to His Prophet, who had come from nothing and who was nothing, then he could also give him all the countries and peoples of the Orient, and of the whole world as well. The youthful power, the youthful enthusiasm had remained unweakened in the Prophet. He accepted the sovereignty over Arabia as a matter of course, and he thought it equally natural that he should rule the world. No sooner was he certain of his domination over Arabia than new, more daring plans occurred to him. His eyes were directed towards the frontiers of Arabia. The great world of Iran and Byzantium lay around Mohammed. After decades of fighting these two opponents had finally made their peace. God was to give both to the Prophet. As usual, Mohammed felt his way cautiously. One day the Prophet sent six messengers out of Medina to the six rulers of the world about Arabia: to the Emperor of Byzantium, to the Emperor of Iran, to the King of Abyssinia, to the Governor of Egypt, to the King of Hirah and to the Duke of Yamamah in Central Arabia. In the letters which were sent to them, the potentates were invited to submit to Islam and to its Prophet. The fate of the messengers has already been described. The rulers of the world paid no attention to them, for they knew too little about the strange changes which had taken place during the past years in Arabia. The Prophet had hardly expected it to be otherwise.

The disbelieving world was to pay dearly for its disdain. For the world and all its people were a present from God to the true faith and to him who revealed it. The messengers who had been sent to the rulers of the world left Medina on 11 May 628.

On that day, the universal power of Islam was founded. On that day, the Prophet began to conquer the world outside Arabia.

THE STATE EXPANDS

What can we call our own other than energy, power and will?

Goethe

Mohammed did not wish to rule Arabia as other tribal chiefs had done before him. Booty was not his goal but merely a means. Now he had come to the end of those means. A state awaited his commands; the great world outside Arabia awaited its new master. This domination had to be organized. Once again Mohammed thought of the people of the Scriptures who were to enter into his domain. Up to that time, Mohammed had only encountered the Jews of Medina. The solution which he had found then had been a brutal one. It had been dictated by the exigencies of the moment and had not been a definite solution. For this reason, Mohammed decided to create rules which were to regulate the life of the Jews and Christians under him.

The Christians of Arabia were not numerous. Nevertheless, an imposing convent, that of St. Catherine, stood on Mt. Sinai. Some Christian Bedouins wandered over the steppes who were at times friendly, and at times hostile to the Prophet. The Prophet issued a decree which was to govern the relationship between the Christian nomads and monks, and the Moslems. The basic ideas of this new law were as follows: No Christian was to be hindered in the profession of his religion. The churches and convents of the Christians were to be held sacred by the Moslems. The marriage of a Christian woman with a Moslem did not prevent the woman from retaining her religion. In case of war between Moslems and inimical Christians, there was no reason to maltreat the vanquished Christians. On the contrary, whoever ill-treated a Christian because of his faith rebelled against the word of the Prophet. This decree is probably the first case in history where an egocentric, fanatic religion recognized and respected the rights of another faith.

At the same time, Mohammed accomplished something of greater importance. This simple Arab, who had not hesitated to send hundreds of his enemies to their death, who had waged wars merely for the sake of pillage, was again the first in the world's history to issue decrees concerning humane warfare. How had the wars of antiquity been fought? How were the wars of the Arabs carried on? The foe was attacked, all the men were killed, their property was taken, the women were ravished and the children sold into slavery. The ancient world knew no other kind of warfare.

Even the Bible only knew war as a complete destruction of the enemy. Samuel, the Prophet, revealed to the Jews: "Now go and smite Amalek, and utterly destroy all that they have, and spare them not; but slay both man and woman, infant and suckling, ox and sheep, camel and ass." (1 Samuel 15,3) And Ezekiel says: "Slay utterly old and young, both maids and little children, and women." (Ezekiel 9,6) This manner of warfare was in keeping with the morality of antiquity, where pity was unknown and mercy was shown to none.

The wars of the Persians and the Byzantines which took place in Mohammed's time were of a similar character. Where a hostile army marched, a desert remained. Mohammed, too, knew what wars of annihilation were, he too knew that they meant killing the men and selling the women and children into slavery. His sudden change of attitude is therefore the more astounding, particularly at a time when he was planning great campaigns and conquests. He discarded all the moral ideas of antiquity and preached humane warfare. Mohammed's aim was not conquest, but the organization of the world.

For the first time in the history of bloody Oriental warfare, a ruler appeared who recognized the value of human life and who publicly declared: "Do not use trickery or treachery in the field. Do not kill children." Mohammed commanded his generals: "When in combat with the army of the enemy, do not oppress the peaceful inhabitants of the enemy's country. Spare the feeble among the women and be compassionate to the sucklings and the sick. Do not destroy the houses of the inhabitants and do not damage their gardens, fields and palm trees." It is more important that Mohammed, not content with giving out this decree, actually saw to it that it was carried out. Humane warfare became an integral part of the Moslem way of thinking.

When Abu Bakr sent the army of the pious against Byzantium, he said to its commander, Yazid, the son of Abu Sufyan, the future Caliph: "Do not oppress the people and do not excite them unnecessarily. Do only that which is good and right and success will reward you. When you meet an enemy, then fight him courageously, but if you win the battle do not kill women or children. Spare the fields and the houses, for men have erected them. If you conclude a treaty, then keep it. In the land of the Christians you will meet pious men on your way, who serve God in the churches and convents. Do not harm them and do not destroy the churches and convents."

Neither before nor after Mohammed have there been many generals in history who were given similar commands by their rulers. On the other hand, the great campaigns against alien lands were still merely vague plans.

The Christians in Arabia were not numerous. However, many Jews lived in the Arabian oases. Mohammed decided to give these Jews, who had but little reason to be friendly towards him, an example of his knowledge of governing. North of Medina, in a region rich with date trees, lies Khaibar. Mohammed had an old score to settle with Khaibar, for the great coalition against him had been organized there. All the Jews and Arabs who had wished to escape the Prophet's persecution had gone to Khaibar. It was a mighty colony and its inhabitants were proud. The city was also afforded protection by the surrounding mountains.

Mohammed was determined to conquer Khaibar. Immediately after the peace-treaty of Hudaibiyah, Mohammed prepared for the campaign. He had in the meantime become an experienced warrior and was a master of the art of warfare. Before he started out, he announced an unusual decree: only those soldiers who had accompanied Mohammed on his pilgrimage to Hudaibiyah were to share in the great loot which was expected. The remaining ones were to content themselves with what they could secure immediately after the battle. This was contrary to the usual custom, but Mohammed was sufficiently strong to force his will upon the fiercest of the Bedouin.

The campaign was difficult. The Jews, bearing in mind the fate of their brothers of Medina, defended themselves heroically. Their former allies, the wild desert tribes, now deserted them and fought on the side of Mohammed, for he was once again one of their own. After an arduous siege, Khaibar fell, and again Mohammed could give his verdict. This time it was no less severe than the former one had been. These Jews were not traitors as the Quraizah had been, and for this reason their lives were spared by the Prophet. But their property and their fields fell to the army. Mohammed divided the loot among the pilgrims of Hudaibiyah. Up to this point there had been nothing unusual in the procedure. It had been a campaign like the others. But this time, only the most pious of the followers had been rewarded with the booty.

It was said, however, that after the fields, meadows and palm trees had been distributed, Mohammed called the new, pious owners to him and had a long, wise conversation with them. The results of this conference were epoch-making. The Jews, who were about to seek out a new home for themselves, were recalled by the new owners. The land on which they were born was given back to them, and they were bound to give to the new owners one half of their income. The Prophet confirmed the agreement and appointed a wise man named Abdallah ibn Rawahah to be appraiser of the crops and to act as overseer of the Jews. And so the rehabilitated Jews were given a sort of governor and judge in their province.

The results of this act were of vast importance. At Khaibar Mohammed put an end to the great pillaging campaigns and fashioned the foundations for a new social relationship. Mohammed had divided the people into two great categories: the Moslem ruling class who waged wars and were permitted to spread the faith, and the sedentaries who did not have to go to war, who were allowed to remain peacefully in their fields and enjoy the protection of the Moslems, and in return had to pay rent and taxes to their new rulers. The impression that thus a new nobility and vassalage was created is incorrect. The disbelievers could at any time join the ranks of the ruling classes by being converted to Islam. It was a law which saved the vanquished from death, destruction and pillage. Up to the present day, this law has remained the corner-stone of all the laws to which the disbelievers were subjected.

As in the case of most conquests, there were many attempts after the victory of Khaibar, on the part of the vanquished, to do away with the new ruler. A Jewess by the name of Zainab appeared in the tent of Mohammed shortly after the victory and was engaged as a cook. Zainab roasted a lamb and poisoned it. Then she set it before the Prophet and his friends. Slowly Mohammed tasted a morsel and quickly spat it out, for he could taste the poison. His friend, Bishr ibn al-Bara, who was very hungry, had eaten before him and died a painful death. The Jewess was thrown into chains and led before the Prophet. "O messenger of God," she said, "I merely wished to convince myself that you were really a prophet. If you were not a prophet you would have eaten of the poisoned meat and would now be dead. But now I know that you are a prophet of God and I believe in you." Although this all-too-obvious defence was ridiculous, and although the Prophet had punished lesser crimes more stringently at an earlier time, he pardoned the Jewess Zainab. For the time of wars and the shedding of blood was over for him. Peace was going to reign in Arabia and the Prophet wished to rule his land with gentleness.

At the same time, the Prophet knew how to forgive an even greater sin. Shortly after the peace of Hudaibiyah, the daughter of the Prophet travelled through the desert on her way from Mecca to Medina. Habbar, a Quraishite and a heathen, attacked her in senseless fury and killed her with his lance. The blood of the Prophet was spilled on the sands of the desert and called out for vengeance. All the desert laws entitled the Prophet to avenge Habbar's act. Some time later the murderer fell into the hands of Mohammed. Habbar threw himself at Mohammed's feet and declared himself ready to embrace Islam, and begged that his life be spared. The Prophet remained silent for a long time, staring at the murderer of his daughter, then he said, "I forgive you. Arise and never again appear before my eyes." Later, Abu Bakr asked his friend: "Why were you silent so long, O Prophet, when the criminal lay at your feet?" The Prophet lifted up his eyes and said reproachfully to Abu Bakr and to the others around him, "I expected that one of you would throw himself upon him and slay him." "Why did you not give us a sign?" asked the pious. "A prophet does not rule by signs," replied Mohammed.

The blood of the Arab had spoken in him and demanded vengeance. But when no one in his surroundings drew his sword, the statesman Mohammed pardoned a wrong-doing which had not been directed against the State. The man Mohammed had learned to control his feelings. Mercy and not blood was to rule the world of Islam.

THE MARCH ON MECCA

Each one must empty himself like a cup.

Morgenstern

Mecca was the sole obstacle which prevented Mohammed from ruling over all Arabia. Unconquered and untamed, the city of Mecca reigned over the desert, and the desert lent it its ear. The numerous stone idols still stood in the courtyard of the Caaba. Mohammed now had to conquer the proud, rich and noble city, for the deserts obey the ruler of Mecca. The preparations for the decisive blow lasted a long time. Mecca was to fall into the hands of the Prophet like a ripe fruit.

The first step towards conquest was the contractual pilgrimage to the Caaba. One year after peace had been made at Hudaibiyah, Mohammed assembled the faithful and set out with a large, armed army for Mecca. When this news had been spread, Mecca was filled with fear and confusion as it had been in the previous year. No one knew what Mohammed's objective was: peace or prayer. At the frontier of Mecca, Mohammed gave orders that the weapons were to be laid down, and garbed as a pilgrim and with his head shaven, he travelled towards Mecca. With firm step he walked through the desert, accompanied by all the *muhajirun*, by all those who once had fled the bright city because of their faith.

In Medina and throughout the period of their exile, they had never ceased to think of their native city. On the dark path which led from contempt to success, from poverty to riches, from nothingness to power, they were often seized with a longing for the great city of the Caaba, for the worthy Quraish assemblies, for the pilgrimages and annual fairs, for the brilliance and wealth of the wonderful city of Mecca.

The Prophet, too, had longed for Mecca. At one time, when he was a poor merchant riding through the desert, the invisible hand of Mecca had protected him from afar. The Prophet had preached Islam for the first time in the streets and squares of Mecca. He had experienced all that a man can in the queen of cities: happiness and unhappiness, poverty and wealth, conflicts, persecution, defeats and victories. Then he was forced to take flight. Throughout the long years of his exile the Prophet had been homesick for his native city. The Prophet was an Arab, and the love for one's native city, for one's native tribe, is rooted in the heart of the Arab. The messenger of God had not been able to tear out this love from his heart. His native city of Mecca had prosecuted, persecuted, battled with and exiled him, and still he loved her.

Now, after many years, the city lay before him once again. He saw the large, square building of the Caaba, saw the hills of the Ummayah and the Makhzum, the house of Khadijah and the fortress of the Hashim. His heart began to beat more quickly, his eyes became hard and direct as he trod through the desert. Mohammed did not return to his native city as a penitent son. The hatred of Mecca had not broken him. Nor did he come home as a victor. The gates of the city were open to him for three days only.

He knew, as no one else did, how to utilize those three days. With great pains he carried out all the ceremonies of the pilgrimage, he circled the Caaba seven times, kissed the holy black stone and visited the well of Zamzam, the inheritance of the Hashim. For the whole desert was to know that Mohammed, the Hashemite, was a true son of the holy city of Mecca.

But this was not the only purpose which connected Mohammed with this trip to Mecca. He had a second, a very sober political task to accomplish. After the pious ceremonies, Mohammed discarded the pilgrim's garb and was married to the Quraishite, Maimunah bint Al-Harith. The bride was fifty-one years of age and doubtless the least attractive among the wives of the Prophet. She had brought her husband neither beauty, nor youth, nor wealth. But the marriage with her brought the power over Mecca nearer to hand.

There were two people in the Quraishite city who were capable of effectively opposing the Prophet. Both were clever military leaders, a fact which Mohammed had learned by experience. They were Khalid ibn-Walid and Amr ibn al-As. The Prophet wished to win over both of them. Maimunah led the way. She was the favourite aunt of Khalid and he, in turn, was the best friend of the able Amr. Both of them were sufficiently wise to have recognized a fact which the old, stubborn Quraishites refused to acknowledge, namely, that the future of the country belonged to Islam. Nor were they unwilling to fight on the side of the stronger. But since Khalid as well as Amr had been opponents of the Prophet for many years, Mohammed had to marry old Maimunah in order to bring about a change of opinion on the part of the two prominent warriors. All the Quraish knew that one could not fight against one's relatives.

Together with Mohammed, Khalid and Amr left the city of Mecca. The fate of Mecca was sealed. The conversion of Khalid meant as much to Mohammed as if he had gained a hundred thousand soldiers. In the same year, Khalid crossed the frontier of Arabia. Under the leadership of Zaid, he set out against a small province of Byzantium called Mu'tah. Zaid fell in battle. Khalid took over the command, and with one wild attack of his cavalry he destroyed the far superior army of his opponent. This was the first conflict between the army of the messenger of God and the fighting forces of the Emperor of Byzantium.

Gradually, softly at first but constantly growing louder, the news was spread in the desert that Mohammed was planning the conquest of Mecca. A pretext for breaking a treaty can readily be found. Somewhere in the desert a few careless Meccans attacked some of the allies of the Prophet. After a few arrows had been exchanged, some of the Moslems remained wounded on the field. The whole affair was insignificant, but it could be regarded as the breaking of the treaty. As a reply, Mohammed announced a campaign against Mecca.

The impending danger was no secret for Mecca. They suspected that Mohammed was planning a campaign and did not know how to go about defending themselves.

Mohammed's importance had changed. He was no longer, as he had been in earlier times, a threat to the faith, wealth and renown of Mecca. He was a faithful follower of the Caaba and the Bedouins believed in him. It did not take much calculation to guess that the three hundred and sixty idols could be replaced by the old god, Allah. On the other hand, for the Meccans themselves, for the noble tribe of the Quraish, an acute danger threatened.

It was to be expected that if Mohammed actually occupied the city he would show but little respect to the Quraishite leaders. The races which had persecuted and hunted him could count on his revenge. This made the chiefs of the Quraish uneasy. They had no exact news of the plans of the Prophet. They thought that the danger could be avoided by means of adroit negotiations, and they decided to send Abu Sufyan to Medina for this purpose. It was certainly not easy for the wealthiest and noblest of the Meccans to go in the role of a suppliant to the city whose ruler had once been a poverty-stricken and despised Hashemite. An Ummayah had never yet appeared before a Hashemite to ask favours, and certainly never before from the poor, exiled *parvenu* Mohammed. Now Abu Sufyan had to take this task upon himself. However, the rich banker thought that his peaceful appearance in Medina would suffice to reawaken the former respect for the house of the Ummayah in the breasts of Mohammed and all the fugitives. A handshake, a courteous smile, a few pleasant words would surely be sufficient. Abu Sufyan felt like a noble lord who, in temporary embarrassment, has to turn to a simple peasant for aid.

But like Mohammed, Abu Sufyan was not to be spared any humiliation. God wished to reward His Prophet. Having arrived in Medina, Abu Sufyan was kept waiting uneasily for hours before he was led into the presence of Mohammed. The Prophet sat in the courtyard of the mosque. He hardly returned the greeting of the fashionable Ummayah. But perhaps that was due to the etiquette of Medina. Abu Sufyan began to make a long speech, suggested that the friendship between Medina and Mecca be strengthened, excused himself in the name of the city for the painful hostile occurrence and declared himself ready to revise the treaty of Hudaibiyah, or, what was more, to accede to some of the Prophet's demands. That was a great deal. It was more than was to be expected from an Ummayah who, as a mighty leader, had for years opposed the Prophet. According to all human speculation, Mohammed would have to give in. The ice had to melt.

The Prophet looked at Abu Sufyan for a time, arose and, without saying a word, left the mosque. It was nothing short of a public slap in the face. Abu Sufyan slowly began to realize that the name of the Ummayah was not a welcome one in Medina. He would have much preferred to mount his camel immediately, declare eternal warfare and ride back to Mecca. But the times in which it would have been permissible to act in such a manner towards the Prophet were definitely over. Heavy at heart, Abu Sufyan decided to continue his labours. He had enough friends and blood-relatives in Medina. They were surely calmer than the obstinate prophet. They would in all probability be more receptive to sensible words.

Like a small, come-down bankrupt, Abu Sufyan now ran from one person to another, knocked on every door and recalled old friendships and relationships, but on all sides he met with a cool reception. His own daughter, who now belonged to the harem of the Prophet, showed him, "the unclean idolater," the door. Abu Bakr, once his friend and equal, had no word left for him. But Umar told him abruptly and frankly: "By God, if I had nothing but a few ants to command, I would never cease fighting you." Even Ali, who could never deny anyone anything, rejected him, saying: "Mohammed has come to a decision and we can do nothing about it." There was no room for doubt in Abu Sufyan's mind as to what that decision might be. He saddled his camel and rode to Mecca. When, exhausted from his trip, he had returned home and had told his wife, Hind, the results of his mission, she listened to him quietly. But when he wished to lie down beside her, she pushed him out of bed with her feet, crying: "I will not share my bed with a coward."

After Abu Sufyan's return, fear and confusion reigned in Mecca. They were all as if paralysed and none knew the way out.

Quietly Mohammed assembled in Medina all the tribes who were allied to him; he equipped his army carefully but did not announce where the expedition was to be led. The goal had to be kept secret, for despite all the loyalty of the desert tribes he was not quite sure if they would participate in a campaign against the Caaba. Nor did he wish the Quraish to learn prematurely that the campaign was directed against them.

The times in which Mohammed went to war with three hundred soldiers were gone. An army of ten thousand men followed the Prophet. It was led by the best leaders of Arabia, Umar, Khalid and Amr. The preparations were discussed in the council of war. The army was no longer a horde of wild soldiers. It consisted of well-armed regiments equipped with coats of mail, which obeyed every word, every command of the Prophet, in so far as they were not wild nomads. The fate of Mecca seemed determined. The poor exile, Mohammed, was about to return as victor to his native city.

Fear and confusion reigned in Mecca. The merchants were split up into numerous parties. They tried to convince themselves that Mohammed was not as yet ready, that he had no intention of marching against Mecca, and that, above all else, he would not dare touch the holy Caaba. They were still discussing and pondering in this fashion when Mohammed had already taken up his position behind the hills near Mecca.

THE RIPE FRUIT

> Mecca, the most brilliant among the cities, the
> favourite treasure of Allah.
>
> *Mohammed*

Ten thousand marched through the desert, and their leader was the messenger of God. They marched aside from the great caravan route, over narrow mountain paths, through steep ravines and over high peaks. No one in the desert was to carry the news to the people of the Quraish that the army had broken camp. Along the caravan route, small detachments of troops trapped the messengers who might hurry off to Mecca, chased them in all directions and confused the senses of the people of the desert. No one knew what Mohammed had planned and against whom his campaign was directed. The army travelled through uninhabited, empty places, and yet the Prophet would not allow them to light a fire, to beat a drum or to sing pious songs. Noiselessly, silently, like a train of shadows, the ten thousand moved through the desert.

Halfway, Mohammed spied a rider behind a hilltop. The rider approached the army. Filled with amazement, Mohammed recognized his uncle, Al-Abbas. Al-Abbas was both cunning and wise. Nothing remained hidden to him. Of all the Quraish he alone was aware of the march of the ten thousand and realized its consequences. Secretly he left the threatened city and determined that the time had come to make use of his relationship with the messenger of God. He rode out to meet Mohammed, got off his camel, knelt down and became converted to Islam. Al-Abbas had delayed long enough until God had finally made him see clearly as to his nephew's mission. For this reason Mohammed despised him thoroughly. "You are the last of the emigrants," he said ironically. Nevertheless, Uncle Abbas had come in time, so that he was able to brag for the rest of his life that he had been among the *muhajirun* and had participated in the campaign against Mecca.

Mohammed did not possess the gift of prophecy, so that he could not foresee that the family of the man he despised most among all the faithful would sit for centuries to come on the throne of the Caliphs, and would produce the greatest Caliph in all Islam, the wise and fabulous Harun Al-Rashid.

Two dynasties were to rule over the world of Islam: the dynasty of the Ummayah, the heirs of Abu Sufyan, and the dynasty of the Abbasides, the heirs of Uncle Abbas.

But Mohammed knew nothing of all this as he marched to do battle with Abu

Sufyan and despised the cunning Abbas. Unmoved, he marched forward until he could finally see the square sanctuary of the Caaba in the distance. For the first time, the army of the Prophet came to a halt, and bivouac fires were lighted, for now everyone in Mecca was to know that the army of the Prophet lay at the door.

The army besieged the city and the city could do nothing against the army. The siege had come as a complete surprise. Abu Sufyan had to mount a donkey in order to ride to the camp of the Prophet. He had no vain illusions, and the pride of the noble Ummayah had disappeared from his face. Now he experienced a simple and by no means aristocratic fear for his life, for the wealth of the house of the Ummayah, and for the flourishing business of the city. Humbly Abu Sufyan rode to the camp of the Prophet. The first to recognize him was Umar. Abu Sufyan had little to expect from him. As a matter of fact, Umar took hold of him by the collar, dragged him into the presence of Mohammed and cried: "O messenger of God, here is Abu Sufyan who, not protected by any treaty, has fallen into our hands through the help of Allah. Permit me to slit his throat." Umar was very much astonished that Mohammed did not seem to be in a hurry to accomplish this. On the contrary, he gave orders that Abu Sufyan was to be kept safely and brought before him again on the next day.

The next day, however, was to be the worst in the long life of Abu Sufyan. When he had again appeared before the Prophet, he was received with the words: "Woe to you, Abu Sufyan, do you not realize that there is no god but Allah?" The proud member of the Ummayah fell at the feet of Mohammed and said: "O Mohammed, you are dearer to me than father and mother. How mild, how gentle, how noble you are! I really believe that Allah is the only god, for otherwise the others might have been of some help." "Woe to you, Abu Sufyan," Mohammed replied, "do you not acknowledge that I am the messenger of God?" This was decidedly too much for old Abu Sufyan. Now he was called upon to acknowledge Mohammed publicly. Again the Ummayah fell on his knees and spoke: "Oh Mohammed, you are dearer to me than all which I possess. I love you more than father and mother, but as far as your being a prophet is concerned, my spirit is not convinced of that." In other times, Mohammed would have stooped down to Abu Sufyan, would have raised him up and begun to argue quietly with him. Now he was silent. But Umar, who stood next to the Prophet, cried out: "There is no better argument than the sword to convince stubborn unbelievers. Thereupon he drew his sword from its sheath, turned to Abu Sufyan and said: "Accept the truth or I will sever your head from your body." Then Abu Sufyan knelt down, became converted to Islam, and recited the act of faith: *"Ashhadu an la illah ila Allah. Ashhadu anna Muhammadan Rasul Allah"*, (I believe that there is no God but Allah. I believe that Mohammed is His messenger). And so Abu Sufyan was converted to Islam without realizing that his son was to be the fifth

Caliph in Islam. Mohammed had received complete satisfaction; he could not have wished for a better reward.

Before Abu Sufyan returned to Mecca, Mohammed decided to demonstrate to him the power of Allah. In a valley between two hills, a review of the troops was held. The simple Bedouins, the auxiliaries, marched at the head. They were followed by the regular regiments, disciplined and in coats of mail, and finally, amid the chosen, by Mohammed, the messenger of God, clad in full armour.

Two of the newly-made converts, Al-Abbas and Abu Sufyan, watched the parade from the top of a small hill. When the Prophet, surrounded by his bodyguard, passed by, Abu Sufyan sighed and said to Al-Abbas, "Truly, the empire of my nephew has assumed noble proportions. He is irresistible."

But Al-Abbas lifted his eyes piously to heaven and said reverently, "It is his power because he is a prophet."

On the same day, Abu Sufyan hurried back to Mecca, assembled the Quraish and told them what he had seen and experienced. The fashionable bankers were depressed. Only Hind, who had been present at the assembly, arose and with her face distorted with anger snatched her husband's beard and cried: "Kill this dirty, useless worm who brings shame upon us!" But this time the energy of the Meccan Xanthippe was of no avail. Only a few of the Quraish, namely those of the house of Makhzum, to which Abu Jahl belonged, were inclined to fight. Among them was Suhail ibn Amr, the unfortunate diplomat of Hudaibiyah. The rest joyfully accepted the terms of peace which Abu Sufyan had brought them from Mohammed. The terms were: "Mohammed will occupy the city of Mecca for all time. But the Quraish who remain peacefully in their houses when the Prophet makes his entrance may be sure of their lives."

On the next day, the triumphal march into Mecca began. Only a small company of heathen, led by the son of Abu Jahl, offered any resistance, and they were conquered with ease. The way to Mecca, the way to the most brilliant of the cities, to the favourite treasure of Allah was open. The Medinese had begun to celebrate their victory, and the *ansari* Sa'd ibn Ubadah shouted out: "Today is the day of the battle, today the sanctuary will be defiled."

No one doubted but that the day of the great revenge had come, that the richest among the cities of Arabia was to be pillaged, that the enemies of the Prophet were to be destroyed, and that, with this, the great act of uniting all Arabia would be complete. But Mohammed and the oldest among the *muhajirun* thought differently. They themselves had come from Mecca. Their love belonged to the city. Every stone, every street, every corner in Mecca was familiar to them and dear because of their many memories. Suddenly they all felt that they were Quraishites again, and the pride of the ancient race awakened in them. Never had the noble city of Mecca been pillaged by strangers, and not even now was a strange army to leave the city laden with plunder. In the long years of their exile, the *muhajirun* had retained something which no emigrants before or after them had retained, their love for their native city.

With wise forethought, Mohammed had only permitted the *muhajirun*, Meccans by birth, to lead the army on that day. On the day following that in which the enemy had been conquered, the messenger of God put on the robes of a pilgrim, mounted a snow-white camel and, accompanied by Abu Bakr, rode towards Mecca. When he had reached the outskirts of the city, the first rays of the sun began to appear. They surrounded Mohammed's head like a halo. The streets of Mecca lay dead and empty of men. The inhabitants had hidden in their houses in fear. No one knew the plans of the Prophet. No one knew if he would spare the fortresses.

Mohammed rode through the streets of Mecca. To his right rose the house of Khadijah, in which he had spent the happiest years of his life. Unseeing he rode past it. He rode straight ahead to the great courtyard of the Caaba. And there Mohammed performed the deed for which he had once left home, family and the holy courtyard of the Caaba itself. Seven times he circled the Caaba, seven times he reverently touched the holy stone with his staff. And then there happened to Mohammed, the messenger of God, the greatest event of his entire life. He got down from his camel, and with his head held high he began to break the idols of stone and wood with his staff. The Moslems followed his example. Soon the mighty Hubal, the three moon virgins and all the three hundred and sixty idols lay in the dust. The deed which Mohammed had announced years before had been accomplished.

As is usual, the newly-made converts were the most active against the old gods. Khalid ibn Al-Walid and Amr ibn al-As raced with their riders through the entire sanctuary. They forced their way into the temples and the sacred fields of the Arabs, smashed the statues of the gods, and killed the few priests who still resisted. Soon nowhere in Mecca nor in any other portion of the sacred territory was a single idol to be found. Even the statues of Abraham and Ishmael were destroyed, and the picture of the Virgin Mary as well, out of "respect for their sanctity," as Mohammed said. An artfully carved wooden dove was broken with Mohammed's own hands.

The signal to begin the pillage did not follow the destruction of the gods as had been expected. Their property was not taken from the Quraish, a fact which displeased even some of the *muhajirun*. When they had been driven out of Mecca, their property had been seized by the Meccans. Now, after the final siege, they felt that they were at least entitled to the return of their confiscated property. But Mohammed forbade that as well. He himself did not demand the return of any of his former property. He did not enter into the house of Khadijah. During his entire stay in Mecca he lived in a tent.

In his heart Mohammed felt that he had acted unjustly. His love for the city of

Mecca threatened to surmount his duties as a conqueror. Had he not once said, "To be a Moslem is to place the community of the faithful above the tribes, and is to obey the community and not the laws of the tribes; for all Moslems are equal and between them there are no races, no tribes and no hatred"? Now, it seemed impossible for him to go against his own tribe, the noble Quraish. He assembled the Moslems and delivered to them a well-thought-out speech: "O you men," he said, "God sanctified Mecca on the day he created heaven and earth. This city will remain sanctified until the day of the resurrection. It is not allowed to any one of the faithful to shed blood in the city or to cut down a tree. It was not permitted to any one before me and it will not be permitted to any one after me. It was only permitted to me, as the executor of God's wrath, to go against the inhabitants of the city. But now this city has again been sanctified. Let those present tell this to those who are not present. Should anyone say to you that Mohammed has ever waged war in Mecca, then reply: 'God permitted it to His messenger but not to you.'"

And as was always the custom with Mohammed, this decision, which had been born of the moment, was decisive for the whole history of Islam. Mecca was given a special position. It was withdrawn from general politics: it was sanctified. The four months of the Quraish were extended by Mohammed to the whole year – for eternity. The sanctity and the peace of the city have been preserved until modern times by Islam. With the law which forbade the shedding of blood or the waging of war in Mecca, the political importance of the city was removed from it. For blood and politics are inseparable in the Orient. Mecca, the city of the direction of prayer, was in the future to be the spiritual and not the political centre of Islam.

The speech of the Prophet and the unexpected mildness with which he appeared in the city made the *ansar*, the native Medinese, uneasy. Once, when the Prophet had been persecuted by all, he had placed himself under their protection and had solemnly separated himself from the Quraish. Medina had taken pity on him, had fought his battles and suffered his sufferings. How were they now to be rewarded? The *ansar* came to the Prophet and recalled to him the words which he had spoken when there had been no one in the desert who wished to have anything to do with him.

Now the Prophet looked gently at the city of his birth and said, "O Mecca, you are the most beautiful of cities and the beloved of Allah. If I had not been driven out by my own tribe, I would never have left you." And the *ansar* replied, "See, Mohammed has captured his native city. Now he will leave Medina." Then Mohammed recalled what the people of Medina had done for him. He also remembered the promise he had made. He placed the duties of the statesman above those of his love for his native city. He called all the *ansar* to him and said, "When you pledged me your fidelity, I too swore to live and die with you. I would not be the messenger of God if I were to leave you now." As a matter of fact, Mohammed remained in his native city for only two weeks before he returned to Medina. Medina remained the capital of the Prophet and of the first four of his followers, who, like himself, had all come from Mecca. They were Abu Bakr, Umar, Uthman and Ali. Soon, behind closed windows and doors, the news was slowly spread in Mecca that the Prophet had not returned to his native city as a blood-thirsty avenger. Gradually the doors were opened, people appeared on the streets, went to the Caaba and were astonished at the great piles of the broken idols. Then they saw the negro, Bilal, the former slave of a cousin of Abu Sufyan, on the roof of the Caaba, and heard him cry out: "Arise for prayer. Prayer is better than sleep." They looked at him and shook their heads. A negro, a slave, was given high honours in Islam and was the first *mu'azzin*. The Prophet did not differentiate between races and people.

The Prophet condemned but a very few of his old Meccan friends to death. And most of those condemned were pardoned by him before the time set for the execution. Only two sentences of death were carried out. One was on a Moslem who had fallen from the true faith and had falsified the Koran, and the other on a woman who had injured the Prophet with her bitter poems. For poems hurt him more than swords.

Now that the victory was complete and the Meccans again dared appear on the streets, the Prophet decided to take a bloodless revenge and invited his former fellow-citizens to a painful performance. Exactly as he had done many, many years before, in the first year of his mission, the Prophet sent criers to the streets and squares of the city – at least so the legend tells us – who called out, "Mohammed ibn Abdallah, of the tribe of the Hashim, requests the people to assemble on Mt. Safa, for he has an important announcement to make to them." And as they had done a long time before the people came to Mt. Safa. Their expressions were neither curious nor proud. Fear and expectation were written on their faces. Before the assembled multitude, the Prophet announced the fundamental teaching of the new faith: "All men are made of dust and will return to dust. For that reason they are all equal in the sight of God, and there is no difference between races, tribes and people, between master and slave. Blood-relationship must be honoured, but much higher still is the community of the faithful, the community of those who believe in one God, in the great Allah."

In contrast to the first meeting which had been held on Mt. Safa, the words of the Prophet now worked miracles. One after another, the Meccans stepped up to Mohammed and were converted. Many old enemies who had insulted or wronged the Prophet came trembling with fear lest the Prophet might not accept their conversion. "Do not be afraid," he said to them, "I am no king but merely the son of a simple Quraishite who ate dried meat in the sun." "You are the son of a noble tribe," insisted the Quraish humbly. The Prophet looked at them contemptuously and said,

"Go, you are free." Among the newly converted was Hind, the wife of Abu Sufyan, the fury of Uhud. She was almost brought by force to the Prophet by the other women, and then repentantly was converted. She, too, was forgiven. Filled with rage, she smashed the idols in her house which had failed to help her.

And so Mecca, like ripe fruit, fell into the hands of the Prophet. But Mohammed had made the defeat simple for his compatriots. When, at a later time, the Meccans were accused of cowardice at Badr, at the ditch and in Mecca, they were allowed to answer upon the advice of the Prophet: "We were not only fighting the army of the Prophet but the angels also who fought by his side. It was only against the angels and not against the *ansar* that we were helpless."

So Mohammed completed the task which he had begun on the same Mt. Safa eighteen years before. His path led through poverty, banishment and persecution, and now it had ended. All Arabia submitted to the will of the Prophet, and with Arabia Mecca as well, Mecca the favourite city of God.

Now his task was to make secure the state which he had created out of nothing.

THE ORGANIZATION OF THE REPUBLIC OF GOD

> O Prophet of God! Torch which lights the world; Sword of God which destroys the heathen!
>
> *Qasidat Banat Su'ad*

Mohammed sat daily in the courtyard of the mosque, received petitioners, gave commands and ruled over the people of the desert. He was surrounded by a number of literate Moslems who wrote down his orders, passed them on and saw to it that he was not disturbed. But the Prophet did not live as a king in the land of the deserts. Islam had no desire to be a worldly kingdom. The sole, unrestrained ruler of the state was God. The laws appeared in His name and in His name the taxes were imposed and judgements given. The Prophet was merely the humble medium through which the words of God were revealed. He made no claims to royal honours or despotic powers for himself. He too bowed to the will of God.

Life in the State of God was theocratically socialistic. All the faithful were equal in the sight of God, all were subject to the same laws, paid the same taxes and fulfilled the same duties. Excepted from this were the unbelievers, the Jews and the Christians. These paid higher taxes but, on the other hand, they were free of the duties imposed upon the Moslems. They did not have to go to war and they were not obliged to shed their blood in God's cause.

The remaining heathen were energetically persecuted. Finally, the Prophet forbade them admission to the Caaba. The old practice of making a pilgrimage to Mecca soon became the motive for many to embrace Islam. The inhabitants of Ta'if alone attempted to bargain with the Prophet. They begged that they might be permitted to keep their idols for another two years or, if that were not possible, for one year or at least six months. When they saw that Mohammed had no intention of relenting, they declared in desperation that Mohammed should send someone to smash their idols for they themselves could not do so. Mohammed entrusted Abu Sufyan with the task. The former enemy submitted to this indignity as he had to so many others, travelled to Ta'if and there solemnly destroyed the idols.

For the first time in their history, the free Bedouins were forced to pay taxes regularly. For them this was the reverse side of the new faith. The Prophet had to lead many a campaign in order to collect the taxes. Their payment was a religious duty and was looked upon as a command of God. The money raised in taxes was to be used for the army and to support the destitute. There was to be no want in the land of God. At times the taxes were paid out by the collectors to the poor then and there, which won over many a friend to this strange institution.

At first the taxes were only collected under difficulties. So, for example, the proud tribe of the Tamin, who lived in the desert, refused to pay taxes. Taxes meant tribute to them and tribute was the lot of the vanquished. They chased away the collectors, but when they heard that the Prophet was equipping an expedition against them they sent the best poets of their tribe to Medina. These appeared before the Prophet, and, in glowing verses, began to describe the injustice which was being done to their tribe. But Mohammed was equally well prepared for poetic campaigns. The court poets of the Prophet stepped forth and sang in enthusiastic praise of the new State and all its institutions. Thereupon the Taminites, in artistic honesty, recognized the superior talents of the poets of the Prophet, and declared themselves willing to pay the taxes in these circumstances.

The Prophet divided the country into a series of provinces. He appointed a prayer leader who was to lead the pious in prayer, and a tax collector who took the poor tax from the faithful, for each province. The office of the prayer leader developed into that of the *qadi* and *imam*, judge and priest; for the word and the spirit were to work together in Islam.

It was only in those countries which had their own lords, like Southern Arabia, that the masters themselves collected the taxes of the Prophet.

Taxes were only one of the many innovations which were created in the State of God. The government of the State required something else which had hitherto been entirely unknown to the desert: officials and police. The prophet had both, but he looked upon the police as an honorary office. Umar was the first to inaugurate payment for them. The duties of the police, the *ihtisab*, were most peculiar. They were not concerned with fights, thefts and similar transgressions. Those were matters to be looked after by the individual families. They merely had to see to it that the religious laws were obeyed, and, since every law was a religious one in the State of God, the tasks of the police were broad in scope. It was their duty to see that no pork was sold in the markets, that the drunkards were properly punished – a thorough whipping was the punishment – and many other things. During the Prophet's lifetime the devotion of the faithful was so ardent that despite their many tasks the police were never too busy. It was only after the death of the Prophet that they had their hands full.

The most significant office in the land of God during Mohammed's time was that of the prayer leader. Only those who were familiar with the Koran and who had been proved in loyalty and military knowledge were chosen for it. Their task was not only to lead in the ceremony of prayer, but also to watch over the life of the tribes and to represent the Prophet. The prayer leader was the governor of the new State.

In Medina, the capital of the State, Mohammed himself was the prayer leader. Five times a day he said the prayers, and no task was so important that he would have neglected his prayers because of it. Now that he was the ruler of all Arabia, the Prophet still refused all external pomp. As had always been the case with him, he had no house of his own, but he lived in the mosque and slept in each of the huts of his wives in turn. It was only for official acts, that is to say for purposes of ceremony, that he had a large and imposing tent built in which to receive the delegates of foreign powers or distinguished visitors. He used none of the wealth which now poured into his treasury for himself. On the other hand, he ordered that the members of the tribes of the Hashim and the Abdul-Muttalibs, who had stood by him in parlous times, were to have free access to the State treasury—that is, to the treasury of the messenger of God. He was also accustomed to give lavish gifts to his other friends, and the *ansar* and *muhajirun* received country places, money and cattle. Begging from the Prophet had become a constant habit on the part of most of the participants in the battles of Badr and Uhud.

It is true that all the Moslems were equal. But the *ansar* and *muhajirun*, who were now all assembled in Medina, made up the recognized aristocracy of the new State. Their hearts and brains were full of the words and deeds of the Prophet. They knew his every footstep, repeated all his sayings and were adept in exchanging their excellent memories for coin of the realm. They were the parasites in the State of God, and after the Prophet's death they made up a closed, pious caste, the members of which lived in the true sense of the word by their memories, and protected their well-earned material zealously. The treasury of the Caliphs often suffered under their pious demands. As a result, most of these parasites left large fortunes behind them.

The Prophet understood the weaknesses of his followers. He knew well which deprivations each one had undergone for his sake and he knew how to give his gifts in accordance with the services rendered. The time had come when the wives of the Prophet were to be repaid for the sufferings of their youth. However, the Prophet was far from giving them the large amounts which they received from the Caliphs after his death. Mention has been made that a few ells of cloth or some musk was a magnificent present. A deed of gift made out to his relations, dated during the last years of the life of the Prophet, has been preserved and reads as follows: "Deed of gift from Mohammed, the messenger of God: Each of my wives is to receive one hundred and eighty measures of wheat. My daughter, Fatimah, is to receive eighty-five measures, and the son of Zaid, forty measures. Witnesses to the deed are Uthman and Abbas." A gift of wheat apparently seemed so important to the Prophet that he required a deed for it with two witnesses.

Deeds, laws, sayings, military plans, all these were now decided in the courtyard of the mosque by the sixty-one-year-old Prophet. He alone possessed all the important posts in the State. He was the supreme judge, leader of the army, law-giver and Prophet, all at the same time. The outlines of the new Islamic legal code were taken from his sayings, commands and documents in Medina. The code was canonical, but even during Mohammed's lifetime it had begun to be divided into *'adat* and *shari'at,* civil law and canon law.

Mohammed interfered but little in the affairs of individual tribes and families. For these purposes the ancient laws of the desert sufficed, and for this reason he allowed the people to retain their *'adat,* their right by custom. The future conquerors of Islam did the same. They permitted the people to be happy after their own fashion. It was only in matters of faith that the *shari'at,* the law of the Prophet, was invoked. The faith embraced practically every aspect of human life. Not only the relationship between man and God is regulated in Islam by faith, but marriage, inheritance, the treatment of subordinates, punishments, and many things more are covered by *shari'at.* All questions which affect the fate of man on earth and in the next world are governed by *shari'at.*

It became more and more the practice in the State of the Prophet to decide all questions according to the judgment of God and the words of the Koran. The judgment of God and His Prophet was nearly always impressive and comprehensible to the people of the desert. For the entire State was, as we have already said, a new sort of tribal community, an expansion of the Arabic tribal point of view over the entire world. The Prophet was an Arab, and unconsciously the primitive life of the desert was reflected in his speeches, sayings and laws.

If the Prophet had been inspired to found a national state, then he would have achieved his aim with the conquest of Mecca. Just a few more campaigns, a few more victories and defeats, and the national state of the Arabs would have been secure. Former heathen, proud Quraishites, natural children of Abu Sufyan, *ansar, muhajirun,* and even former blood enemies now fought side by side for the Prophet's cause. The founder of a national state could have looked upon his work as finished. But a national state was not Mohammed's idea. Since the very first day of his mission he had announced Islam as a universal sovereignty.

And since the capabilities of the Prophet as statesman, general and propagandist were developed in accordance with the exigencies of the moment, it did not seem at all impossible to the faithful that the former merchant of Mecca should some day hold the reins of universal power securely in his hands. But before Mohammed could undertake the first step towards conquering the non-Arabian world, there was still one danger to be removed, which had suddenly sprung up in the sand and which might easily have undermined the proud edifice of the State of the Prophet.

THE FALSE PROPHETS

> Man is judged by his pen.
> *Mohammed*

How did Mohammed secure the immense power which he possessed? The only explanation was that he was actually the messenger of God. It was not difficult to make such a claim. But how a man, having made such a statement, should also have the good fortune to succeed was a question which now occupied the imagination of the entire Arabian world. At first accepted with ridicule and doubt, and later on regarded with astonishment, a strange rumour began to permeate the deserts, the mountains and the distant oases: Mohammed is not the only prophet of God. There are other powerful and inspired persons, who also have a Koran and reveal the word of God. The people of the desert took up this news with interest. That prophets could be mighty was seen by the example set by Mohammed, and the people were curious to see what the ruler of Medina would do in view of the sudden appearance of competitors. A conflict between prophets in Arabia had never yet been experienced.

At that time three men were disputing the messenger of God's right to claim the leadership of the world. Three men arose in the desert and declared that they were prophets of the Almighty.

The best-known and the most dangerous of the three was Aihalah ibn Ka'b, called al-Aswad, the Black One. Al-Aswad was a clever and ambitious man. For a time he had been a Moslem, then, having abandoned the Prophet, he became an idolater and finally declared that he was the Prophet of God. Mohammed disdainfully called Aihalah the weather-vane.

Al-Aswad was rich. He had great influence in Yemen, where he had led a regiment for a time. According to the pious Moslems, he was possessed of the spirits of black magic. He accomplished wonders, conjured up spirits from the lower world and prophesied terrible things – in short, he did everything which he thought a prophet should do, and he met with success.

Like Mohammed, al-Aswad sought power. But unlike the Prophet of Medina, he did not discard black magic. The domain of the "black one" was Yemen, the "happy Arabia," which only a short time before had acknowledged Mohammed's supremacy. One day al-Aswad killed Mohammed's governor, Shahr ibn Badhan, married his widow Mersban and travelled to San'a, the capital of Yemen. On the way he performed miraculous deeds and gave some sleight-of-hand performances. Like Mohammed, he too began to exercise worldly power.

The danger of a rival prophet came to Mohammed as a surprise. Never before had he even given thought to such a possibility. He was weighed down with affairs of State; he was equipping an army to march against Byzantium; he felt that his internal strength was on the wane and now he was supposed to devote time to the criminal claims of a liar, a conjurer and a magician.

Mohammed did not minimize the danger. If people began to doubt that he was unique as a prophet, then the entire structure of the State would be undermined. Islam stood or fell with the claim that he was the only prophet in the world. His competitor, the desert spirit of the black magician, would have to disappear. Mohammed called two Moslems whose loyalty to the Prophet was assured by the fact that they were involved in an old blood-feud with the other prophet. The faithful were called Rais and Firas. Upon Mohammed's command, they were now to fulfil the blood-duty. They went to San'a and arrived at the house of Mersban, the wife of al-Aswad; and late at night she made it possible for them to enter the bedroom of the "black one." Firas plunged a dagger deep into the throat of al-Aswad. The magician jumped up and cried for help. Thereupon his wife, Mersban, stepped out of the house and told the watch: "Heavenly enchantment has descended upon my husband, do not disturb him." But the heavenly enchantment was soon laid to rest. The murderers cut off al-Aswad's head. On the next day, San'a and all of Yemen were once again in the hands of the Prophet. The dangerous ghost had vanished.

But little is known about the other two prophets. The pious chroniclers who usually put down every word, every step of Mohammed so that posterity might benefit, have practically nothing to say about Mohammed's competitors. But their sparse reports are filled with glowing hatred.

Another of the competitors was Tu'aihah ibn Khuwailid. His activities were much more grotesque than dangerous. Quite accidentally, without any desire on his own part, he was given the reputation by his tribal brothers of having prophetic powers. The witty and unscrupulous Tulaifiah decided to turn the accident to good account. He wrote a Koran, gave out silly revelations and enjoyed the respect which was shown him. It has been said that later, when he realized the danger which threatened him because of his jokes, he became penitent and was converted to Islam. He amused himself greatly over his Koran verses. Some of these have been preserved down to our day. In the world of Islam they are a source of ridicule and amusement. In fact, the verses were not very edifying, and that they secured adherents for their author ably shows how insecure Mohammed's footing must have been in the beginning. Mohammed had a third competitor, who did not disappear until the time of Mohammed's death. In Yamamah, in a distant Arabian province, there lived the tribe of the Benu Hanifah. To this tribe belonged a man named Abu Sumamah Harun ibn Halib, who was called Musailimah, the little Moslem, by the Islamic chroniclers. Musailimah was old, clever and cunning: Mohammed's laurels gave him no peace. He was the first in Arabia to discover a very simple trick, which consisted of placing an egg into a bottle without breaking it. His dexterity astonished the people of the Banu Hanifah. A man who could do such wonders was without doubt a messenger of God. With the aid of these primitive miracles, Musailimah collected a number of followers to whom he preached his own Koran, and married the prophetess Sajah who had tried to rival him. Little is known about his teaching. Apparently he was a monotheist, believed in Allah and, in addition, was an adherent of Christian asceticism. It is known that he only permitted intercourse, even among married people, when it was for purposes of procreation. However, the main portion of his teaching seemed to concern the soul, a teaching which was remarkable in that the soul was assigned a modest dwelling-place below the intestines.

The demands of Musailimah were not exactly modest. His premise was that God had sent each race its own prophet and that he was the prophet of Yamamah. He had no thought of entering into rivalry with Mohammed, for he carefully revealed in his own Koran the following: "We have given thee, Musailimah, many people; keep these people for yourself. Be careful and do not strive for too much. And do not enter into any competition." As for the rest, Musailimah declared himself ready to acknowledge Mohammed but demanded in return that Mohammed should appoint him his successor. He suggested that the Islamic article of faith should be changed to read, "Mohammed is the messenger of God and Musailimah is his successor." Mohammed was interested in this remarkable Yamamite. It has been said that he even instructed Ali to visit him. After his visit to Yamamah, Ali told the Prophet: "I swear by every grain of sand in the desert of Dahna that Musailimah is an impostor." Perhaps Ali was not disinclined to be Mohammed's successor himself.

Be that as it may, one day Musailimah sent a solemn embassy to the city of the Prophet. Rich presents were brought by it and also a letter for Mohammed. The letter read: "From Musailimah, the messenger of God, to Mohammed, the messenger of God, greeting. Come, colleague, and let us share the world. Half shall be yours and half shall be mine." Mohammed's answer has also been preserved. "Mohammed, the messenger of God to Musailimah, the Liar. Peace be to him who obeys the truth. The world belongs to God alone."

But Mohammed did not undertake any campaigns against his rivals. At that time he had more important things to do. He was preparing to attack Byzantium. And from that time nothing further was heard from the prophet of Yamamah.

But when the day's work was done, Musailimah, the Liar of God, arose, and with him were the people of the Banu Hanifah and many more people of the desert. They all believed in the heretic creed: "Mohammed is the messenger of God and Musailimah is his successor." In reply to this, the army of the faithful came to Yamamah, conquered the heretics and killed Musailimah, the Liar of God. And so the *fata Morgana* disappeared, the demonic ghost of the false prophet, who wished to rival Mohammed's power over the world.

All three prophets were fascinated by Mohammed's meteoric career, for his star stood high in the Arabian heavens. All three saw his ascent and were eager to imitate it. A man appears before the people, speaks in rhymed verse, declares himself to be the messenger of God, collects followers, destroys his enemies, and in about ten years' time is changed from a persecuted pariah to the ruler of Arabia. It was most tempting to try and imitate the example: that is why all three prophets took the same course. They were better prepared than Mohammed. They could profit by his experiences, and then, too, they were well-versed in black magic, which Mohammed abhorred. Nevertheless, all three succumbed. For among the countless wanderers, magicians, prophets and possessed people who have crossed the sands of Arabia since the beginning of time, Mohammed was the only one who did not perform miracles, magic or tricks. He had come with the word, he had believed in the word and chose the spirit for the foundation of his power. There was but one way in the Whole World and Mohammed was the only one who could tread it. Viewed externally, the way to success seemed to be quite simple, and yet it was inimitable, unrepeatable like the verses of the Koran, like the spirit which led Mohammed to victory. No one could repeat the way and no one knew whither the path of Islam would lead its people.

AGAINST BYZANTIUM

Do not be annoyed by little things if you are on the way to big things.

Hebel

Mohammed had come into closer contact with the "people of the Scriptures," the Jews and the Christians. The stories of Medina and Khaibar have shown us how he settled his differences with Jewry. Now it was the time for a decisive meeting with the Christians. As he had attempted to do with the Jews, Mohammed at first tried to regard the Christians as an allied religious community. During the conflicts between Byzantium and Persia, Mohammed had declared in favour of Heraclius, the Emperor of Byzantium. When the Christians were beaten by the Persians in 622, Mohammed said, "It is true that the Byzantines were defeated. But they are certain to be victorious in a few years. Then the faithful will rejoice." Mohammed also looked upon the Christian ruler of Abyssinia as a co-religionist. The decision of the Negus, "their faith does not differ that much from our own," was entirely Mohammed's point of view.

In Medina, Mohammed attempted to annex Christianity to Islam. In the year 623 he inaugurated fast days and holidays which coincided with the Easter of the Christians. Gradually the Prophet had to acknowledge his error. He began to be more vociferous in his damnation of those who credited God with having a son, and as early as the fourth year of the Hidshra he abolished the "Christian" holidays. When he elevated the pilgrimage to Mecca to the highest law of Islam, the rupture between him and the Christians was complete.

Once again, and probably for merely formal reasons, he turned to the Christian potentates of the world at that time and invited them to recognize him as the Prophet. This invitation was actually a declaration of war.

The gradual break with Christianity had its reasons. There were enough Christians in Arabia who, like the Jewish rabbis, were capable of contradicting the Prophet in learned discourse. Whereas the disputes with the Jewish rabbis resulted in the banishment of the Jews, the situation was now far more difficult. The Christians were not powerless, for they could seek support from the mighty Christian kingdoms which stretched out to the frontiers of Arabia. The Christians were now the same danger to Mohammed that he had once been to the Meccans when he had been an ally of the Negus. The individual smaller and weaker tribes had been easily converted to Islam. Sometimes they went over to the protection of Islam of their own free will. But the Christian rulers were by no means inclined to give up their faith and their independence. They refused to follow the Prophet or to be obedient to him and chose the only possible way out; they gradually emigrated to Christian Byzantium.

In the Syrian frontier territory of Arabia, a compact Christian colony had been established in the course of the years. In addition to their hatred of the Prophet, which they had brought with them from their native country, they also had a clear opinion of his power. The leaders of this colony were the Medinese Christian sectarians, Abu Amir and the Bedouin chief, Adi. In Syria, Abu Amir created a sort of competitive undertaking against Islam. He built a mosque and collected around him the dissenters who had left the city of the Prophet.

Through these Christian emigrants, Byzantium learned of the great empire which had suddenly come into being in the desert. It heard of the new prophet who had unified the people of the desert, and of the demands which this prophet made. But the Christian empire paid but little heed to the stories of the pious fugitives. The Christians had enough troubles of their own and did not seriously believe that the wild, poverty-stricken Arabia could grow to be a danger to the mighty empire. They armed the allied tribes, collected an army and even discussed a plan of sending a punitive expedition into the interior of the country. They could not possibly decide to do more than that at the time. They left it to the emigrants to make their own arrangements. And these pious Christian emigrants actually understood how to profit by their knowledge of Arabian conditions.

Abdallah ibn Ubayy still lived in Medina, and there were still a sufficient number of *munafiqun* carrying on their activities in secret, who had not yet adjusted themselves to conditions as they were. Although outwardly these men bowed to the power of the Prophet, they did so because of their lack of decision. It needed but one push to move them to action. They were easily won over to clever intrigue and treachery. Soon numerous threads were being spun between the chiefs of the *munafiqun* and the leaders of the Christian colony, negotiations were under way, plots were prepared, and the "hypocrites" awaited their opportunity to fall upon Mohammed from the rear. Soon Abu Amir reported to the Christian Emperor that a campaign of the Byzantine army could, with the help of the allied *munafiqun* in Medina, easily overthrow the despotism of the false prophet. It sounded most attractive. It would be possible to annex Arabia to the empire with but little risk of failure. Heraclius decided to start a campaign. He assembled his army on the edge of the desert, to the east of the Dead Sea. This occurred in the late summer of 630.

Mohammed knew of the doings of the emigrants. The proposed campaign of the Emperor Heraclius was also no secret to him. But he was still better informed about the secret intrigues of the "hypocrites," about the plans of Ibn Ubayy and the hopes of the *munafiqun*. He did not overestimate their importance. He knew Abdallah, and so he was aware that the old, rich man was not capable of coming to any definite decision. Mohammed decided to demonstrate the power of all the faithful in the eyes of the Emperor of Byzantium, who had not replied to his letters and who now threatened to invade his land.

He knew that there could be no peace between Byzantium and himself, between two bearers of the idea of a universal state. The hour would come when the Moslems would vanquish the Christian empire. The ageing Prophet wished to show his warriors the way in time, and so he decided to meet the Byzantine emperor in open battle. This plan was daring indeed. The power of his country compared with that of Byzantium was like the power of an Indian Maharaja compared with that of the British Empire. On the one hand, here stood a world-power, which had just victoriously terminated a bloody conflict lasting ten years, and which now extended itself over three continents, Africa, Asia and Europe. On the other, there was a wild, poor country which had just been educated by one man alone to a consciousness of nationalism. The powers were unevenly distributed. The contemporaries of Mohammed could not know that the giant Byzantium had feet of clay. Nor did Mohammed know this, and yet he summoned his army to set out against Byzantium, on the first of the long series of Islamic campaigns which were to destroy the Christian world of the Orient and incorporate the eastern world with Islam.

The Prophet himself had shown his troops the way to universal domination. He led his own as Moses had once led the Jews into the Promised Land. But both prophets were permitted to see the goal only from a distance.

In the summer of the year 630 the steppes lay completely dried out, and heavy sand covered the palm trees. The fields were burned, the oases were thirsty and the camels, who were now mostly skin and bone, lay motionless in the shadow of the trees, which had turned yellow. Intently the Bedouins gazed into the distance; and out of that distance sounded the call of the Prophet, summoning them to a holy war.

It was not easy to move the people to take part in a campaign during that summer: a campaign which promised neither loot nor wealth, and which meant marching through the dead desert to the Dead Sea. It was even more difficult to equip the army properly which followed the call of the Prophet. War was to be waged against Byzantium, against the best-schooled soldiers of the Orient. It was necessary to modernize the army of the Prophet in every department. It is said that Abu Bakr gave up his entire fortune for this purpose and that Uthman alone gave up seventy thousand pieces of gold. After great efforts had been made and certain progress had been accomplished, the army set out for the campaign.

At its head, on a white camel, rode the Prophet. It was only six years ago that he had set out for his first battle, with hardly three hundred men at his command. Today, he was followed by thirty thousand warriors, ten thousand horses and twelve thousand camels. Times had changed. As usual, Abdallah ibn Ubayy, who was on oath to accompany the army, had failed to join up. He had followed the army as far as the boundaries of Medina, and had then turned round with his followers and returned to the city. Mohammed did not trust the powerless intriguer very far. But Ali and the few others of the faithful who had remained behind to guard Medina were, without doubt, able to maintain discipline in the State.

The army of the faithful passed through endless deserts and over sun-burned steppes. A dusty, burning sky hung over the head of the Prophet. No well, no oasis showed itself in the distance. Exhausted, the army followed the messenger of God. Further and further Mohammed led his army through wilderness and desert towards the enigmatic land of the north. The march was difficult, the oppressive heat impeded the warriors. Never before had the desert seemed so endless.

Finally the ruins of the dead desert city, Al-Hijr, appeared out of the sea of sand. Clear, ice-cold water flowed under the ruined walls. There the exhausted army could have rested and refreshed itself.

Mohammed rode at the head of the army. He was the first to see the ruins and the cooling wells. Wise and far-seeing as he was, he decided to put his army to the hardest of all tests. It does not take much to set out against the enemy in the hope of booty, to gain a victory and then to cheer the Prophet. The greatest virtue of a soldier is blind obedience which does not fail when the commands of the leader mean neither victory nor rich booty. Knowing this, Mohammed forbade his army to drink even as much as one drop of the water of the well of Al-Hijr. When the army lay around the well, crazed with thirst and half-dead from exhaustion, and no one, not even the least tamed of the Bedouins, dared to place a drop of water in his mouth, then Mohammed knew that his authority over the army was unlimited. The time of the improvised attacks of pillage was over, the army of the Moslems had become a well-disciplined fighting power.

The army continued its march across the desert. On the next day, God had pity on His faithful and sent down rain from heaven. And the Prophet revealed: "In this manner does God reward the obedience of the faithful."

The army was on the march for fourteen days before it reached Tabuk, the frontier of the Arabian world. There the Prophet climbed on a sand hill, turned his face towards the north and said: "There lies the land Sham, Syria; here is the boundary of Arabia. Here we will await the enemy."

Tabuk is rich and fertile. The army of the pious camped for twenty days in the oasis without the enemy showing himself. Heraclius had not sent out an army. Byzantium avoided the opponent who had suddenly made his appearance, by overlooking him. For Byzantium Mohammed's army was merely a desert mirage. They hoped that the mirage, made up of thirty thousand heads, would disappear of its own accord if it was not confronted. In the meantime dukes and nobles of the neighbouring countries made their appearance, carefully weighed the opposing forces, gave no rein to their admiration and were converted to the faith. They saw more clearly than their distant emperor. A few reconnoitring expeditions, sent out in an attack upon one of the fortresses, taught Syria a rapid lesson. It knew now what the new opponent was like.

Byzantium did not stir. The big city on the Bosphorus remained silent. At times news was received that Byzantium was assembling a gigantic army. It was carefully noted and the necessary preparations undertaken.

When the twenty days were over, and when the Prophet saw that there was no one in the country who was willing to measure his forces with his own, he gave orders for the return march, acting upon the advice of his generals. The army returned to Medina with rich loot. In the next year a new campaign was to extend the newly-made conquests. The Prophet remembered those who had refused to march into battle with him, and he imposed heavy penalties upon them. They were placed under a ban and no Moslem was allowed to associate with them or to talk with them. It required much begging before the Prophet released the cowards from the ban.

A short time after the return of the army, Mohammed's enemy, the hypocrite Abdallah ibn Ubayy, died in Medina. The party of the *munafiqun* collapsed with the death of its leader. Now Mohammed no longer had any enemies in the country. However, in order to change the last of the *munafiqun* into friends, he ordered that the chief of the hypocrites was to be buried with all honours. He himself followed behind the coffin, and at the request of the relatives he prayed for the forgiveness of Ubayy's sins. The honest Umar was hurt by the Prophet's prayer for the hypocrite. When he asked Mohammed about it when they were alone, the Prophet laughed shamefacedly and said, "You may pray for the hypocrites or not, just as you will, but even if you pray seventy times for them they will still not find forgiveness."

Umar was pleased with this satisfactory answer. But the Prophet had achieved his end. From then on there were no more *munafiqun* in Medina.

THE END

If you believe in Mohammed, know, then, that
Mohammed is dead.

Abu Bakr

The days of Mohammed were drawing to a close: his work had been accomplished. He left behind him a united country and had shown his faithful the way to the future. The Prophet was now sixty-three years old. Feebleness and the infirmities of old age were upon him.

Poisonous vapours rose from the damp fields of Medina. Death ruled in the city and threatened those who had not inherited immunity against the fever-laden air. Mohammed realized his condition. He wished to keep his word which he had once given to the people of Medina: "I will live with you and I will die among you."

The messenger of God grew weaker and weaker. It was only with difficulty that he fulfilled his duties as statesman and prophet, and he did not wish the people to know of his illness. Knowing that his end was near, he undertook one more pilgrimage, the last of his life, to Mecca.

The final pious journey of the Prophet became a magnificent farewell from his native city of Mecca. Surrounded by an immense number of the faithful and accompanied by their leaders, the Prophet rode into the great courtyard of the Caaba. With his own hands, he sacrificed sixty-three camels, the number corresponding to the years of his age. Then he fulfilled all the old rites of the pilgrimage, shaved his head, reverently circled the Caaba and prayed to his God. Having distributed among the faithful the locks of hair which had been shorn from his head, he mounted his camel and preached his farewell sermon. Each day he repeated his sermon so that it might become impressed on the minds of his people, and each day he began it as follows: "Listen to my words, for I am but a man like you, and I do not know if we will see each other in this place again." He continued to tell the people about the only God, about the laws of the new religion, about good conduct both at home and in public and about the little things in life. He spoke of honesty and politeness, for nothing is too slight in the eyes of God. When he had preached this sermon for the last time, Mohammed received his last revelation in the presence of the people, the well-known verse of the Koran: "Today shall those who disbelieve in your religion despair; do ye not then fear them, but fear me – today is perfected for you your religion, and fulfilled upon you is my favour, and I am pleased for you to have Islam for a religion."

"These words," so say Arabian chroniclers, "were the seal and termination of the law. No further revelation followed." Finally the Prophet lifted up his hands and asked: "Did I fulfil that which God commanded me to do?" "You have fulfilled it," answered the crowd. "God too has fulfilled his promise," said Mohammed.

When all the solemn rites had been completed, Mohammed returned to Medina, to the city of his fame and his death. The daily work was taken up anew, and again he made his daily appearances, supported by the arms of his friends, in the mosque. He continued to issue orders and to build up the army. As had been done the year before, another campaign was to be started against Byzantium. The hypocrite party had disappeared, the state treasuries were filled now that the tax-collecting had been centralized. Quietly and confidently the new army was being equipped. Mohammed appointed the twenty-year-old Usamah as leader of the army. He was the son of Zaid, who had fallen in the first battle against the Byzantines when Khalid led the army, and now he was to avenge his father's death. Solemnly Mohammed handed over to him the standard which signified that he was in command, took his leave from the men and prayed for victory. He himself could not accompany them on this occasion for his strength was failing.

In the night, when the army had gone out of the city and lay encamped near Medina, the Prophet was taken with a severe attack of tropical fever, *febris subcontinua*. Exhausted and with eyes closed he lay upon his bed. Only his lips were moving. Suddenly, towards midnight, he got up and, shaking with fever, staggered out of the house and wandered alone with swaying steps through the streets of Medina. No one noticed him: only an old slave aided his uncertain steps.

Finally the Prophet arrived at a great open place, the cemetery of Medina. His old friends and soldiers lay here. They had worked at his side and now they had gone before him. They had accompanied the Prophet in countless campaigns, in times of persecution, misery and victory, and had been witnesses of so many of his holy conversations. Now they lay in the cemetery of Medina, and the feverish, dying Prophet thought of them. He knelt down in the empty dark place and cried bitterly. He beat his breast and prayed for his dead companions. Perhaps he cried and prayed in the dark solitary night for his parents, who had died as heathen and for whom he had never been able to pray publicly. "All who die as heathen are destined for hell, even my parents," the Prophet had once said in one of his sermons. Now he knelt and cried and prayed for all who had gone the way with him and who had ended the way before him. Mohammed stood alone in the cemetery of Medina, and only his companion, the old slave, heard the crying of his master. At last he arose, peered through the darkness at the graves of his friends, at the city of Medina, and said, "Rejoice, ye inhabitants of the grave; the dawn which awakes you is more peaceful than that which greets the living." Swaying and shaking, he moved along the deserted streets of the city, and ill, weak and feverish he entered the mosque.

His illness increased from day to day, but Mohammed did not give in. He continued his visits to the mosque and spent his nights with each of his wives in turn. His strength began to leave him, and messengers had already been sent out in secret to the army in the desert with orders for its immediate return. Old friends and companions poured into Medina from all parts of the country, for the news had spread like lightning that the Prophet was near death.

The Prophet was lying in the hut of Maimunah, the least attractive of his wives, when he was seized by a particularly violent attack of fever. He felt that his end was near and asked for all his wives to come to him, so that he might speak a friendly word to each. Then he asked their permission to be allowed to spend his remaining days in the hut of his favourite wife, Aisha. He now lay there in fever and in suffering. Aisha nursed him, kissed his restless eyes and stroked his beard. Fatimah, the only living daughter of Mohammed, came to him, and gently he whispered words of farewell into her ear.

Mohammed became very restless on the second day of the struggle with death. He had himself placed in a bath-tub and had water played upon him from seven hoses, and for a short time it renewed his strength. Carried by Ali and Fadl, the son of his uncle Al-Abbas, he was taken to the mosque, where he asked Abu Bakr to lead in prayer in his place. Then he himself prayed for the faithful who had fallen at Uhud and in the many other battles, after which he arose and spoke for the last time to his friends. Again he cautioned the fugitives and the auxiliaries, the *muhajirun* and the *ansar* to keep together, and said: "The number of the Moslems will increase, but your number will constantly decrease. Stay close to one another, for you were my family."

He gave out his last three orders. They were: "Chase all the idolaters out of Arabia, give the newly-made converts the same rights as your own and pray without ceasing." When he had done this, the messenger of God arose and asked: "Moslems, is there anyone among you whom I have injured?" A simple man of the people got up and said that the Prophet had once borrowed three silver dinars from him to give to the poor, and that he had forgotten to return them. "It is better to blush here than in the next world," the Prophet said, and paid the man his three pieces of silver with interest. In this manner the messenger of God took his leave from the congregation of the faithful.

His decline was rapid. One fainting spell followed another. In his few conscious moments the Prophet did not cease to talk about the new campaign against Byzantium. The plans of the statesman and the visions of the prophet had not yet come to an end. The victory over Byzantium was to establish a world-power and to unite Islam and Christianity. Not even in the last throes of death did Mohammed stop announcing his plans for the future and giving orders concerning them.

He was to be permitted to speak to the people once more. When Abu Bakr had led the prayers on Friday, the rumour had spread that Mohammed was already dead. Confusion covered the city. In order to pacify the crowds, Mohammed had himself carried out to the people and, in a trembling voice, he spoke to them: "Was there ever a prophet before me who lived forever? I return to Him who sent me. My last command is that you love one another, help one another and do pious deeds. That alone is important, and all else leads to destruction. I will now precede you, but remember that you will follow me."

Again the fever raged in the body of the Prophet. The slight improvement was followed by a relapse. The fever became worse and worse and the Prophet felt his end approaching. He commanded that all his slaves be set free and that the money which was in the house be given to the poor. He sank into a feverish sleep. Softly Aisha placed his head on her knee, stroked him and moistened his face with cooling water. Finally she tried a talismanic formula. She took the right hand of the messenger of God and stroked his face with it while she said, "O God of the people, remove the evil. For you are the Healer and there is no healing but your healing, and your healing does not permit the illness to linger." Mohammed's hand moved; once again he opened his eyes and said, "O Allah, let it be so, among the companions in Paradise." Mohammed was dead.

The Prophet died on Monday, the 12th day of the Arabic month of Rabi 'ul-awwal, on 8 June, 632. He was buried in Aisha's hut on the spot where he had died. The hut became part of the mosque.

The news of Mohammed's death spread like wild-fire throughout the city. At first none would believe it. The people were stunned. Many of the Moslems had thought that the Prophet was immortal, and to them his death meant the end of Islam. A vast crowd assembled before the hut of Aisha. The people cried and wailed. It appeared as if the old hatred between the parties would break forth anew, and none knew what was now to happen to the Republic of God. The Prophet had left no successor. It seemed as if his death was the death of Islam.

Suddenly a door opened, and Abu Bakr, the oldest of the *muhajirun*, stepped out of Aisha's hut. He lifted up his hand and said:

"If you believe in Mohammed, know then that Mohammed is dead.
If you believe in God, know that God lives and cannot die."

Abu Bakr took over the inheritance of the Prophet with a firm hand. The day after

Mohammed's death, he was made the first Caliph, which means, Representative of the Messenger of God, Shadow of God on Earth, Ruler of the Faithful.

Twenty-five years after the death of the Prophet, Syria, Egypt, North Africa, Persia and Mesopotamia belonged to Islam.

After five hundred years, Islam ruled Byzantium, India and Russia; steppes, deserts and continents. Victoriously it stood at the gates of Vienna.

The merchant of Mecca had reached his goal.

IV.

THE WORLD AFTER THE PROPHET

The foundation of Mohammed's empire was the spirit,

   and that is why it outlived its founder.

The Caliphs continued the way of the Prophet.

Where did the way lead?

How will it end?

A TRAGIC END

Ideas do not live if they have no opportunity to fight.

Thomas Mann

It was the year 1924. Deep, impenetrable night lay over the great city on the Bosphorus. The imperial palace lay within a garden surrounded by thick marble walls. Once, many centuries ago, a new ruler had ridden into the brilliant city on the Bosphorus. He had slain Romanus Palaeologus, the last emperor of Byzantium, the ruler of the Roman Empire of the Orient. The new ruler had crossed over a mountain of dead bodies into the church of Santa Sophia, had dipped his hand in the blood of the enemy and pressed his bloody palm on one of the walls of the church. The imprint of this heavy, barbaric hand was to be the symbol of the new empire.

Now a reproduction in gold of the outlines of that hand decorates the marble door of the old palace. In the month of March 1924, a deathly silence reigned over the palace. Silently the few attendants wandered through the splendid halls. Somewhere in some distant room an old gentleman with grey hair lay asleep. The palace, the gold seal on the door and the memories of the ancestor with the heavy, bloody, barbaric hand belonged to this man. His name was Abdul-Majid ibn Abdul-Aziz Khan. His title was Ruler of the Faithful, Shadow of God on Earth, Governor of the Messenger of God.

Somewhere in the shadows of the great silence, Abdul-Majid was thinking of the host of his powerful ancestors, who once had borne the same title as he did, and who had taken it by force and retained it in fame and honour throughout the centuries.

One day, young, strong and wild Turkish nomads had appeared out of the depths of the Middle Asiatic-Mongolian steppes and had advanced to the borders of the Islamic Empire. They became the swords of the Caliphate, conquered Asia Minor and brought about the fall of the Byzantine Empire.

With ease they snatched the power out of the hands of the tired, helpless Arabian Caliph.

The domination over the State of God, the protection of Islam and the holy places and the representation of the messenger of God on earth were all taken over by Al-i-Osman, the famous house of Osman.

Again centuries had passed. The empire expanded, and with it grew the power, the fame and the grandeur of the proud Caliphs on the Bosphorus, the rulers of Stamboul.

And now the last of the long line of rulers, Abdul-Majid ibn Abdul-Aziz Khan, lay somewhere in one of the rooms of the big palace. His empire was still large. The pious souls of three hundred million belonged to him, and his name was praised every Friday in the mosques. His was the office of representative of the Prophet, but his might and his power had been lamed. Actually he only ruled over the palace, over the green gardens on the Bosphorus and over the insignia of the Caliphate. A blond, strict general, whose plans no one could fathom, now governed over the cities and the country his fathers once ruled. The name of the general was Mustafa Kemal Pasha.

The Caliph lay lost in thought. While the row of his ancestors passed by him, a sudden knock was heard on the door. An officer, a representative of Mustafa Kemal, entered. He wished to speak to the Caliph. Energetic steps resounded through the darkness of the palace. Clad only in his nightshirt, the Shadow of God on Earth, the Governor of the Messenger of God was led through the palace. The officer remained standing in the large, empty throne room where once the Islamic pope had received the homage of the world. The trembling old man had to mount the throne. With a quaking voice he read in the darkness of the night a document which the officer had presented to him. "I, Abdul-Majid, relinquish for myself, and in the name of the entire house of Osman, all the rights to the Caliphate and the Sultanate as well as the spiritual and temporal power of Islam." Only a few old and feeble attendants listened to his words. The palace was empty. The voice of the Shadow of God on Earth sounded tired in the threatening emptiness of the magnificent room.

On the next day the Caliph left the territory of the Turkish Republic, and he was followed by the entire house of Osman. The world of Islam, the three hundred million Moslems in India, Turkey, Russia and Egypt learned that a Caliph, a representative of Mohammed on earth, no longer existed.

This occurred in the Palace of Stamboul on 3 March, 1924.

No one was slain that night in the palace. But the idea which had appeared in dream-like visions to a merchant of Mecca had died. The State of God, the idea of the unity of mankind in Islam, was dead. There was no one on earth to represent the word of Mohammed.

For thirteen hundred years the Caliphs, the spiritual heirs of the Prophet, had ruled the world of Islam. They had been building on the edifice of God and they had not been able to complete their task. An ambitious general and an active officer seemed sufficient to destroy the work of centuries, to abolish the labours of the merchant of Mecca.

Did they really destroy his teaching? Is his idea really dead? Had the Prophet preached in Mecca for nothing? Had people for more than a thousand years turned their faces in vain towards Mecca and cried out: "There is no God but Allah and Mohammed is His Prophet?" What remained of the idea? Who represents it today in the world of the Orient?

The career of Islam will furnish the answer.

THE FATE OF AN IDEA

> Only small things in life succeed, all the rest is
> tragic.
>
> *Keyserling*

Mohammed launched the idea of a State of God into the world. What happened to the idea? Abu Bakr had not been able to secure the inheritance of the Prophet without a struggle. The death of Mohammed had split the ranks of the faithful in Medina. The tribe of the Hashim, the flesh and blood of Mohammed, demanded that one of their own – in this case, Ali – should take over the inheritance. The same demands were made by the *ansar* who had protected the Prophet. They too proposed a candidate, the Khazarite Sa'd ibn Ubadah. In the most dramatic of circumstances Abu Bakr had succeeded in securing the acknowledgment of both parties to his claim. An example of the chaos which reigned in Medina immediately after the Prophet's death is the fact that the faithful had forgotten to bury him. His burial did not take place until thirty-six hours after his death, when decomposition had begun to set in. Abu Bakr used those thirty-six hours to create the Arabian Caliphate.

Mohammed's death was not the signal for general confusion in Medina alone. All the desert tribes turned from Islam and refused to pay taxes. But Abu Bakr had not been the oldest friend and ally of the Prophet for nothing. Mohammed's spirit continued to live in Abu Bakr. A few campaigns sufficed to restore the unity of the state. Thereafter Abu Bakr proceeded to execute the will of the Prophet – the conquest of the world. At first this world was represented by Iran and Byzantium. Abu Bakr sent out armies against both.

In March of the year 633, less than a year after the death of the Prophet, the army of the first Caliph crossed the boundaries of Iran. The leader of this army was Khalid ibn al-Walid and he commanded eighteen thousand men. In Iraq he fought against the army of the Persian governor, Hormuzd. This battle ended in a victory for Islam. In less than a year, half of Mesopotamia belonged to the Caliphs.

The second Syrian campaign followed. Again Khalid led the army and vanquished the superior army of Byzantium at Yarmuk. The knowledge of this mighty victory reached Abu Bakr as he lay upon his death-bed. Abu Bakr had only ruled for two years, and everything he had done was merely carrying out the plans and intentions of the Prophet. "Mohammed's shadow fell upon the earth through Abu Bakr," said the biographers of the latter. The only thing he did of his own accord was the creation of the form of the state, and that, after all, was also in keeping with Mohammed's idea. Islam was to be an elective monarchy. Abu Bakr, knowing how to exclude Ali and his people, ordered that Umar, the most energetic of the Moslems, was to be his successor.

Umar was the St. Paul of Islam. He gave to the idea of a State of God definite outlines and far-reaching form. Finance, government, justice, all the elements which Mohammed had merely indicated were created and developed by Umar. Surrounded by the *muhajirun* and the *ansar* in Medina, Umar ruled over a gigantic empire. His active past when he had been a smuggler, merchant and soldier was of great use to him now. He was versed in questions of government and he decided everything himself, even the smallest matter. He ruled for ten years, without rest or pause. His armies moved victoriously into the land of the unbelievers. At Qadisiyah, in the heart of Iraq, a decisive battle took place between Persia and Islam. The battle raged for three days. On the fourth night, "the night of woe," the Arabs won the upper hand. When they were about to pursue the Persians, one of the Moslems cut off the trunk of the Persian lead-elephant. The pain transported the animal into a frenzy, and it charged the Persians and was followed by all the other elephants. A panic burst forth in the ranks of the Persian troops. Rustem, the regent of the Persian kingdom, was slain in battle, and the tiger-skin ornamented with diamonds, the imperial standard of Iran, fell into the hands of the victors.

The way to Persia lay open. The fires of Zoroaster burned for but a few years longer. The waves of Islam put them out. In the year 651, deserted by all, Jesdegerd III, the last emperor of Iran, fell at the hands of an assassin. "For us the Arabs were nothing but beggars and vagabonds. God willed that we were to know them as warriors," were said to have been his last words.

The victory of Islam over Syria and Palestine was even more rapid than that over Persia. It was only with great difficulty that the old Emperor Heraclius could defend the Holy Land of the Christians and the city of Jerusalem. The Moslems advanced on all sides. In the year 636, the sick and dying emperor left the Holy City. He carried the Holy Cross with him and no longer thought of rescue. Only a few years later, Umar, dressed in poor clothing and mounted on an old red-haired camel, and surrounded by victorious generals bedecked with gold, entered into Jerusalem. On his right rode the Patriarch of Jerusalem, and Umar gave orders that he was to be shown kingly honours, for tolerant laws were to protect the Christians. As a matter of fact, not a single inhabitant of the city of Jerusalem was killed because of his faith.

When the Crusaders vanquished the city centuries later, not a single Moslem, woman or child, was spared. A terrible blood bath crowned the victory of the Crusaders. When Jerusalem had been conquered by Islam, Umar built a great mosque on the site of the old temple. This became the third holiest mosque in Islam.

The conquest of Egypt was equally rapid. Amr ibn al-As, the poet, diplomat and satirist, advanced with four thousand men into the valley of the Nile. The population received him with shouts of joy, for he brought them liberation from the sectarian conflicts and from the burden of taxes. Alexandria alone made an attempt at resistance. When Heraclius had died and the Byzantine court began to quarrel bitterly about his heir, the cunning Arabian poet was able to enter the brilliant capital of the great Alexander victoriously.

The conqueror of Alexandria, the proud Amr, sent long reports of the brilliance of his victory to the barbaric desert city of Medina. He wrote: "I have conquered a mighty city with twelve thousand places of amusement and forty thousand Jews."

The vast amounts of gold and wealth which now poured in from all sides to the court of the Caliph changed nothing in his patriarchal mode of living. But Umar was not penurious. As a matter of fact he enabled the new aristocracy of Medina to enjoy an excellent and carefree existence. Pensions and grants were distributed among the faithful. The Caliph himself was satisfied with the bare necessities of life. The puritanical teachings of Mohammed had taken root in his soul. So, for example, the only reason why he deposed the great warrior Khalid ibn al- Walid, who had won many victories for Islam, was because he did not lead a moral life. When he heard that Sa'd, the conqueror of Persia, wished to build himself a castle at Kufah, he wrote to him: "I have heard that you wish to build a palace like those of Khosrau. Have you perhaps the intention of placing a guard at the doors of your palace so that the petitioners who come to you may be kept out?" When this letter was received, the palace was destroyed. If a general, who had just won some important siege, appeared bedecked with some of the precious jewels that were part of the conquered booty, the Caliph would pick up a stone from the ground and throw it at the general in anger. Discipline, modesty and prayer were to be the virtues of the new State.

In politics, Umar applied the inflexible principle of *tafdil*, the pre-eminence of the pious *ansar* and *muhajirun* over the rest of the community of the faithful. Only those who had lived side by side with the Prophet were worthy of ruling the new State. Under the Caliphate of Umar, the widespread family of the *ansar* and the *muhajirun* became the governmental clique of the new State. Generals, prayer leaders and provincial governors came from their ranks; they received the major portion of the booty, and they regarded the State of God as the sole domain of the auxiliaries of the messenger of God. Those in search of wealth and booty who had joined Mohammed, anyone who had participated in the desert pillagings under Mohammed's leadership, or those who had been wounded at Badr or Uhud, could now lead a parasitical life protected by pious memories.

Gold, wealth and rewards of all sorts were the wages of the pious. The ancient ideas of the Arabian aristocracy were completely changed. The noble families of Mecca which had failed to join the Prophet at the proper time were ground into the dust. The community of the pious ruled over the gigantic state, over the wealth and over the army. The believing Medinese looked with contempt at the newly-converted gentlemen of Mecca, the former enemies of Badr and Uhud. Apparently the power of Mecca had been crushed for all time. In addition, the pious of Medina had the greatest of advantages; they could choose the leader of the new State, the Caliph, out of their own ranks. Slowly the members of the ruling caste of Medina were changed into parasites living on the State treasury. Only a few realized how great a responsibility rested upon their shoulders after the death of the Prophet. Most of them knew that they could now secure rich rewards for the sacrifices they had once made. Umar was one of the few who continued to lead Islam along the way of the Prophet and to develop the idea which had once inspired Mohammed.

When Umar was the victim of an attack by a Christian worker in 644, he did not name his successor but upheld the idea of an elective monarchy. Six of the oldest associates of the Prophet were to elect a new Caliph out of their ranks.

The choice of the six wise men was not a happy one. They elected Uthman, the son-in-law of the Prophet. Uthman was old, pious, easily influenced and thoroughly unsuited for executive duties. However, he merits attention because it was due to him that the Koran was brought into its final shape. He collected the verses of the divine book and deleted much which the inhabitants of Medina would have liked to have preached as God's words. Many of his fellow citizens disliked him because of this.

Old Uthman was the tragic turning point of Islam. He too believed in the idea of a State of God, in the eternal equality of men, and in the governing of the puritanical, pious Republic of God by the pupils of the Prophet. And yet it is his fault that the State of God did not retain its original character for hundreds of years.

Uthman came from a fashionable house in Mecca. He was a blood-relative of the Ummayah and, like the Prophet, loved Mecca, the city of his birth. And his love for Mecca culminated in his love for his ancient and noble family. When his reign began, more and more of his down-trodden, poor and disdained relatives came from Mecca to Medina. They were all pure, full-blooded Ummayahs. The old man could not withstand the influence of his relatives, and he believed them when they said that they were convinced Moslems.

Under the protection of Uthman, the Ummayah once again dared to appear in public. They were sorry for their sins. The Caliph could not help himself, and appointed his nephews as governors of the provinces and gave them other political power. This meant his decline. The pious executive caste in Medina felt the ground slipping away from under them. The worst enemies of the Prophet, the sons of Hind, had come into power. The pious *muhajirun* and the *ansar* did not wish to share their rule over Islam with them. It was almost as bad as sliding back to heathendom if, only a few years after his death, the Prophet's bitterest enemies were to have leading positions in Islam. A storm of indignation arose in Medina and destroyed the Caliph.

When Uthman had been elected it had been expected that he would make the usual speech of acceptance. Many people had come together in the mosque and respectfully made way for the venerable Uthman as he went up to the pulpit. Uthman remained there for half an hour, looked at the crowd and did not say a word. Finally the faithful became impatient, and after prolonged hesitation the feeble old man in the pulpit brought forth a daring sentence: "Every beginning is difficult." Much to the surprise of the crowd, he left the pulpit after having said these words, and went home.

It now appeared that not only the beginning was difficult for old Uthman but that his end would be more so. One day a number of Bedouins appeared before his house and reviled him because he had permitted the Ummayah to come into power. They then entered into his room and pressed him to abdicate. Although Uthman was a weak person, he knew how to keep his dignity. Without paying any attention to the intruders he kept on reading in the Koran. Without any further ado he was murdered. The few Meccans who tried to defend him were forced to flee from the city.

The pious clique of Medina now gave the office of Caliph to their worthiest representative, Ali, the cousin of the Prophet, the leader among the faithful. And so for the first and last time, the dream of the Hashim was fulfilled in Islam. A cousin of the Prophet received Mohammed's inheritance. Three times Ali had been prevented from ascending the throne, but he had never ceased to look upon himself as the rightful heir. The Caliphs, who had taken the throne from him, sought to indemnify him richly. His wealth was great, and the more it grew the larger was the number of the followers who gathered around him. Now, when it was a question of safeguarding their power against the Meccan usurpers, the faithful crowded around him. In the provinces of the new empire, where Ali had sent the most pious of the Medinese as governors, he was refused recognition. Aisha, the mother of the faithful, set out against him at the head of a large army. Civil war became an actuality in Islam. In a bloody conflict, known as the "battle of the camels," Ali was victorious over the rebels. Aisha was taken prisoner and brought to Medina with all honours. When Ali was ready to take over the office of the Caliphate, a new name appeared on the horizon of Arabian politics. The name was that of Mu'awiyah ibn Abu Sufyan, the governor of Syria. Everything that the pious executive caste in Medina hated was personified in Mu'awiyah. He was a Meccan and of the Ummayah, and the son of Abu Sufyan and Hind. It was only through Uthman's weakness that he had secured a leading position in the government. His piety was more than questionable, and his hatred of the Medinese limitless. On the other hand, Mu'awiyah was a born aristocrat who was accustomed to rule and knew the art of ruling. He incorporated in himself all the traits of the Quraish and was now reaching out his greedy hands towards the throne of the Caliphate.

The courageous and pious Ali was not an equal match for him. Near Siffin on the Euphrates, Mu'awiyah met the army of the *ansar* and the *muhajirun*. The army of Ali was far superior to that of the insurgent. The battle lasted for three days and Ali was victorious. Thereupon the army of Mu'awiyah bound copies of the verses of the Koran to their lances, and this evidence of piety was enough to bring the army of the pious to a halt. Ali did not dare to wage war against the word of God. He consented to negotiations and came out second best. On the great battlefield of Siffin the idea of the State of God was defeated through the trickery of an Ummayah.

Once more the idea of the Prophet attempted to oppose the sober world of politics. On the battlefield of Siffin, a party of the very holiest, to whom the idea of a just State of God was sacred, separated itself from the army of Ali. "We wish to set out upon the path of God," they said, and they were known as Kharijites, that is, the wanderers. In the turmoil of the civil war they were soon the only ones who retained the pure faith. In spirit and in deed they were the direct descendants of the Prophet.

On 21 January, 661, Caliph Ali fell at the hands of a fanatic. Without difficulty Mu'awiyah took over the Caliphate, the leadership over the world of the hated Hashemites. It is one of the most ironic facts in history that it was the house of the Ummayah, the most bitter opponents of Mohammed, which drew the greatest amount of profit out of the work of the Prophet. For with the ascent of the Ummayah the Caliphate became hereditary.

Three movements sought to save the idea of a free State of God. First it was the Kharijites, the noblest among the faithful, then the pious clique of Medina which was greedy for power, and finally the direct heirs of the Prophet, the descendants of Ali. All three movements were drowned in blood by the first two Caliphs of the Ummayah. The democratic puritans of Islam, the last representatives of the pure faith, the Kharijites, fought fanatically. They were decisively opposed and in the end almost completely annihilated. Only a few succeeded in preserving their beliefs for the benefit of future generations.

An equally tragic fate awaited the fellow-fighters of the Prophet. At the last moment, when the army of the new Caliph was approaching Medina, they regained their courage. Honourable old men, *muhajirun* and *ansar*, threw themselves into the fray with youthful ardour. Suddenly, they recalled the time when the Prophet himself led them into battle. Rarely had anyone fought with such fanatical energy and hatred

as at the gates of Medina. The old men had perhaps forgotten the art of living honourably but they did know how to die heroically. The steps of the great courtyard of
the Prophet's mosque were covered with the blood of the oldest friends of the messenger of God. Despite the heroic defence, the Caliph was victorious. His riders used
the mosque as a stable for their horses.

The grandchildren of the Prophet, the sons of Ali, Hassan and Hussain, also fell in
the hopeless battle with the Ummayah. The host of the Alides was destroyed, the *shi'a
Ali* – the party of Ali – was excluded from the throne for all time. However, they
never desisted throughout the entire history of Islam to fight for their rights. Even
today the name of Mu'awiyah or that of Yazid, his successor, is considered the worst
possible curse on the lips of a pious Shi'ite.

The civil war lasted for forty years. When it was ended the house of the Ummayah
ruled in the land of the Prophet. The court of the Caliph became that of an emperor.
Palaces, ceremonies, feasts, orgies, wine and beautiful women filled the life of the
Caliph, the Shadow of God on Earth, the Governor of the Messenger of God.

The idea of a State of God seemed vanquished.

But it still lived.

THE PARADISE OF THE PIOUS

The Koran? What poor astronomy and yet,
what great poetry!

Pushkin

Heroic generations arose in Islam. An utter disregard for death and the keenest determination were the marks of this religion. The sober, rationalistic Bedouins developed into fanatical fighters for the faith. Islam knew how to instil heroic courage and absolute devotion into all the peoples it had ever ruled. Arabs, Persians, Berbers and Turks, all were united in a warlike fanaticism.

The Bedouin is loath to risk his life unless he may expect a suitable reward. It was therefore perhaps Mohammed's most important task to reach and inflame the simple sons of the desert. The ideal of the Bedouin was the teaching about the life beyond, the teaching of Paradise, of the retribution of sin, and of the reward which awaited the martyr and fighter for the faith. Mohammed had known how to bequeath this ideal to the Bedouins and to make it one of their most treasured possessions.

The rhythmic verses, which in glowing colours describe the rewards for the pious, inflamed the enthusiasm of the people of the Orient. The naive belief in the literal interpretation of these descriptions made the plundering Bedouin tribes into an army which was both eager to fight and eager to be sacrificed. The picture of the next world, which Mohammed had painted for them, stirred the sentimental Orient. The words which Mohammed had spoken at Badr: "Only a thrust of the sword of the enemy separates us from Paradise," were repeated with any number of variations. They longed for martyrdom, for the lightning-like transformation into the revelations of God's book. It was no longer the more sober, religious teaching but the sudden development of a belief in Paradise which led the army of Islam from victory to victory, and developed the peaceful, vital religion into a fighting confession of faith.

Let us hear what the Koran itself has to say to the Bedouins and how it brought them under its domination:

"The life of this world is but a possession of deceit" (3,182) ... it is nothing but a sport and a play; but verily, the abode of the next world, that is life (29,64). Death is but a transition from one world to another. Count not those who are killed in the way of God [that is, in war] as dead, but living with their Lord; provided for, rejoicing in what God has brought them of His grace" (3,164).

The soul of man is immortal and yet the belief in this immortality was difficult to the Arab. "They say, 'What! when we have become bones and rubbish are we to be raised up a new creature?' Say, 'Be ye stones, or iron, or a creature, the greatest your breasts can conceive!' Then they shall say, 'Who is to restore us?' Say, 'He who originated you at first'" (17,52–3)

"Could they not see that God who created the heavens and the earth is able to create the like of them . . . yet the wrongdoers refuse to accept it, save ungratefully! (17,101). And we sent down from the heaven water as a blessing and caused to grow therewith gardens and the harvest grain . . . and we quickened thereby a dead land; thus shall the resurrection be!" (50,11). The belief in immortality is derived by the Koran from the simplest manifestations of life. "Have ye considered the fire which ye strike? Do ye produce the tree that gives it, or do we produce it?" (56,70–72).

When the resurrection was to take place, no one knew. Nor was it necessary to worry about it. The day will come suddenly and like a bolt of lightning. But the pious are to have a sign: "And then thy Lord proclaimed that he would surely send against them till the resurrection day those who would wreak them evil torment (7,166). When the earth shall quake with its quaking and the earth shall bring forth her burdens ... on that day she shall tell her tidings because the Lord inspires her (99,1). On the day ye shall see it, every suckling woman shall be scared away from that to which she gave suck; and every pregnant woman shall lay down her load; and thou shalt see men drunken though they be not drunken (22,2). When the sun is folded up, and when the stars do fall, and when the mountains are moved . . . and when the seas shall surge up (81,1–4,6). But expect thou the day when the heaven shall bring obvious smoke (44,9). And the trumpet shall be blown, and those who are in the heavens and in the earth shall swoon, save whom God pleases. Then it shall be blown again, and lo! they shall stand up and look on" (39,68).

A great ravine will open up and a keen, sharp sword, as-Sirat, will be placed over it. Every man must cross over the sharp sword. The pious will be able to do so easily. But woe to the sinners! They will fall into the deep and neither wealth nor power can save them. For the Day of the Last Judgment begins.

"What can they expect but that God should come unto them in the shadow of a cloud, and the angels too? (2,206). And ye shall see three sorts; and the men of the right hand – what right lucky men! And the men of the left hand – what unlucky men! And the foremost will be foremost! (56,7–11). And thou shalt see each nation kneeling, each nation summoned to its book. Today ye are rewarded for that which ye have done (45,27). On the day when God shall assemble the apostles and shall say, 'How were ye answered?' they will say, 'We have no knowledge; verily, thou art He who knoweth the unseen.' When God says, 'O Jesus, son of Mary! Remember my favours towards thee and towards thy mother, when I aided thee with the Holy Ghost, till thou didst speak to men in the cradle and when grown up' (5,108–9).

And the day when the enemies of God shall be gathered together into the fire, marshalled along; until when they come to it, their hearing and their eyesight and their skin shall bear witness against them of that which they have done . . . (41,16). He who brings a good work shall have ten like it; but he who brings a bad work shall be recompensed only with the like thereof, for they shall not be wronged" (6,161).

Accompanied by light and surrounded by light, the pious and the martyrs will go to the gates of Paradise. "In it are rivers of water without corruption, and rivers of milk, the taste whereof changes not, and rivers of wine delicious to those who drink; and rivers of honey clarified (47,16,17). Those who believe and who have fled and been strenuous in the way of God . . . verily, those who fear God shall dwell amidst gardens and springs: Enter ye therein with peace in safety! And we will strip off whatever ill-feeling is in their breasts; as brethren on couches face to face (15,47). Verily, the righteous shall be in pleasure; upon couches they shall gaze; thou mayest recognize in their faces the brightness of pleasure (83,23). Around them shall go eternal youths with goblets and ewers and a cup of flowing wine; no headache shall they feel therefrom, nor shall their wits be dimmed (56,171) . . . and girls with swelling breasts of the same age as themselves (78,33). And made them virgins, darlings of equal age for the fellows of the right (56,35). And the men of the right – what right lucky men! Amid thornless Lote trees . . . and Talh trees with piles of fruit and outspread shade" (56, 26).

Hell has seven portals and a new torment awaits the sinner behind each one of them. But the *munafiqun* who hypocritically accepted the true faith will receive the worst tortures.

One would have to read the numerous verses of the Koran dealing with heaven and earth, reward and punishment, in order to conceive their extraordinary powers of persuasion. Obviously the Bedouin, who knew nothing but poor idols and the poverty-stricken life of the desert, accepted them as revelations from God. The Islamic soldiers' willingness to sacrifice their lives was born out of these verses, born of the words of God, which painted these terrifying pictures.

But Islam was not only destined for soldiers and warriors alone. The fearful pictures had a definite purpose. They were to affect the imaginations of the simple children of the desert. Their aim was not conflict but peace, the final peace of a world tamed by the rules of a common faith. The Bedouin, who went to war in hopes of booty and Paradise, knew but little of this peace. Hope and life hereafter sufficed for them. But it did not suffice for the messenger of God. He thought of the peace of the world. And so, out of the verses of the Koran, out of the State which he ruled, and out of the people who were around him, he created the mighty edifice of universal peace – Islam.

THE PRACTICAL ISLAM

Wander along the path of God!
Mohammed

The faith of the Prophet covered man as the sheath the sword. Unnoticeably, but always more closely it surrounded the faithful and determined every act, every step of man, his State, his wars, his wives and his judgment.

The edifice of Islam rests on four dogmas, and man has five duties towards God. The four dogmas are: belief in God, belief in the Prophet, belief in the equality of men, and belief in a life hereafter. Whoever confesses to this faith has the following practical commands to obey: prayer, fasting, the giving of alms, the pilgrimage to Mecca, and the belief in the unity of God.

All the Moslems of the world make up one community. Their unity is expressed externally by the *qibla*, the direction towards Mecca while at prayer. The faithful may not wage war amongst themselves nor may they hate one another. On the other hand, religious wars, *jihad*, are a religious duty. Every one of the faithful must spread the faith, either by means of the sword or by preaching. But the religious wars are to be directed principally against the heathen. The conversion of the Jews and Christians by force is forbidden. "Verily those who believe, and those who are Jews, and the Sabaeans, and the Christians, whosoever believes in God and the last day, and does what is right, there is no fear for them, nor shall they grieve," says *Sura* 5, verse 73 of the Koran. The Moslems must obey the ten commandments of the Christians and the Jews. Above all else, Islam is the practical teaching of how to live one's life, and as such it seeks to embrace and direct all man's actions. Everything which can happen to man, everything that he can do, falls into five categories in Islam: *Fard, Sunna, Mubah, Makruh* and *Haram*.

Fard is that which is commanded, that which is unavoidable in order to find favour in the eyes of God, as, for example, the giving of alms. *Sunna* is doing good, meritorious acts in the sight of God. But it is not a sin to omit such acts. There are many examples of this in the life of the Prophet, who did not make a commandment of everything that he himself did. Whoever wishes to receive particular rewards may live as the Prophet did, for God will be gracious to him for it. *Mubah* are the deeds which are indifferent to both God and man. Their number is not large and they bring neither reward nor punishment. *Makruh* is the evil, but not the forbidden. One can commit it without fear of God's punishment. But the pious will omit it. *Haram*, finally, is sin, express violation of God's commands. Whoever commits *Haram* may be sure of God's punishment.

These five categories of human deeds embrace everything conceivable. When Islam was at its height one distinguished, for example, whether the wearing of gold rings was *sunna* or *mubah*, and when a copious meal ceases being *mubah* and becomes *makruh*.

Every incident of daily life, the manner of the five daily ablutions, marital hygiene, intercourse with superiors or subordinates, how to salute older people, all these were covered by the five categories. The source for the judging of human actions went directly back to the Prophet and was based on his statements, his deeds and his examples. But their interpretation was unusually tolerant. Much that was outside the framework was nevertheless tolerated. Had not the Prophet said: "Do not judge what you cannot understand"? One of the consequences of this basic thought is the treatment of the insane in Islam. They may speak irrationally and act in the same way, but who knows what lies behind that incomprehensibility?

The relationship between man and God needs no intermediary. There was no priesthood and no hierarchy. Even visits to the mosques, which are always open, were not always obligatory. On the contrary, beautiful women are counselled not to go into the mosques lest they attract the glances of the pious to themselves. Monasticism of every kind is expressly forbidden in Islam. The dervish sects which flourished at a later period had a difficult time in making their teaching conform to the basic dogmas of Islam. It is remarkable, and evidence of the tolerance of Islam that it brought forth so few sects. Slight deviations which result in the creating of sects in other religions were never an incitement to dissension in Islam.

The entire canonical law of Islam, for example, is divided into four directions or schools: Hanifites, Shafiites, Hambalites and Malikites. And although the schools differ in many ways, they each recognize the full value of one another. The primacy of free interpretation is established in Islam as in no other religion. Even today any Moslem may belong to any one of the four schools. In the courtyard of the Caaba, the faithful erected four pulpits for the four equal preachers of each of the-different schools. A Moslem argues about the interpretation of the teaching of the Prophet, acts according to his own judgment and allows the final decision to be made in the next world.

Only very little is important and insisted upon. Whoever believes in the confession of faith, in giving alms, in fasting and in the pilgrimage can safely err in all other matters. It does not make a heretic of him. The only large sect in Islam, the Shi'ites, are concerned not so much with differences of opinion in faith as with a political difference, the succession of the Prophet. The Shi'ites are of Ali's party, the defenders of legitimacy, the inheritance of the temporal power in the house of Ali. Ali's demands were not recognized by his opponents, and until this day the world of Islam still quarrels over whether the first Caliphs ruled legally, or whether the temporal power belongs to the heirs of Ali. To the Shi'ites all the Caliphs were despots and the enemies of the true faith. The Shi'ite only recognizes the so-called imamate of Ali.

The Islamic State of the Sunni, the party of the overwhelming majority in Islam is, theoretically speaking, a republic of the wise. On principle Islam does not recognize a hereditary monarchy. The chief of the State is the Caliph, the representative of the Prophet, and his office is not an hereditary one. The theory of the Islamic State requires that each new Caliph be chosen from among the learned who know the Koran. After his election, the power of the Caliph is unbounded. He rules over the life and death of all the faithful, makes laws and combines in his person both spiritual and temporal power. He is the chief leader in prayer and the commander-in-chief of the army of Islam.

But he has difficult duties to perform. He must defend the people of the faith in all the world. He must wage wars, especially religious wars which serve to expand Islam. His spiritual power is super-state, super-national, like that of the Pope. Islamic scholars demand the fulfilment of strange things from the Caliph. According to some interpretations, it is his duty to see to it that no virgins remain unmarried in his State. If no man can be found for a virgin, she may demand of the Caliph that he free a slave and give him to her for a husband. Unbounded as the power of the Caliph is, it can be withdrawn from him if he commits *haram*, that is if he violates a command of the Koran.

A decision of the wise men sufficed to dethrone a Caliph. As a matter of fact, down to our own day, every dethronement was always accompanied by the judicial verdict of the wise men. Through the recognition of the elective principle, through the possibility of unseating every Caliph, Islam succeeded in combining an absolute lifelong theocratic dictatorship with an extensive republican democracy. True, this was only so in principle, for frequently dethronements occurred for purely political reasons. It is remarkable that Islam, at least in theory, was a happy synthesis of dictatorship and democracy.

It is a peculiarity of Islam that it can always infuse the new into the traditional. It recognizes warfare, yet at the same time requires that it be carried on humanely, and elevates war to a religious duty. It recognizes slavery, yet at the same time restricts the power of the master by means of one of Mohammed's statements: "As far as the slave is concerned, give him to eat that which you yourselves eat, and clothe him with the clothes you yourselves wear." The manumission of slaves is also looked upon as sunna, a pious action pleasing in the eyes of God.

It is impossible to explain in a few pages the practical importance of Islam, its manner or the spirit which enlivens it. As an example, let us examine the problems of women, and their position in Islam. Islam permits polygamy. A Moslem may marry four wives. But this right is bound up with a particular condition. "You may have two, three or four wives, but not more," says the Koran. "If you cannot treat your wives justly and equally then take only one." It is the duty of the husband not to prefer one wife to another. In addition it is law that the wife must live under the same conditions in the house of her husband as she did in the house of her parents. If a man cannot treat his wife in the manner to which she has been accustomed at home, then the woman may demand a divorce.

A wife may have her own fortune and the handling of it. If she does not wish to or cannot do so herself, she entrusts its handling to her parents, not to her husband. There are numerous reasons why a woman can seek and obtain a divorce. Ill-treatment, neglect, even poverty of the husband are looked upon as grounds for divorce. But the Prophet recommends: "If a divorce is threatened, send a wise man into the house of the married couple so that he may try to effect peace." A peculiar law forbids the remarrying of the divorced people with each other until each of the parties has contracted another marriage. Islam does not recognize religious marriages. Marriage is a private matter which is not subject to religious ceremonies. On the other hand, a marriage contract is advisable and is usually drawn up. "When a woman fears that a man may treat her badly, then it is not a sin for her to conclude an agreement, for the soul of man is inclined to be miserly."

In all matters of private law, the wife is the equal of the husband; and the veiling of a woman is by no means a religious edict, but merely a bad custom of later development. In the beginnings of Islam, women played an important role in public life. For example, Aisha, the favourite wife of the Prophet, led an army in battle. Fatimah, Mohammed's favourite daughter, took an active part in disputes concerning inheritance, and her daughter, Zainab, openly opposed the Caliph.

In the first century of the existence of Islam, there lived in Mecca a woman named Kumad who was well-known and feared as a student of law. A number of women were famed as poets and students, as for example Buran, the wife of the Caliph Ma'mun. In the 5th century of the Hidshra there lived in Baghdad a woman named Shaihah Chukda who was also called *Fakhr-an-Nisa*, which means "the fame of women." She was a learned professor and lectured on literature, poetry and rhetoric before large audiences in the great mosque of Baghdad.

This suffices to give an idea of the true picture of the enslaving of women in Islam. But the position of women is only an example. In all phases of life, Islam, practically applied Islam, is actuated by the same spirit. It is no wonder that it became firmly implanted in the world of the Orient, and that even in our day it energetically continues its growth. The word of the Prophet about the expansion of Islam is ardently obeyed by his followers today.

THE CALIPHATE

The mortal sways in its foundations, but the immortal begins to shine more brightly and recognizes itself.

Novalis

Despite all the confusion of the civil war, the State of the faithful grew without ceasing. The Ummayads not only held celebrations in their capital, Damascus, but they also waged wars, conquered new provinces and spread the word of God. The Abbasides, too, the descendants of Uncle Abbas, who later relieved the Ummayads, did the same. The Moslem State grew and so did the fame of the brilliant capital of the Abbasides, Baghdad.

At the zenith of the Caliphate, the State of God embraced Spain, North Africa, Egypt, Arabia, Asia Minor, Syria, Mesopotamia, Palestine, Persia, the Caucasus and Turkistan. It seemed as if the *imperium romanum*, the unity of the people under one law, was suddenly resurrected in the Eastern part of the world.

But it is not only externally, not only in its vast dimensions, that the Islamic state can be compared with the Roman Empire. Islam subjugated lands which had once been made fertile by Graeco-Roman culture. Now, under the influence of the tired, ancient cultural people of the Orient, Hellenism lay dying. Islam, the youthful people of the Arabs, took up this culture and continued it. The heir of Rome in the Middle Ages was not wild, barbaric Europe but the empire of the Caliphs. The *pax romana* of the Emperor Hadrian was newly erected by the Arabs. From the Pyrenees to the boundaries of India, Islam created a unified culture, a unified world-picture. Law, language, religion, economic forms, all things which mould man internally and destine his life, were unified. Islam assimilated the bearers of the Hellenistic culture, the Greeks and the Byzantines. The stunted spiritual values of the senile Romans awakened to a new life. The streets of the Arabian cities and their dress were gradually given an almost classic stamp. The classic spirit was creatively propagated by Islam. It was mainly by these devious paths that Europe received its knowledge of the old world and with it the impetus for the Renaissance. This historical service of the Arabs must not be forgotten. To a great extent, Western Europe owes its later cultural flowering to Islam.

The democratic spirit of the creator was mirrored in the existence of the people. Economically, the empire of the Caliphs was a land of small rustic settlements. The tolerant laws regarding the Jews and the Christians, and the century-long internal peace brought the peasants of all confessions an unusual advancement, and so created a fertile ground for a rich cultural development. Entire territories, which up to that time had been deserted and barren, were opened up to agrarian development by the Islamic peace. The empire of the Caliphs was like a huge granary. The satisfied lower classes, the homogeneity of widely spread territory which extended itself over three continents, the government which had been organized with an almost Roman thoroughness, and the tolerant, lively legal code, all these together built the foundation of a new wealth which developed out of the unusual upward trend of commerce. Islam occupied and ruled over all the focal points of the old-world commerce. The routes between East and West, between Europe and India now belonged to Islam. It was impossible for the world of the Middle Ages to carry on trade on a large scale without having to pass through an Islamic customs station. Egypt, Mesopotamia, Turkistan, all the well-known trade routes to Europe, China and India belonged to the empire of the Caliphs. Nearly over-night, in less than a decade, great towns sprang up in which the ancient Quraish spirit celebrated universal triumphs. Baghdad, Cairo, Basrah and Bucharah were the central points of the commerce of the world. This world-commerce had been organized with a sort of modern rationalization. A network of banks with ample capital was created, and in the tenth and eleventh centuries bank cheques were familiar objects. The trade routes were in splendid condition and provided with signposts giving the distances. One could travel without danger throughout the most distant regions of the Caliphates. For peace and right ruled on earth in those times, as in Rome at the time of Hadrian.

When the people are not hungry and the merchants are rich, a third factor is not lacking. Culture begins to bear rich and luscious fruit. Islam was well disposed towards the development of the spiritual life. "Seek learning even if you must travel to China," was a well-known saying of the Prophet. These words were held in high honour in the world of Islam. Every teaching, every phase of the spiritual life had a right to existence and to tolerance. There were but very few exceptions to this general rule.

It was due to Islam that the idea of universal education first came into being during the height of its development. The first university in the world was founded in Cairo, the first high school in which various sciences were given equal stress. This university, al-Azhar, still exists as the seat of Islamic religious education. Mathematics, poetry, philology, logic, jurisprudence, all the philosophical and natural sciences were furthered in this university, at the court of the Caliph and in the palaces of the rich. Islam embraces a wealth of races and people. Each race knew how to contribute its own specific note to the common culture of Islam. The mathematically sober mind of the Arabs, which had only occupied itself with logical thinking, found a welcome addition in the imaginative, mystically confused poetical ideas of the Aryan Persians,

Greeks, Jews, Bedouins and Egyptians. Even the wild Berbers brought their contribution to the great development of Islamic culture. It is almost impossible to discern today what goes back to Persian, Arabian or Greek origins in this culture.

At a time when Europe was still in a very primitive state of existence, the empire of the Caliphs possessed an unusual amount of knowledge. This knowledge had been stored up in books. Books about every branch of learning, history, medicine, astronomy, cookery and geography appeared in great numbers. The first impetus was given to this by translations. At the beginning of the 2nd century of the Hidshra the works of Aristotle, Plutarch, Euclid, Galen, Theodorus and Hieron of Alexandria, as well as other Greek works, were translated into Arabic. Indian influences were also felt. The development of architecture gave rise to the invention of trigonometry. Textbooks of geometry and algebra were freely distributed.

A well-stocked library was the pride of every Arabian household. The large individual libraries were astonishing even to modern conceptions. So, for example, the Ummayad Caliphs of Cordoba possessed a library of four hundred thousand manuscripts. Ya'qub al-Kindi, a worthy philosopher and writer, died of despair when his library had been confiscated. Usamah ibn Munqidh, a rough Arabian warrior, called the loss of his library the greatest misfortune of his long life.

The ban on painting directed creative efforts towards architecture. On the foundation of the classic Graeco-Roman type of architecture developed the fairy-like buildings of Islam, which perhaps are among the most beautiful architectural monuments in the world. The Taj Mahal in India, the Alhambra, the great mosque of Cordoba give evidence of a perfected *Lebensstil*.

What did the world of Europe mean to the Arab? From the time of the closest intellectual connection between East and West, the time of the Crusades, a remarkable document has been preserved: "The Memoirs of an Arabian General (the Usamah ibn Munqidh mentioned above) of the Crusaders and Europeans." Usamah had frequently come across Europeans. His book gives an interesting picture of the opinion of a civilized Arab of the people of the West. "No one," says Usamah, "can see anything but animals in the Franks (Europeans) who are most courageous in war, which is an instinct of animals. Other than courage they have no human traits and that is why the knight, the warrior, is the greatest man among them. Other people are not considered as humans by them. The Franks who have just come from their country are much coarser and simpler than those who have spent some time among us. The Franks know neither self-respect nor jealousy. It will happen that a man and a woman will walk on the street and meet a strange man. If the woman begins to talk with the strange man, her husband will let her stand there and continue on his way. If a Frank surprises his friend with his wife he merely says, 'If this happens again we shall have a serious quarrel.'

"The Franks do not shave their bodies. On some spots, the growth of their hair assumes the size of a second beard. If they see the Moslems bathing, they are so attracted that they not only have their own bodies shaved, but they have their wives shaved all over by Moslem barbers." In numerous examples, Usamah describes primitive conceptions of law, barbaric living conditions and the customs of the crusaders who had not yet acclimatized themselves to the Orient. His opinion is summed up in the sentence: "They have no feeling of honour, and yet they are courageous, although courage is only inspired by honour and through the fear of losing one's honour." The verdict of the warrior Usamah was the verdict of the Islamic world.

The cultural flowering of Islam lasted for centuries. The fall of the Ummayads and the ascent of the throne by the Abbasides in the year 750 had no evil consequences for this culture. The internal confusion, which was caused now and then by the insurrections of the Alides or by the occasional separation of one of the provinces, also did not affect it. And yet the mighty world, born of the word of Mohammed, has disappeared and has almost been forgotten. Practically nothing remains to remind us of the great period of the Caliphates, of the time when the world of the Orient had undertaken the mighty experiment of uniting mankind.

The beginning of the decline was unnoticed.

In the interior of the Central-Asiatic steppes a new, greedy and young people had sprung up, the Turks. Slowly Turkish tribes forced their way into the empire of the Caliphate. At first obedient mercenaries of the Caliphs, they gradually won more and more power. Turkish tribal leaders took the Caliphate for themselves. The country was suddenly plunged into political confusion. Persian and Arabian governors founded independent principalities. The immeasurable ocean of the Islamic world suddenly began to show political shadows.

But that was still not the decline. The land of the Caliphs was still rich and powerful, the universities still flourished, the poets wrote their poems and commerce continued.

In the Eastern part of the world a wild warrior arose, a brutal man with small, slit-like eyes. This warrior set the avalanche into motion and the avalanche ruined the Caliphate. The name of the warrior was Genghis Khan and the avalanche which he started was the Mongolian invasion. The Mongols came like a scourge of God, and where their horses grazed the grass no longer grew. Hulagu, the Mongolian wolf of the steppes, conquered Baghdad, pulled the mantle of the Prophet from the shoulders of the Caliph and trod the relic into the ground. The Caliph was slain and Baghdad plundered. The Asiatic world has not yet recovered from the terror of the Mongolian storm. Under the blows of Genghis Khan, the cities and villages became barren and the canals dried up. Deserts spread themselves out and the land faded.

Then there came a second and more severe blow. Only a few experienced its original vehemence, and yet it was the cause of the final disappearance of the Caliphate. The originator of this disappearance did not know that he had dealt a decisive blow, nor had he the remotest idea of waging war upon the land of the Caliphs.

One day Christopher Columbus discovered America. No one in the world realized that this meant that the last word had been spoken over the Caliphate. The eyes of the world were turned towards the new continent. World-trade found new outlets, new routes. Prices began to fall, the caravans which had brought wealth to Arabia no longer made their way through the desert, the customs stations had little to do and the great trade routes, now no longer in use, began to decay. No one knew from whence the crisis had come or when it would end. The people were filled with unrest. They began to be impoverished, the country to grow wild.

The decline of the spiritual life set in at the same time. The beginning was the well-known "Closing of the Bab al-Ijtihad," the Door of Recognition. The Moslem authorities determined that they had reached the peak of the comprehensible and that further research seemed unnecessary. The rapid downfall of the sciences followed. The domination of the Arabs was at an end. Wild peoples, the Berbers in the West, the Turks in the East, were leading Islam. It was only in Persia, which had gradually become the central point of the Shi'ites, that a new spiritual life began to spring up, and, naturally enough, on a national Persian foundation.

The Caliph, the heir of the one who had been slain in Baghdad, travelled to the shores of the Nile. There, under the protection of the Sultan of the Mamelukes, he lived a shadowy existence until the newly-arising Islamic power, the Ottoman empire of the Turks, took over the Caliphate. Once again they succeeded in combining great territories of Islam under the rule of the governor of the messenger of God, the Caliph of all the faithful. The Ottoman Caliphate spiritually led the Moslems of the entire world with the exception of the Moroccans and the Shi'ites. Politically it combined portions of North Africa, Egypt, Arabia, Syria, Palestine, Mesopotamia, Asia Minor and the Balkans under the rule of the Sultan-Caliph. But this last Caliphate, robbed of its spiritual foundation, also declined after a short flowering. The Islamic Ijtihad, the Door of Recognition, the main element of the spiritual existence, was apparently exhausted. The political Caliphate of the Turks crumbled gradually but inevitably.

Abdul-Hamid, the last Caliph of historical grandeur, the last to incorporate spirit and power in his own person, made one more attempt to give new life to the word of the Prophet, to the representation of the messenger of God. This last attempt, called Pan-islamism, failed. In the world war Moslems fought with one another, Moslems marched under Christian leadership against the army of the Caliph. The unity of Islam, the word which the Prophet had once preached, had disappeared.

The blond Turkish general, Mustafa Kemal, had given the *coup de grace* to a mortally wounded institution.

But is the idea of Islam, is the word of the Prophet really dead?

The idea lives and the Prophet did not pray in vain. The Caliphate and the splendour of the Islamic world were not the only means of expression of Islam. The idea showed itself to be more vital than its expression.

The man who today incorporates the idea of the Prophet is called Abdul-Aziz ibn Abdar-Rahman ibn Faisal ibn Sa'ud, King of Najd, of Assyria, of Hejaz, *imam* of the Wahhabites.

THE RESURRECTION

For years I was alone without any other assistance, with the exception of the help of God, and that is why I would appear clean before him.

Ibn Sa'ud

Islam emerged from the war and the confusion of the last decades, a vanquished cause. It had lost its unity. It was no longer a power, it had no Caliph and, what was worse, there was no one who could be Caliph. For there is a basic idea in Islam which says that "the mantle of the Prophet can only be worn by him who can protect the people of the Prophet throughout all parts of the world." There was no such person in modern Islam. For this reason the Caliphate had to remain unoccupied.

Arabia, the birthland of Islam, had once again become its central point. Islam had returned to its motherland, to the vast deserts of Arabia. And suddenly, through its contact with the old, sacred ground, it awakened to a new power, to new life. How did this happen?

During the time of the flowering of the Caliphate, Arabia had gradually sunk to an unimportant province, and it played a secondary role in the great politics of the Caliphate. It is true that the Caliph bore the title "Protector of the Holy Places," and that he annually sent a piece of cloth with valuable embroidery on it to the Caaba. But Islam itself had grown beyond the confines of Arabia.

Still, Mecca and the holy territory remained the focal point of the cult of Islam. There was the holy Caaba, and to it thousands of the faithful made their annual pilgrimages, and there the tribe of the Prophet, the Hashim, held independent sway under their tribal leader, the sherif of Mecca.

After the collapse of the Caliphate, this sherif attempted to become the head of Islam. But something stronger came in between – the movement of the Wahhabites.

About 1700, there lived in Arabia a wise man named Abdul-Wahhab. He founded the sect of Wahhabites. Numerous plainly visible threads bound his sermons with those "I the Kharijites who had been annihilated by the Ummayad Caliphs, and so bound them up with the original, unadulterated words of the Prophet. Abdul-Wahhab declared war upon official Islam. He fought the Sultan-Caliph, and he fought the learned additions and the lying alterations in the unique words of the Prophet.

246

He believed in the Koran, held to the words of the Prophet and defended the pure, unspoiled, basic idea of Islam. At his side stood the dynasty of Ibn Sa'ud, a noble Arabian family, who created a Wahhabite state in Najd with Dar'iya as its centre. The State of the Wahhabites declared war on the ruler of the faithful, the Sultan of the Osmans. This declaration of war resembled that of Mohammed against the Emperor of Byzantium: a dwarf confronting a giant. After a few preliminary victories – the Wahhabites even occupied Mecca for a time – the army of the Turks became victorious, and it had not been expected otherwise. Ibn Sa'ud was decapitated in Stamboul as a rebel and a heretic. But his heirs, together with the rest of the Wahhabites, founded a small principality in Najd, in which the original, unchanged teachings of the Prophet became maxims of state. Of course no one in the world of Islam bothered about the State of the Wahhabites, about their true teaching, and about the spirit of the Islamic ideas which they had revived. For two hundred years nothing was heard of them, except that they lived according to their teaching and maintained their community unimpaired.

When the world war was over, when the Caliph had been driven away and Islam had fallen into apathy, there suddenly and unexpectedly arose out of the deserts of Arabia, out of the distant Ar-Riyadh, Abdul-Aziz ibn Sa'ud, the master of the Wahhabites, who called himself King of Najd. No one knew who Ibn Sa'ud was.

He is the only Moslem ruler in the world who has maintained the pure word of the Prophet, who has given it new life and new strength. When Ibn Sa'ud was still a boy, the dynasty to which he had belonged had been expelled out of Ar-Riyadh by the neighbouring race of the Rashid. Young Sa'ud collected a troop of twenty men, travelled through the desert to Ar-Riyadh, stole his way into the palace of the Rashid, and slew the sleeping sultan, thus regaining the power over Najd for himself and his tribe. With this act, his rise began which, in the course of time, made him ruler over two-thirds of Arabia, protector of the Holy Places and the most important man of present-day Islam.

Together with the faithful Wahhabites he attacked Mecca, drove out the sherif, occupied the Caaba in 1925 and became the most popular man in Islam. Today, Abdul-Aziz ibn Sa'ud is the ruler of Hejaz, Assyria and Najd. He is the religious and spiritual leader of the Arabs.

Ibn Sa'ud repeated the deeds of the Prophet. He recalled God's words to mankind. And these words proved themselves to be sufficiently alive to create and rule a state in the 20th century as they did in the seventh. Ibn Sa'ud created a religio-social brotherhood called Ikhwan. This Ikhwan movement supports the Wahhabite empire today. The teaching of Ikhwan is pure Islam, just as the Prophet and the Kharijites had preached it. Ibn Sa'ud does nothing that the Prophet would not have done and fulfils all the duties which the prophet fulfilled. Every luxury, music, theatre, coffee, even tobacco, are forbidden in the empire of the Wahhabites. Every word of the Koran is law, and the slightest misinterpretation is heresy. The equality of mankind in the eyes of God has been reintroduced practically. Monotheism is law. Adoration, even the veneration of the Caaba, the holy stone, is forbidden to the Wahhabites. The sober, straight, only way of truth, the way the Prophet trod, is known to them.

On this way Ikhwan only knows of two things: prayer and exercise. Prayer and exercise, in which prayer is exercise and exercise is prayer, created the land of the Wahhabites and gave life to the dying body of Islam.

The incomparable thing about the ascetic teaching of Ikhwan is that it knows no intolerance. This accounts for its all-embracing position in the world of Islam. Shi'ites, Sunni, even Jews and Christians are tolerated by Ikhwan. Like Mohammed, Ikhwan recognizes the weakness of mankind and does not condemn it. They are merely the older, wiser brothers and not the punishing judges of humanity. Ibn Sa'ud is the ruler of a new state, and this state has been changed into the new core of the resurrection of Islam.

The war of conquest of the first Caliphs and the emigration of entire tribes to newly-acquired territories had emptied the desert. Many hundred years have elapsed since then, and, following the primitive laws of Semitic emigration, the desert has collected new strength, has developed a new surplus population which now, like the Semites in the times of Babylon, Assyria and the Caliphate, wishes to penetrate the magic circle of the sand. Again there stands at the head of the over-populated desert a great leader who, like Mohammed, is actuated by a great yet simple, primitive and eternal vision.

But times today have changed materially. No longer do three hundred soldiers decide the fate of history. Ibn Sa'ud knows that. The new victory of an old idea requires new methods.

The new methods of the new ruler of Arabia are remarkable. Ibn Sa'ud is accomplishing that which no one before him has succeeded in doing – not even Mohammed. He makes the Bedouins sedentary. He has created a disciplined, sedentary population out of the wild nomads, and holds them fast in his hand. The Bedouin, who up till now has bothered himself but little about the commands of the Koran, has not only become sedentary but pious. The *imam*, the ruler of the holy places, gives him land and water and requires nothing from him that he does not ask from every Wahhabite, namely prayer and exercise.

Through this the wild desert of Arabia has been given a new face. Again it has become a flowering state out of nothing. The once wild and dangerous roads of Arabia, where behind each stone a robber awaited the traveller, are more peaceful and less dangerous than the roads of Europe. Flourishing villages spring up in Arabia. For the first time in his history, the Arab has begun to conquer the desert. The campaign against the desert is led by Ibn Sa'ud, for the people who conquer the desert are in turn won over to the true faith. And so the State of God, the new State, is growing up in the desert. The State is led according to the words of the Prophet and is, at the same time, a modern state, with telephones, telegraph, aeroplanes and motors. In short, it has everything that the world of Europe had produced in order to make their liberation easier for the people of Asia. Prayer, exercise and the word of the Prophet are the foundations of the State which today, barely ten years after its founding, occupies a territory three times as large as Germany.

Thus the eternal world-history repeats itself, and a new State has arisen in the land of the Prophet. Thus the word of the Prophet is awakened to new life, to new strength in its primitive home.

The eyes of all the Islamic people are directed today with eager expectation towards Mecca, towards the city of the Caaba, towards the city of Ibn Sa'ud, the centre of the new Islamic power.

Slowly Ibn Sa'ud goes his way. It is the way of the Prophet. The people of Islam know it, feel it. A new reform has set in, which is both salvation and fulfilment at one and the same time.

Islam is still the most vital world-religion, the religion most capable of expansion. It is still on the offensive, conquers new territories and makes believers out of the heathen. Africa and India are the expansion fields of Islam. It knows neither races nor classes, and that leads the castes of India and the negros of Africa to it. The number of converts increases from year to year. Islamic missionaries are even active in Europe.

Islam, having returned to its native land, touches the holy stone of the Caaba, and suddenly new forces are developed in it. Now as then, its goal is the goal of Mohammed, the goal of Kharijites, the goal of the pious warriors: the conquest of the world.

The Islamic Orient experiences strange changes today. In the midst of these changes stands the word of the Prophet. Out of the confusion and defeats, out of the disappointments and humiliations, a new power has arisen which the world of Europe has not yet fully understood. This power is modern Islam. Again it collects the people about it, girds its loins for the fray, builds and changes, conforms to the new world and to the new methods.

As in the days of the Prophet, there stands, in the foreground of this development and the great Arabian land, the holy, ancient city of Mecca, and a stern soldier who gives new strength and reality to the words of God.

The new Orient, the new Islam, the great brotherhood of Ikhwan, all are preparing for the fight of the spirit, the fight of the sword, preparing for the sacred fight of Islam.

ENDNOTES

1 "Reading the Koran" must be understood in the sense that, according to Muslim tradition, a few Suras had already been written down and that in the incident described someone had brought Umar's sister some pages with parts of a newly revealed Sura.

2 *Hidshra*, "flight". The flight from Mecca denotes the beginning of the Islamic calculation of time, that is 16th July, 622 = 1st Muharram 1 A.H. (A.H. = after the Hidshra). This calendar is still used today. The year 2014 A.D. = 1435 A.H.

3 It is interesting that the best selling and critically acclaimed Turkish scholar Yaşar Nuri Öztürk points out that it is not sanctioned by the Koran to beat a wife. The word *darb*, traditionally translated as "to beat", can take on up to twenty different meanings in Arabic, one of them being "to beat". Therefore, when it stipulates in Sura 4.34 that a husband ought to "admonish his wife first, then refuse to share her bed, and then to beat her" (lightly or otherwise), the translation is erroneous. Erroneous, simply because the prophet himself did not beat his wife Aisha, instead sent her to her parents. Note that one of the twenty meanings of *darb* is "to send on a trip" or "to send away" (until one decides what to do).
See Öztürk, *Islam nasıl yozlaştırıldı*, Istanbul 2005, Yeni Boyut Publishing. Quoted from the German translation *Der verfälschte Islam*, Düsseldorf 2007, page 107.

BOOKS BY ESSAD BEY
BY THE SAME PUBLISHER

Coming in 2014:

Stalin – Career of a Fanatic
(First published in 1932)
ISBN 978-3-929345-68-1

Nicholas II. Prisoner of the Purple
(First published in 1936)
ISBN 978-3-929345-69-8

Already available:

Twelve Secrets in the Caucasus
(First published in 1931)
ISBN 978-3-929345-37-7

Blood and Oil in the Orient
(First published in 1932)
ISBN 978-3-929345-36-0

Lightning Source UK Ltd.
Milton Keynes UK
UKOW04f1853170117
292300UK00012B/549/P